STATA SURVEY DATA
REFERENCE MANUAL
RELEASE 9

A Stata Press Publication
StataCorp LP
College Station, Texas

Stata Press, 4905 Lakeway Drive, College Station, Texas 77845

The suggested citation for this software is

StataCorp. 2005. *Stata Statistical Software: Release 9*. College Station, TX: StataCorp LP.

Table of Contents

Cross-Referencing the Documentation

When reading this manual, you will find references to other Stata manuals. For example,

[U] **26 Overview of Stata estimation commands**
[R] **regress**
[D] **reshape**

The first is a reference to chapter 26, *Overview of Stata estimation commands* in the *Stata User's Guide*, the second is a reference to the `regress` entry in the *Base Reference Manual*, and the third is a reference to the `reshape` entry in the *Data Management Reference Manual*.

All the manuals in the Stata Documentation have a shorthand notation, such as [U] for the *User's Guide* and [R] for the *Base Reference Manual*.

The complete list of shorthand notations and manuals is as follows:

[GSM]   *Getting Started with Stata for Macintosh*
[GSU]   *Getting Started with Stata for Unix*
[GSW]   *Getting Started with Stata for Windows*

[U]   *Stata User's Guide*

[R]   *Stata Base Reference Manual*

[D]   *Stata Data Management Reference Manual*

[G]   *Stata Graphics Reference Manual*

[P]   *Stata Programming Reference Manual*

[XT]   *Stata Longitudinal/Panel Data Reference Manual*

[MV]   *Stata Multivariate Statistics Reference Manual*

[SVY]   *Stata Survey Data Reference Manual*

[ST]   *Stata Survival Analysis and Epidemiological Tables Reference Manual*

[TS]   *Stata Time-Series Reference Manual*

[I]   *Stata Quick Reference and Index*

[M]   *Mata Reference Manual*

Detailed information about each of these manuals may be found online at

http://www.stata-press.com/manuals/

Title

intro — Introduction to survey data manual

Description

This entry describes this manual and what has changed since Stata 8. See the next entry, [SVY] **survey**, for an introduction to Stata's survey commands.

Remarks

This manual documents the survey data commands and is referred to as [SVY] in references.

Following this entry, [SVY] **survey** provides an overview of the survey commands. This manual is arranged alphabetically. If you are new to Stata's survey data commands, we recommend that you read the following sections first:

[SVY] **survey**	Introduction to survey commands
[SVY] **svyset**	Declare survey design for dataset
[SVY] **svydes**	Describe survey data
[SVY] **svy**	The survey prefix command
[SVY] **svy postestimation**	Postestimation tools for svy

Stata is continually being updated, and Stata users are continually writing new commands. To find out about the latest survey data features, type `search survey` after installing the latest official updates; see [R] **update**.

What's new

Stata 9 substantially extends Stata's survey analysis and correlated-data analysis facilities by adding two popular methods of computing standard errors—balanced repeated replications (BRR) and survey jackknife.

Stata 9 also adds complete support for multistage sampling and poststratification.

A new, unified syntax is used for declaring the design of survey data and for fitting models. For an overview of all survey facilities, see [SVY] **survey**.

All the old syntax continues to work under version control, but if you use the old syntax, the new features will not be available.

This section is intended for previous Stata users. If you are new to Stata, you may as well skip it.

1. The existing command `svyset` for declaring the survey design has new syntax that supports a host of new features in Stata's survey-analysis facilities.

   a. BRR and jackknife variance estimators have been added to the previously available linearization variance estimator. Moreover, use of BRR or jackknife (or linearization) can now be specified either when you `svyset` or at estimation time.

   b. Multistage designs can now be declared, and they may have primary, secondary, and lower-stage sampling units. The linearization variance estimator takes complete advantage of the information contained in multistage designs.

1

c. Stratification is now allowed within all stages, making variance estimates more efficient wherever stratification can be exploited.

d. Poststratification is now available and, like stratification, also makes variance estimates more efficient. Poststratification adjusts weights, improves variance estimates, and accounts for biases when demographic or other groupings are known.

e. Finite-population corrections are allowed at all stages.

f. Sampling weights are supported with all three variance estimators.

For details, see [SVY] **svyset**. The previous `svyset` syntax continues to work under version control.

2. The new prefix command `svy:` is how you tell estimators that you have survey data. You no longer type `svyregress`; you type `svy: regress`. This is not just a matter of style; `svy` really is a prefix command, and, in fact, you can even use it as a prefix on estimation commands you write. In addition, `svy:` provides a standard, unified syntax for Stata's accessing survey features, and `svy:` is easy to use because it automatically applies everything you have previously `svyset`, including the design.

The following estimators can be used with `svy:` prefix:

Descriptive statistics

`svy: mean`	Population and subpopulation means
`svy: proportion`	Population and subpopulation proportions
`svy: ratio`	Population and subpopulation ratios
`svy: total`	Population and subpopulation totals
`svy: tabulate oneway`	One-way tables for survey data
`svy: tabulate twoway`	Two-way tables for survey data

Regression models

`svy: regress`	Linear regression
`svy: ivreg`	Instrumental variables regression
`svy: intreg`	Interval regression
`svy: logistic`	Logistic regression, reporting odds ratios
`svy: logit`	Logistic regression, reporting coefficients
`svy: probit`	Probit regression
`svy: mlogit`	Multinomial logistic regression
`svy: ologit`	Ordered logistic regression
`svy: oprobit`	Ordered probit regression
`svy: poisson`	Poisson regression
`svy: nbreg`	Negative binomial regression
`svy: gnbreg`	Generalized negative binomial regression
`svy: heckman`	Heckman selection model
`svy: heckprob`	Probit regression with selection

Previously existing survey-estimation commands, such as `svyregress`, `svymean`, and `svypoisson`, continue to work as they did before, but only if your survey design is declared using `version 8:` `svyset` or if you are working with an old Stata 8 dataset. For a mapping from old estimation commands to the new syntax; type `help svy8` from within Stata. (The new `svy:` works with datasets that were `svyset` under an earlier version of Stata.)

In addition to the three variance estimators and support for multistage sampling, the new `svy:` prefix provides other enhancements, including

a. The `subpop()` option allows more flexible selection of subpopulations, which is to say, more general `if` conditions are now allowed.

b. Strata with only one sampling unit (sometimes called singleton PSUs) are now handled better—the coefficients are now reported, but with missing standard errors. `svydes` can now be used to find and describe these strata; see [SVY] **svydes**.

c. With BRR variance estimation, a Hadamard matrix can be used in place of BRR weights and Fay's adjustment may be specified; see [SVY] *brr_options*.

3. The new command `svy: proportion` replaces `svyprop`. (By the way, the new command `proportion` can be used without the `svy:` prefix; see [R] **proportion**.) Unlike `svyprop`, `svy: proportion` is an estimation command and computes a full covariance matrix for all the estimated proportions, allowing postestimation features, such as tests of linear and nonlinear combinations of proportions ([R] **test** and [R] **testnl**) or the creation of linear and nonlinear combinations with confidence intervals ([R] **lincom** and [R] **nlcom**).

4. The new commands `ratio`, `total`, and `mean`, when used with the `svy:` prefix, use casewise deletion and estimate full covariance matrices.

5. The new command `svy: tabulate oneway` makes it easy to get one-way tabulation.

6. The new `estat` command computes and reports additional statistics and information after estimation with `svy:` prefix:

a. `estat svyset` reports information on the survey design.

b. `estat effects` computes and reports the survey design effects—DEFF and DEFT—and the misspecification effects—MEFF and MEFT—in any combination for each estimated parameter.

c. `estat effects` can also compute DEFF and DEFT for subpopulations using simple random-sample estimates either from the overall population or from the subpopulation. `estat effects` replaces and extends the `deff`, `deft`, `meff`, and `meft` options previously available on survey estimators.

d. `estat lceffects` computes and reports the survey design effects and misspecification effects for any linear combination of estimated parameters.

e. `estat size` reports the sample and population sizes for each subpopulation after `svy: mean`, `svy: proportion`, `svy: ratio`, and `svy: total`.

For details on `estat` after survey estimation, see [SVY] **estat**.

7. Existing command `svydes` has several new features and options:

a. New option `stage()` lets you select the sampling stage for which sample statistics are to be reported.

b. New option `generate()` identifies strata with a single sampling unit.

c. New option `finalstage` replaces `bypsu` and reports observation sample statistics by sampling unit in the final stage.

8. The new options `stdize()` and `stdweight()` to the commands `svy: mean`, `svy: ratio`, `svy: proportion`, `svy: tabulate oneway`, and `svy: tabulate twoway` allow for direct standardization of means, ratios, proportions, and tabulations using any of the three survey variance estimators.

9. Programmers of estimation commands can get full support for estimation with survey and correlated data almost automatically. This support includes correct treatment of multistage designs, weighting, stratification, poststratification, and finite-population corrections, as well as access to all three variance estimators. For a discussion, see [P] **program properties**.

10. This manual now has a glossary that defines commonly used terms in survey analysis and explains how these terms are used in the manual; see [SVY] **glossary**.

Also See

Complementary: [U] **1.3 What's new**

Background: [R] **intro**

Title

> **survey** — Introduction to survey commands

Description

The *Survey Data Reference Manual* organizes the commands alphabetically, making it easy to find individual command entries if you know the name of the command. This overview organizes and presents the commands conceptually, that is, according to the similarities in the functions that they perform.

The following list of commands may have been updated since the release of Stata 9. For an updated list, type the following in an up-to-date Stata:

```
. help survey
```

Survey design tools

svyset	Declare survey design for dataset
svydes	Describe survey data

Descriptive statistics

svy: mean	Estimation of population and subpopulation means
svy: proportion	Estimation of population and subpopulation proportions
svy: ratio	Estimation of population and subpopulation ratios
svy: total	Estimation of population and subpopulation totals
svy: tabulate oneway	One-way tables for survey data
svy: tabulate twoway	Two-way tables for survey data

Regression models

svy: regress	Linear regression for survey data
svy: ivreg	Instrumental variables regression for survey data
svy: intreg	Interval regression for survey data
svy: logistic	Logistic regression, reporting odds ratios, for survey data
svy: logit	Logistic regression, reporting coefficients, for survey data
svy: probit	Probit regression for survey data
svy: mlogit	Multinomial logistic regression for survey data
svy: ologit	Ordered logistic regression for survey data
svy: oprobit	Ordered probit regression for survey data
svy: poisson	Poisson regression for survey data
svy: nbreg	Negative binomial regression for survey data
svy: gnbreg	Generalized negative binomial regression for survey data
svy: heckman	Heckman selection model for survey data
svy: heckprob	Probit regression with selection for survey data

Survey data analysis tools

svy	Overview of the svy prefix command
svy brr	Balanced repeated replication for survey data
svy jackknife	Jackknife estimation for survey data
svy postestimation	Overview of postestimation commands for survey data analysis
estat	Postestimation statistics for survey data
ml for svy	Maximum pseudolikelihood estimation for survey data
svymarkout	Mark observations for exclusion based on survey characteristics

Survey data concepts

variance estimation	Variance estimation for survey data
subpopulation estimation	Subpopulation estimation for survey data
direct standardization	Direct standardization of means, proportions, and ratios
poststratification	Poststratification for survey data

Remarks

Remarks are presented under the headings

> *Overview*
> *Survey design tools*
> *Descriptive statistics*
> *Regression models*
> *Survey data analysis tools*
> *Survey data concepts*

Overview

Stata's facilities for survey data are centered around the svy prefix command. Once the design characteristics of a survey dataset are identified with the svyset command, the svy prefix can be used with supported estimation commands in essentially the same way as the corresponding command for nonsurvey data. For example, where you would normally use the regress command to fit a linear regression using nonsurvey data, use svy: regress for your survey data.

Why should you use the svy prefix command rather than, say, the mean command for means or regress for linear regression? To answer this question, we need to discuss some of the characteristics of survey design and survey data collection because these characteristics affect how we must perform our analysis if we want to "get it right".

Survey data are characterized by the following:

1. sampling weights, also called probability weights—pweights in Stata's syntax

2. cluster sampling

3. stratification

These factors arise from the design of the data collection procedure. Here's a brief description of how these design features affect the analysis of the data:

1. *Sampling weights.* In sample surveys, observations are selected through a random process, but different observations may have different probabilities of selection. Weights are equal to (or proportional to) the inverse of the probability of being sampled. Various postsampling

adjustments to the weights are sometimes made, as well. A weight of w_j for the jth observation means, roughly speaking, that the jth observation represents w_j elements in the population from which the sample was drawn.

Omitting weights from the analysis results in estimates that may be biased, sometimes seriously so. Sampling weights also need to be taken in account when estimating standard errors, and for purposes of testing and inference.

2. *Clustering.* Individuals are not sampled independently in almost all survey designs. Collections of individuals (for example, counties, city blocks, or households) are typically sampled as a group, known as a *cluster.*

   There may also be further subsampling within the clusters. For example, counties may be sampled, then city blocks within counties, then households within city blocks, and then finally persons within households. The clusters at the first level of sampling are called *primary sampling units* (PSUs)—in this example, counties are the PSUs. In the absence of clustering, the PSUs are defined to be the individuals or, equivalently, clusters each of size one.

   Sampling by cluster implies a sample-to-sample variability of the resulting estimator that is usually greater than that obtained through sampling individually, and this variability must be accounted for when estimating standard errors, testing, or performing other inference.

3. *Stratification.* In surveys, different groups of clusters are often sampled separately. These groups are called *strata.* For example, the 254 counties of a state might be divided into two strata, say, urban counties and rural counties. Then ten counties might be sampled from the urban stratum, and fifteen from the rural stratum.

   Sampling is done independently across strata; the stratum divisions are fixed in advance. Thus strata are statistically independent and can be analyzed as such. When the individual strata are more homogenous than the population as a whole, the homogeneity can be exploited to produce smaller (and honestly so) estimates of standard errors.

To put it succinctly: it is important to use sampling weights in order to get the point estimates right. We must consider the weighting, clustering, and stratification of the survey design to get the standard errors right. If our analysis ignores the clustering in our design, we would likely produce standard errors that are smaller than they should be. Stratification can be used to get smaller standard errors for a given total amount of data.

▷ Example 1: A preview of survey data analysis with Stata

We have (fictional) data on American high school seniors (12th graders), and the data were collected according to the following multistage design. In the first stage, counties were independently selected within each state. In the second stage, schools were selected within each chosen county. Within each chosen school, a questionaire was filled out by every attending high school senior. We've entered all the information into a Stata dataset called `multistage.dta`. The survey design variables are as follows:

1. `state` contains the stratum identifiers

2. `county` contains the first-stage sampling units

3. `ncounties` contains the total number of counties within each state

4. `school` contains the second-stage sampling units

5. `nschools` contains the total number of schools within each county

6. `sampwgt` contains the sampling weight for each sampled individual

Here we load `multistage.dta` into memory and use `svyset` with the above variables to declare that this data is survey data.

```
. use http://www.stata-press.com/data/r9/multistage
. svyset county [pw=sampwgt], strata(state) fpc(ncounties) || school, fpc(nschools)
      pweight: sampwgt
          VCE: linearized
    Strata 1: state
       SU 1: county
      FPC 1: ncounties
    Strata 2: <one>
       SU 2: school
      FPC 2: nschools
```

Now that the data are `svyset`, we can use the `svy` estimation commands to perform our analysis. In the following, we estimate the mean of `weight` (in lbs.) for each subpopulation identified by the categories of the `sex` variable (male and female).

```
. svy: mean weight, over(sex)
(running mean on estimation sample)

Survey: Mean estimation

Number of strata =        50      Number of obs     =      4071
Number of PSUs   =       100      Population size   = 8.0e+06
                                  Design df         =        50

        male: sex = male
      female: sex = female
```

		Linearized		
Over	Mean	Std. Err.	[95% Conf. Interval]	
weight				
male	175.4809	1.116802	173.2377	177.7241
female	146.204	.9004157	144.3955	148.0125

Based on the above results, we are 95% confident that the average weight of male high school seniors is between 173.2 and 177.7 pounds.

Here we use the `test` command to test the hypothesis that the average male is 30 pounds heavier than the average female; however, based on the results we cannot reject this hypothesis at the 5% level.

```
. test [weight]male - [weight]female = 30
Adjusted Wald test
 ( 1)  [weight]male - [weight]female = 30
        F(  1,     50) =      0.23
             Prob > F =      0.6353
```

◁

Survey design tools

Before using svy, first take a quick look at [SVY] **svyset**. Use the svyset command to specify the variables that identify the survey design characteristics and default method for standard error estimation. Once set, svy will automatically use these design specifications until they are cleared or changed, or a new dataset is loaded into memory.

The svydes command describes the survey design and is useful in, among other things, tracking down strata with only one sampling unit.

Descriptive statistics

svy: mean, svy: ratio, svy: proportion, and svy: total produce estimates of finite-population means, ratios, proportions and totals. svy: mean, svy: ratio, and svy: proportion can also estimate standardized means, ratios, and proportions. Estimates for multiple subpopulations can be obtained using the over() option.

svy: tabulate can be used to produce one-way and two-way tables with survey data and can also produce tests of independence for two-way contingency tables.

Regression models

Many commands in Stata are used to fit regression models to data, for example regress for linear regression, poisson for Poisson regression, logistic for logistic regression, etc. A subset of these *estimation commands* are supported by svy, that is, they may be prefixed by svy: in order to produce results appropriate for complex survey data. Whereas poisson is used with standard, nonsurvey data, svy: poisson is used with survey data. In what follows we refer to any estimation command unprefixed by svy: as the standard command. A standard command prefixed by svy: is referred to as a svy command.

Most standard commands (and all standard commands supported by svy) allow pweights and the cluster(*varname*) option, where *varname* corresponds to the *psu* variable that you svyset. If your survey data exhibit only sampling weights and/or first-stage clusters, you can get by with using the standard command with pweights and/or cluster(). Your parameter estimates will always be identical to those you would have obtained from the svy command, and the standard command uses the same robust (linearization) variance estimator as the svy command with a similarly svyset design.

Most standard commands are also fit using maximum-likelihood methodology. When used with independently distributed, nonweighted data, the likelihood to be maximized is reflective of the joint probability distribution of the data given the chosen model. With complex survey data, however, this interpretation of the likelihood is no longer valid, as survey data are either weighted, not independently distributed, or both. With survey data, (valid) parameter estimates are obtained using the independence-assuming likelihood and weighting if necessary. Since the probabilistic interpretation no longer holds, the likelihood here is instead called a *pseudolikelihood*. See Skinner (1989, section 3.4.4) for a discussion of maximum pseudolikelihood estimators.

Below we highlight the other features of svy commands.

1. svy commands handle stratified sampling, but none of the standard commands do. Since stratification usually makes standard errors smaller, ignoring stratification is usually conservative. So, not using svy with stratified sample data is not a terrible thing to do. However, to get the smallest possible "honest" standard-error estimates for stratified sampling, use svy.

2. svy commands use t statistics with $n - L$ degrees of freedom to test the significance of coefficients, where n is the total number of sampled PSUs (clusters) and L is the number of strata in the first stage. Some of the standard commands use t statistics, but most use z statistics. If the standard command uses z statistics for its standard variance estimator, then it also uses z statistics with the robust (linearization) variance estimator. Strictly speaking, t statistics are appropriate with the robust (linearization) variance estimator; see [P] _robust for the theoretical rationale. But, using z rather than t statistics only yields a nontrivial difference when there is a small number of clusters (< 50). If a regression model command uses t statistics and the cluster() option is specified, then the degrees of freedom used are the same as that of the svy command (in the absence of stratification).

3. svy commands produce an adjusted Wald test for the model test, and test can be used to produce adjusted Wald tests for other hypotheses after svy commands. Only unadjusted Wald tests are available if the svy prefix is not used. The adjustment can be important when the degrees of freedom $n - L$ are small relative to the dimension of the test. (If the dimension is one, then the adjusted and unadjusted Wald tests are identical.) This fact along with point 2 make it important to use the svy command if the number of sampled PSUs (clusters) is small (< 50).

4. svy: regress differs slightly from regress and svy: ivreg differs slightly from ivreg in that they use different multipliers for the variance estimator. regress and ivreg use a multiplier of $\{(N - 1)/(N - k)\}\{n/(n - 1)\}$, where N is the number of observations, n is the number of clusters (PSUs), and k is the number of regressors including the constant. svy: regress and svy: ivreg use $n/(n - 1)$ instead. Thus they produce slightly different standard errors. The $(N - 1)/(N - k)$ is ad hoc and has no rigorous theoretical justification; hence, the purist svy commands do not use it. The svy commands tacitly assume that $N \gg k$. If $(N - 1)/(N - k)$ is not close to 1, you may be well advised to use regress or ivreg so that some punishment is inflicted on your variance estimates. Note that maximum likelihood estimators in Stata (e.g., logit) do no such adjustment, but rely on the sensibilities of the analyst to ensure that N is reasonably larger than k. Thus the maximum pseudolikelihood estimators (e.g., svy: logit) produce exactly the same standard errors as the corresponding maximum likelihood commands (e.g., logit), but p-values are slightly different because of point 2.

5. svy commands can produce proper estimates for subpopulations through use of the subpop() option. Use of an *if* restriction with svy or standard commands can yield incorrect standard error estimates for subpopulations. Often an *if* restriction will yield exactly the same standard error as subpop(); most other times, the two standard errors will be slightly different; but, in some cases—usually for thinly sampled subpopulations—the standard errors can be appreciably different. Hence, the svy command with the subpop() option should be used to obtain estimates for thinly sampled subpopulations. See [SVY] **subpopulation estimation** for more information.

6. svy commands handle zero sampling weights properly. Standard commands ignore any observation with a weight of zero. Usually, this will yield exactly the same standard errors, but sometimes they will differ. Sampling weights of zero can arise from various postsampling adjustment procedures. If the sum of weights for one or more PSUs is zero, svy and standard commands will produce different standard errors, but usually this difference is very small.

7. You can svyset iweights and let these weights be negative. Negative sampling weights can arise from various postsampling adjustment procedures. If you want to use negative sampling weights, then you must svyset iweights instead of pweights; no standard command will allow negative sampling weights.

8. The svy commands compute finite population corrections (FPC).

9. After a `svy` command, `estat effects` will compute the design effects DEFF and DEFT and the misspecification effects MEFF and MEFT.

10. `svy` commands can perform variance estimation that accounts for multiple stages of clustered sampling.

11. `svy` commands can perform variance estimation that accounts for poststratification adjustments to the sampling weights.

Survey data analysis tools

Stata's suite of survey-data commands is governed by the `svy` prefix command. `svy` runs the supplied estimation command while accounting for the survey design characteristics in the point estimates and the variance estimator. The three available variance estimation methods are balanced repeated replication (BRR), the jackknife, and first-order Taylor linearization. By default, `svy` computes standard errors using the linearized variance estimator—so called because it is based on a first-order Taylor series linear approximation. In the nonsurvey context, we refer to this variance estimator as the *robust* variance estimator, otherwise known in Stata as the Huber/White/sandwich estimator; see [P] **_robust**.

The `svy brr` and `svy jackknife` prefix commands can be used with those commands that may not be fully supported by `svy` but are compatible with BRR and the jackknife; see [SVY] **svy brr** and [SVY] **svy jackknife**.

All the standard postestimation commands (e.g., `estat`, `lincom`, `nlcom`, `test`, `testnl`) are also available after `svy`.

`estat` has specific subroutines for use after `svy`. `estat svyset` reports the survey design settings used to produce the current estimation results. `estat effects` and `estat lceffects` report a table of design and misspecification effects for point estimates and linear combinations of point estimates, respectively. `estat size` reports a table of sample and subpopulation sizes after `svy: mean`, `svy: proportion`, `svy: ratio`, and `svy: total`.

The `ml` command can be used to fit a pseudolikelihood model. When maximum pseudolikelihood is carried out using `ml`, the weighting during estimation and postestimation linearization is performed automatically, provided that the user specifies the appropriate survey options to `ml`; see [R] **ml** for details.

`svymarkout` is a programmer's command that resets the values in a variable that identifies the estimation sample, dropping observations for which any of the survey-characteristic variables contain missing values. This tool is most helpful for developing estimation commands that use `ml` to fit models using maximum pseudolikelihood.

Survey data concepts

The variance estimation methods used by Stata are discussed in [SVY] **variance estimation**.

See [SVY] **subpopulation estimation** for an explanation of why you should use the `subpop()` option instead of the *if* and *in* options.

The weight adjusting methods for direct standardization and poststratification are discussed in [SVY] **direct standardization** and [SVY] **poststratification**.

For more detailed introductions to complex survey data analysis, see Scheaffer, Mendenhall, and Ott (1996), Stuart (1984), Williams (1978), and Levy and Lemeshow (1999). Advanced treatments and discussion of important special topics are given by Cochran (1977), Korn and Graubard (1999),

Särndal, Swensson, and Wretman (1992), Shao and Tu (1995), Skinner, Holt, and Smith (1989), Thompson (2002), and Wolter (1985).

Acknowledgments

Many of the svy commands were developed in collaboration with John L. Eltinge, Bureau of Labor Statistics. We thank him for his invaluable assistance.

We thank Wayne Johnson of the National Center for Health Statistics for providing the NHANES II dataset.

We thank Nicholas Winter, Department of Government, Cornell University, for his diligent efforts to keep Stata up to date with mainstream variance estimation methods for survey data, and for providing versions of svy brr and svy jackknife.

William Gemmell Cochran (1909–1980) was born in Rutherglen, Scotland, and educated at the Universities of Glasgow and Cambridge. He accepted a post at Rothamsted before finishing his doctorate. Cochran emigrated to the United States in 1939 and worked at Iowa State, North Carolina State, Johns Hopkins, and Harvard. He made many major contributions across several fields of statistics, including experimental design, the analysis of counted data, sample surveys and observational studies, and was author or co-author (with Gertrude M. Cox and George W. Snedecor) of various widely used texts.

References

Binder, D. A. 1983. On the variances of asymptotically normal estimators from complex surveys. *International Statistical Review* 51: 279–292.

Cochran, W. G. 1977. *Sampling Techniques*. 3rd ed. New York: Wiley.

——. 1982. *Contributions to Statistics*. New York: Wiley.

Eltinge, J. L. and W. M. Sribney. 1996a. svy1: Some basic concepts for design-based analysis of complex survey data. *Stata Technical Bulletin* 31: 3–6. Reprinted in *Stata Technical Bulletin Reprints*, vol. 6, pp. 208–213.

——. 1996b. svy4: Linear, logistic, and probit regressions for survey data. *Stata Technical Bulletin* 31: 26–31. Reprinted in *Stata Technical Bulletin Reprints*, vol. 6, pp. 239–245.

Fuller, W. A. 1975. Regression analysis for sample survey. *Sankhyā, Series C* 37: 117–132.

Garrett, J. M. 2001. sxd4: Sample size estimation for cluster designed samples. *Stata Technical Bulletin* 60: 41–45. Reprinted in *Stata Technical Bulletin Reprints*, vol. 10, pp. 387–393.

Godambe, V. P. ed. 1991. *Estimating Functions*. Oxford: Clarendon Press.

Gonzalez J. F., Jr., N. Krauss, and C. Scott. 1992. Estimation in the 1988 National Maternal and Infant Health Survey. In *Proceedings of the Section on Statistics Education, American Statistical Association*, 343–348.

Hansen, M. and F. Mosteller. 1987. William Gemmell Cochran. *Biographical Memoirs, National Academy of Sciences* 56: 60–89.

Johnson, W. 1995. Variance estimation for the NMIHS. Technical document. Hyattsville, MD: National Center for Health Statistics.

Kish, L. and M. R. Frankel. 1974. Inference from complex samples. *Journal of the Royal Statistical Society* B 36: 1–37.

Korn, E. L. and B. I. Graubard. 1990. Simultaneous testing of regression coefficients with complex survey data: Use of Bonferroni t statistics. *The American Statistician* 44: 270–276.

——. 1999. *Analysis of Health Surveys*. New York: Wiley.

Kott, P. S. 1991. A model-based look at linear regression with survey data. *The American Statistician* 45: 107–112.

Levy, P. and S. Lemeshow. 1999. *Sampling of Populations*. 3rd ed. New York: Wiley.

McDowell, A., A. Engel, J. T. Massey, and K. Maurer. 1981. Plan and operation of the Second National Health and Nutrition Examination Survey, 1976–1980. *Vital and Health Statistics* 15(1). Hyattsville, MD: National Center for Health Statistics.

McDowell, A. and J. Pitblado. 2002. From the help desk: It's all about the sampling. *Stata Journal* 2: 190–201.

Särndal, C.-E., B. Swensson, and J. Wretman. 1992. *Model Assisted Survey Sampling*. New York: Springer.

Scheaffer, R. L., W. Mendenhall, and L. Ott. 1996. *Elementary Survey Sampling*. 5th ed. Boston: Duxbury Press.

Scott, A. J. and D. Holt. 1982. The effect of two-stage sampling on ordinary least squares methods. *Journal of the American Statistical Association* 77: 848–854.

Shao, J. 1996. Resampling methods for sample surveys (with discussion). *Statistics* 27: 203–254.

Shao, J. and D. Tu. 1995. *The Jackknife and Bootstrap*. New York: Springer.

Skinner, C. J. 1989. Introduction to Part A. In *Analysis of Complex Surveys*, ed. C. J. Skinner, D. Holt, and T. M. F. Smith, 23–58. New York: Wiley.

Skinner, C. J., D. Holt, and T. M. F. Smith, eds. 1989. *Analysis of Complex Surveys*. New York: Wiley.

Stuart, A. 1984. *The Ideas of Sampling*. 3rd ed. New York: Macmillan.

Thompson, S. K. 2002. *Sampling*. 2nd ed. New York: Wiley.

Watson, G. S. 1982. William Gemmell Cochran 1909–1980. *Annals of Statistics* 10: 1–10.

Williams, B. 1978. *A Sampler on Sampling*. New York: Wiley.

Wolter, K. M. 1985. *Introduction to Variance Estimation*. New York: Springer.

Also See

Complementary:	[R] **estat**, [R] **jackknife**, [R] **lincom**, [R] **ml**, [R] **nlcom**, [R] **predict**, [R] **predictnl**, [R] **test**, [R] **testnl**
Background:	[P] **_robust**

Title

> **brr_options** — Additional options for BRR variance estimation

Syntax

brr_options	description
SE	
hadamard(*matrix*)	Hadamard matrix
fay(*#*)	Fay's adjustment
mse	use MSE formula for variance estimation
nodots	suppress the replication dots
†saving(*filename*, ...)	save results to *filename*
†verbose	display the full table legend
†noisily	display any output from *command*
†trace	trace the *command*
†title(*text*)	use *text* as the title for results
†reject(*exp*)	identify invalid results

†These options are not shown in the dialog boxes for estimation commands.

Description

svy accepts additional options when performing balanced repeated replication (BRR) variance estimation.

Options

> SE

hadamard(*matrix*) specifies the Hadamard matrix to be used to determine which PSUs are chosen for each replicate.

fay(*#*) specifies Fay's adjustment. The sampling weight of the selected PSUs for a given replicate is multiplied by 2−#, where the sampling weight for the unselected PSUs is multiplied by #. fay(0) is the default and is equivalent to the original BRR method. fay(1) is not allowed since this results in unadjusted weights.

mse specifies that svy compute the variance using deviations of the replicates from the observed value of the statistics based on the entire dataset. By default, svy computes the variance using deviations of the replicates from their mean.

nodots suppresses display of the replication dots. By default, a single dot character is printed for each successful replication; however, 'x' is displayed if *command* returns with an error, and 'e' is displayed if at least one of the values in the expression list is missing.

saving(), verbose, noisily, trace, title(), reject(); see [SVY] **svy brr**.

14

Also See

Complementary: [SVY] **svy**, [SVY] **svy brr**

Title

> **direct standardization** — Direct standardization of means, proportions, and ratios

Description

Direct standardization is an estimation method that allows for the comparison of rates that come from different frequency distributions. The `mean`, `proportion`, and `ratio` commands can estimate means, proportions, and ratios using direct standardization. This entry discusses direct standardization for survey data.

See [SVY] **poststratification** for a similar estimation method given population sizes for strata not used in the sampling design.

Remarks

In direct standardization, estimated rates (means, proportions, and ratios) are adjusted according to the frequency distribution of a standard population. The standard population is partitioned into categories, called standard strata. The stratum frequencies for the standard population are called standard weights. In the standardizing frequency distribution, the standard strata are most commonly identified by demographic information such as age, sex, and ethnicity.

Stata's `mean`, `proportion`, and `ratio` estimation commands have options for estimating means, proportions, and ratios using direct standardization. The `stdize()` option takes a variable that identifies the standard strata, and the `stdweight()` option takes a variable that contains the standard weights.

Note that the standard strata (specified using `stdize()`) from the standardizing population are not the same as the strata (specified using `svyset`'s `strata()` option) from the sampling design. In the output header, "Number of strata" is the number of strata in the first stage of the sampling design, and "N. of std strata" is the number of standard strata.

In the following example, we use direct standardization to compare the death rates between two districts of London in 1840.

▷ Example 1: Standardized rates

Table 3.12-6 of Korn and Graubard (1999, 156) contains enumerated data for two districts of London for the year 1840–1841. The `age` variable identifies the age groups in 5-year increments, `bgliving` contains the number of people living in the Bethnal-green district at the beginning of 1840, `bgdeaths` contains the number of people who died in Bethnal-green that year, `hsliving` contains the number of people living in St. George's Hanover-square at the beginning of 1840, and `hsdeaths` contains the number of people who died in Hanover-square that year.

16

```
. use http://www.stata-press.com/data/r9/stdize
. list, noobs sep(0) sum
```

age	bgliving	bgdeaths	hsliving	hsdeaths
0-5	10739	850	5738	463
5-10	9180	76	4591	55
10-15	8006	38	4148	28
15-20	7096	37	6168	36
20-25	6579	38	9440	68
25-30	5829	51	8675	78
30-35	5749	51	7513	64
35-40	4490	56	5091	78
40-45	4385	47	4930	85
45-50	2955	66	2883	66
50-55	2995	74	2711	77
55-60	1644	67	1275	55
60-65	1835	64	1469	61
65-70	1042	64	649	55
70-75	879	68	619	58
75-80	366	47	233	51
80-85	173	39	136	20
85-90	71	22	48	15
90-95	21	6	10	4
95-100	4	2	2	1
unknown	50	1	124	0
Sum	74088	1764	66453	1418

We can use svy: ratio to compute the death rates for each district in 1840. Since this dataset is identified as census data, we will create an FPC variable that will contain a sampling rate of 1. This will result in zero standard errors, which are interpreted to mean no variability, which is appropriate since our point estimates came from the entire population.

```
. gen fpc = 1
. svyset, fpc(fpc)

      pweight: <none>
          VCE: linearized
    Strata 1: <one>
        SU 1: <observations>
       FPC 1: fpc

. svy: ratio (Bethnal: bgdeaths/bgliving) (Hanover: hsdeaths/hsliving)
(running ratio on estimation sample)

Survey: Ratio estimation

Number of strata =        1        Number of obs    =       21
Number of PSUs   =       21        Population size  =       21
                                   Design df        =       20

        Bethnal: bgdeaths/bgliving
        Hanover: hsdeaths/hsliving
```

	Ratio	Linearized Std. Err.	[95% Conf. Interval]	
Bethnal	.0238095	0	.	.
Hanover	.0213384	0	.	.

```
Note: Zero standard error due to 100% sampling rate detected for FPC in the
      first stage.
```

The death rates are 2.38% for Bethnal-green and 2.13% for St. George's Hanover-square. These observed death rates are not really comparable since they come from two different age distributions. We can standardize based on the age distribution from Bethnal-green. In this case, `age` identifies our standard strata, and `bgliving` contains the associated population sizes.

```
. svy: ratio (Bethnal: bgdeaths/bgliving) (Hanover: hsdeaths/hsliving),
> stdize(age) stdweight(bgliving)
(running ratio on estimation sample)

Survey: Ratio estimation

Number of strata =          1        Number of obs    =        21
Number of PSUs   =         21        Population size  =        21
N. of std strata =         21        Design df        =        20

          Bethnal: bgdeaths/bgliving
          Hanover: hsdeaths/hsliving
```

	Ratio	Linearized Std. Err.	[95% Conf. Interval]	
Bethnal	.0238095	0	.	.
Hanover	.0266409	0	.	.

```
Note: Zero standard error due to 100% sampling rate detected for FPC in the
      first stage.
```

Note that the standardized death rate for St. George's Hanover-square 2.66% is larger that the death rate for Bethnal-green.

For this example, we could have used `dstdize` to compute the death rates; however, `dstdize` will not compute the correct standard errors for survey data. Furthermore `dstdize` is not an estimation command, so `test` and the other postestimation commands are not available.

◁

❏ Technical Note

Note that the values in the variable supplied to the `stdweight()` option are normalized so that (1) is true; see *Methods and Formulas*. Thus the `stdweight()` variable can contain population sizes or population proportions for the associated standard strata.

❏

Methods and Formulas

The following discussion assumes that you are already familiar with the topics discussed in [SVY] **variance estimation**.

In direct standardization, a weighted sum of the point estimates from the standard strata is used to produce an overall point estimate for the population. This section will show how direct standardization affects the ratio estimator. The mean and proportion estimators are special cases of the ratio estimator.

Suppose that you used a complex survey design to sample m individuals from a population of size M. Let D_g be the set of individuals in the sample that belong to the gth standard stratum and $I_{D_g}(j)$ indicate if the jth individual is in standard stratum g

$$I_{D_g}(j) = \begin{cases} 1, & \text{if } j \in D_g \\ 0, & \text{otherwise} \end{cases}$$

Also let L_D be the number of standard strata and π_g be the proportion of the population that belongs to standard stratum g

$$\sum_{g=1}^{L_D} \pi_g = 1 \tag{1}$$

In subpopulation estimation, π_g is set to zero if none of the individuals in standard stratum g are in the subpopulation. In this case, the standard stratum proportions are renormalized.

Let y_j and x_j be the items of interest and w_j be the sampling weight for the jth sampled individual. The estimator for the standardized ratio of $R = Y/X$ is

$$\widehat{R}^D = \sum_{g=1}^{L_D} \pi_g \frac{\widehat{Y}_g}{\widehat{X}_g}$$

where

$$\widehat{Y}_g = \sum_{j=1}^{m} I_{D_g}(j)\, w_j y_j$$

with $\widehat{X}_g$ similarly defined.

For replication-based variance estimation, the standardized replicate values are used in the variance formulas.

The score variable for the linearized variance estimator of the standardized ratio is

$$z_j(\widehat{R}^D) = \sum_{g=1}^{L_D} \pi_g I_{D_g}(j) \frac{\widehat{X}_g y_j - \widehat{Y}_g x_j}{\widehat{X}_g^2}$$

This score variable was derived using the method described in [SVY] **variance estimation** for the ratio estimator.

For the `mean` and `proportion` commands, note that the mean estimator is a ratio estimator with the denominator variable equal to one ($x_j = 1$) and the proportion estimator is the mean estimator with an indicator variable in the numerator ($y_j \in \{0, 1\}$).

References

Demnati, A. and J. N. K. Rao. 2004. Linearization variance estimators for survey data. *Survey Methodology* 30: 17–26.

Deville, J.-C. 1999. Variance estimation for complex statistics and estimators: linearization and residual techniques. *Survey Methodology* 25: 193–203.

Korn, E. L. and B. I. Graubard. 1999. *Analysis of Health Surveys.* New York: Wiley.

Shah, B. V. 2004. Comment [on Demnati and Rao (2004)]. *Survey Methodology* 30: 29.

Also See

Complementary:	[SVY] **svy**, [SVY] **svyset**
Related:	[SVY] **svy: mean**, [SVY] **svy: total**, [SVY] **svy: proportion**, [SVY] **poststratification**
Background:	[SVY] **survey**

Title

> *eform_option* — Displaying exponentiated coefficients

Description

An *eform_option* causes the coefficient table to be displayed in exponentiated form: for each coefficient, e^b rather than b is displayed. Standard errors and confidence intervals are also transformed. Display of the intercept, if any, is suppressed.

An *eform_option* is one of the following:

eform_option	description
eform(*string*)	use *string* for the column title
eform	exponentiated coefficient, *string* is "exp(b)"
irr	incidence-rate ratio, *string* is "IRR"
or	odds ratio, *string* is "Odds ratio"
rrr	relative-risk ratio, *string* is "RRR"

These options are not allowed with svy: mean, svy: proportion, svy: ratio, svy: tabulate, or svy: total.

Remarks

▷ Example 1

Here is a simple example of the or option with svy: logit. Note that the confidence interval (CI) for the odds ratio is computed by transforming (by exponentiating) the endpoints of the the CI for the corresponding coefficient.

```
. use http://www.stata-press.com/data/r9/nhanes2d
. svy, noheader: logit highbp female black, or
(running logit on estimation sample)
```

highbp	Odds Ratio	Linearized Std. Err.	t	P>|t|	[95% Conf. Interval]	
female	.693628	.048676	-5.21	0.000	.6011298	.8003593
black	1.509155	.2089569	2.97	0.006	1.137872	2.001586

◁

Also See

Complementary: [SVY] **svy: logit**, [SVY] **svy: mlogit**, [SVY] **svy: nbreg**,
[SVY] **svy: ologit**, [SVY] **svy: poisson**

Title

> **estat** — Postestimation statistics for survey data

Syntax

Survey design characteristics

    estat svyset

Design and misspecification effects for point estimates

    estat <u>eff</u>ects [, *effects_options*]

Design and misspecification effects for linear combinations of point estimates

    estat <u>lceff</u>ects *exp* [, *effects_options*]

Subpopulation sizes

    estat size [, *estat_size_options*]

Display covariance matrix estimates

    estat vce [, *estat_vce_options*]

effects_options	description
deff	report the DEFF design effects
deft	report the DEFT design effects
<u>srs</u>subpop	report design effects assuming SRS within subpopulation
meff	report the MEFF design effects
meft	report the MEFT design effects

estat_size_options	description
obs	report the number of observations (within subpopulation)
size	report the subpopulation sizes

estat_vce_options	description
<u>cov</u>ariance	display as covariance matrix; the default
<u>c</u>orrelation	display as correlation matrix
<u>eq</u>uation(*spec*)	display only specified equations
<u>b</u>lock	display submatrices by equation
<u>d</u>iag	display submatrices by equation; diagonal blocks only
<u>f</u>ormat(%*fmt*)	display format for covariances and correlations
<u>noli</u>nes	suppress lines between equations

Description

estat svyset reports the survey design characteristics associated with the current estimation results.

estat effects displays a table of design and misspecification effects for each estimated parameter.

estat lceffects displays a table of design and misspecification effects for a linear combination of the parameter estimates.

estat size displays a table of sample and subpopulation sizes for each estimated subpopulation mean, proportion, ratio, or total. This command is only available after svy: mean, svy: proportion, svy: ratio, and svy: total.

estat vce displays the covariance or correlation matrix of the parameter estimates of the previous model. See [R] **estat** for examples.

Options for estat effects and lceffects

deff and deft request that the design-effect measures DEFF and DEFT be displayed.

Note that options deff and deft are not allowed with estimation results that employed direct standardization or poststratification.

srssubpop requests that DEFF and DEFT be computed using an estimate of SRS (simple random sampling) variance for sampling within a subpopulation. By default, DEFF and DEFT are computed using an estimate of the SRS variance for sampling from the entire population. Typically, srssubpop is used when computing subpopulation estimates by strata or by groups of strata.

meff and meft request that the misspecification-effect measures MEFF and MEFT be displayed.

Options for estat size

obs requests that the number of observations used to compute the estimate be displayed for each row of estimates.

size requests that the estimate of the subpopulation size be displayed for each row of estimates. The subpopulation size estimate equals the sum of the weights for those observations in the estimation sample that are also in the specified subpopulation. The estimated population size is reported when a subpopulation is not specified.

Options for estat vce

covariance displays the matrix as a variance–covariance matrix; this is the default.

correlation displays the matrix as a correlation matrix rather than a variance–covariance matrix. rho is a synonym for correlation.

eq(*spec*) selects the part of the VCE to be displayed. If *spec* = *eqlist*, the VCE for the listed equations is displayed. If *spec* = *eqlist1* \ *eqlist2*, the part of the VCE associated with the equations in *eqlist1* (row-wise) and *eqlist2* (columnwise) is displayed. * is shorthand for all equations. eq() implies block if diag is not specified.

block displays the submatrices pertaining to distinct equations separately.

diag displays the diagonal submatrices pertaining to distinct equations separately.

format(%*fmt*) specifies the display format for displaying the elements of the matrix. The default is format(%10.0g) for covariances and format(%8.4f) for correlations. See [U] **12.5 Formats: controlling how data are displayed** for more information.

nolines suppresses lines between equations.

Remarks

▷ Example 1

Using data from the Second National Health and Nutrition Examination Survey (NHANES II) (McDowell et al. 1981), let's estimate the population means for total serum cholesterol (tcresult) and for serum triglycerides (tgresult).

```
. use http://www.stata-press.com/data/r9/nhanes2
. svy: mean tcresult tgresult
(running mean on estimation sample)
Survey: Mean estimation
Number of strata =        31      Number of obs     =      5050
Number of PSUs   =        62      Population size  = 5.7e+07
                                  Design df         =        31
```

	Mean	Linearized Std. Err.	[95% Conf. Interval]	
tcresult	211.3975	1.252274	208.8435	213.9515
tgresult	138.576	2.071934	134.3503	142.8018

We can use estat svyset to remind us of the survey design characteristics that were used to produce these results.

```
. estat svyset
     pweight: finalwgt
         VCE: linearized
   Strata 1: strata
       SU 1: psu
      FPC 1: <zero>
```

estat effects reports a table of design and misspecification effects for each mean we estimated.

```
. estat effects, deff deft meff meft
```

	Mean	Linearized Std. Err.	Deff	Deft	Meff	Meft
tcresult	211.3975	1.252274	3.57141	1.88982	3.46105	1.86039
tgresult	138.576	2.071934	2.35697	1.53524	2.32821	1.52585

estat size reports a table that contains sample and population sizes.

```
. estat size
```

	Mean	Linearized Std. Err.	Obs	Size
tcresult	211.3975	1.252274	5050	56820832
tgresult	138.576	2.071934	5050	56820832

estat size can also report a table of subpopulation sizes.

```
. svy: mean tcresult, over(sex)
(output omitted )
. estat size
        Male: sex = Male
      Female: sex = Female
```

Over	Mean	Linearized Std. Err.	Obs	Size
tcresult				
Male	210.7937	1.312967	4915	56159480
Female	215.2188	1.193853	5436	60998033

◁

▷ Example 2: Design effects with subpopulations

When there are subpopulations, estat effects can compute design effects with respect to one of two different hypothetical SRS designs. The first hypothetical design is one in which simple random sampling is conducted across the full population; this is the default. An alternate hypothetical design is one in which simple random sampling is conducted entirely within the subpopulation of interest. This alternate design is used when the srssubpop option is specified.

Deciding which design is preferable depends on the nature of the subpopulations. If we can imagine identifying members of the subpopulations before sampling them, the alternate design is preferable. This case arises primarily when the subpopulations are strata or groups of strata. Otherwise, we may prefer to use the default.

Here is an example using the default with the NHANES II data.

```
. use http://www.stata-press.com/data/r9/nhanes2b
. svy: mean iron, over(sex)
(output omitted )
. estat effects, deff deft
        Male: sex = Male
      Female: sex = Female
```

Over	Mean	Linearized Std. Err.	Deff	Deft
iron				
Male	104.7969	.557267	1.36097	1.16661
Female	97.16247	.6743344	2.01403	1.41916

Thus the design-based variance estimate is about 36% larger than the estimate from the hypothetical SRS design including the full population. We can get DEFF and DEFT for the alternate SRS design using the srssubpop option.

```
. estat effects, srssubpop
       Male: sex = Male
     Female: sex = Female
```

	Over	Mean	Linearized Std. Err.	Deff	Deft
iron					
	Male	104.7969	.557267	1.348	1.16104
	Female	97.16247	.6743344	2.03132	1.42524

Because the NHANES II did not stratify on sex, we think it problematic to consider design effects with respect to simple random sampling of the female (or male) subpopulation. Consequently, we would prefer to use the default here, although the values of DEFF differ little between the two in this case.

For other examples (generally involving heavy oversampling or undersampling of specified subpopulations), the differences in DEFF for the two schemes can be much more dramatic.

Consider the NMIHS data, and compute the mean of `birthwgt` over `race`:

```
. use http://www.stata-press.com/data/r9/nmihs
. svy: mean birthwgt, over(race)
 (output omitted)
. estat effects, deff deft
     nonblack: race = nonblack
        black: race = black
```

	Over	Mean	Linearized Std. Err.	Deff	Deft
birthwgt					
	nonblack	3402.32	7.609532	1.44376	1.20157
	black	3127.834	6.529814	.172041	.414778

```
. svy: mean birthwgt, over(race)
 (output omitted)
. estat effects, srssubpop
     nonblack: race = nonblack
        black: race = black
```

	Over	Mean	Linearized Std. Err.	Deff	Deft
birthwgt					
	nonblack	3402.32	7.609532	.826842	.909308
	black	3127.834	6.529814	.528963	.727298

Since the NMIHS survey was stratified on race, marital status, age, and birth weight, we believe it reasonable to consider design effects computed with respect to simple random sampling within an individual race group. Consequently, in this case, we would recommend the second scheme; i.e., we would use the `srssubpop` option.

◁

▷ Example 3: Misspecification effects

Misspecification effects assess biases in variance estimators that are computed under the wrong assumptions. The survey literature (e.g., Scott and Holt 1982, 850; Skinner 1989) defines misspecification effects with respect to a general set of "wrong" variance estimators. `estat effects` considers only one specific form: variance estimators computed under the incorrect assumption that our *observed* sample was selected through simple random sampling.

The resulting "misspecification effect" measure is informative primarily in cases where an unweighted point estimator is approximately unbiased for the parameter of interest. See Eltinge and Sribney (1996a) for a detailed discussion of extensions of misspecification effects that are appropriate for *biased* point estimators.

Note the difference between a misspecification effect and a design effect. For a design effect, we compare our complex-design-based variance estimate with an estimate of the true variance that we would have obtained under a hypothetical true simple random sample. For a misspecification effect, we compare our complex-design-based variance estimate with an estimate of the variance from fitting the same model without weighting, clustering, or stratification.

`estat effects` defines MEFF and MEFT as

$$\text{MEFF} = \widehat{V}/\widehat{V}_{\text{msp}}$$

$$\text{MEFT} = \sqrt{\text{MEFF}}$$

where $\widehat{V}$ is the appropriate design-based estimate of variance and $\widehat{V}_{\text{msp}}$ is the variance estimate computed with a misspecified design—ignoring the sampling weights, stratification, and clustering.

Here we request that the misspecification effects be displayed for the estimation of mean zinc levels using our NHANES II data.

```
. use http://www.stata-press.com/data/r9/nhanes2b
. svy: mean zinc, over(sex)
  (output omitted)
. estat effects, meff meft
        Male: sex = Male
      Female: sex = Female
```

	Over	Mean	Linearized Std. Err.	Meff	Meft
zinc					
	Male	90.74543	.5850741	6.28254	2.5065
	Female	83.8635	.4689532	6.32648	2.51525

If we run `ci` without weights, we get the standard errors that are $(\widehat{V}_{\text{msp}})^{1/2}$.

```
. sort sex
. ci zinc if sex == "Male":sex
```

Variable	Obs	Mean	Std. Err.	[95% Conf. Interval]
zinc	4375	89.53143	.2334228	89.0738 89.98906

```
. display [zinc]_se[Male]/r(se)
2.5064994
. display ([zinc]_se[Male]/r(se))^2
6.2825393
. ci zinc if sex == "Female":sex
```

Variable	Obs	Mean	Std. Err.	[95% Conf. Interval]
zinc	4827	83.76652	.186444	83.40101 84.13204

```
. display [zinc]_se[Female]/r(se)
2.515249
. display ([zinc]_se[Female]/r(se))^2
6.3264774
```

◁

▷ Example 4: Design and misspecification effects for linear combinations

Let's compare the mean of total serum cholesterol (tcresult) between men and women in the NHANES II dataset.

```
. use http://www.stata-press.com/data/r9/nhanes2
. svy: mean tcresult, over(sex)
(running mean on estimation sample)

Survey: Mean estimation

Number of strata =        31          Number of obs    =      10351
Number of PSUs   =        62          Population size  = 1.2e+08
                                      Design df        =         31

        Male: sex = Male
      Female: sex = Female
```

Over	Mean	Linearized Std. Err.	[95% Conf. Interval]
tcresult			
Male	210.7937	1.312967	208.1159 213.4715
Female	215.2188	1.193853	212.784 217.6537

We can use estat lceffects to report the standard error, design effects, and misspecification effects of the difference between the above means.

```
. estat lceffects [tcresult]Male - [tcresult]Female, deff deft meff meft
 ( 1)  [tcresult]Male - [tcresult]Female = 0
```

	Coef.	Std. Err.	Deff	Deft	Meff	Meft
(1)	-4.425109	1.086786	1.31241	1.1456	1.27473	1.12904

◁

Saved Results

estat svyset saves in r():

Scalars
- r(stages)   number of sampling stages

Macros
- r(wtype)   weight type
- r(wexp)   weight expression
- r(wvar)   weight variable name
- r(ssu#)   variable identifying sampling units for stage #
- r(strata#)   variable identifying strata for stage #
- r(fpc#)   FPC for stage #
- r(brrweight)   brrweight() variable list
- r(jkrweight)   jkrweight() variable list
- r(vce)   from vce() option
- r(mse)   from mse option
- r(poststrata)   poststrata() variable
- r(postweight)   postweight() variable
- r(settings)   svyset arguments to reproduce the current settings

estat effects saves in r():

Matrices
- r(deff)   vector of DEFF estimates
- r(deft)   vector of DEFT estimates
- r(deffsub)   vector of DEFF estimates for srssubpop
- r(deftsub)   vector of DEFT estimates for srssubpop
- r(meff)   vector of MEFF estimates
- r(meft)   vector of MEFT estimates

estat lceffects saves in r():

Scalars
- r(estimate)   point estimate
- r(se)   estimate of standard error
- r(df)   degrees of freedom
- r(deff)   DEFF estimate
- r(deft)   DEFT estimate
- r(deffsub)   DEFF estimate for srssubpop
- r(deftsub)   DEFT estimate for srssubpop
- r(meff)   MEFF estimate
- r(meft)   MEFT estimate

estat size saves in r():

Matrices
- r(_N)   vector of numbers of nonmissing observations
- r(_N_subp)   vector of subpopulation size estimates

estat vce saves in r():

Matrices
- r(V)   VCE or correlation matrix

Methods and Formulas

estat is implemented as an ado-file.

Design effects

estat effects produces two estimators of design effect, DEFF and DEFT.

DEFF is estimated as described in Kish (1965)

$$
\text{DEFF} = \frac{\widehat{V}(\theta)}{\widehat{V}_{\text{srswor}}(\widetilde{\theta}_{\text{srs}})}
$$

where $\widehat{V}(\theta)$ is the design-based estimate of variance for a parameter θ, and $\widehat{V}_{\text{srswor}}(\widetilde{\theta}_{\text{srs}})$ is an estimate of the variance for an estimator $\widetilde{\theta}_{\text{srs}}$ that would be obtained from a similar hypothetical survey conducted using simple random sampling (srs) without replacement (wor) and with the same number of sample elements m as in the actual survey. For example, if θ is a total Y

$$
\widehat{V}_{\text{srswor}}(\widetilde{\theta}_{\text{srs}}) = (1-f)\frac{\widehat{M}}{m-1}\sum_{j=1}^{m} w_j\left(y_j - \widehat{\overline{Y}}\right)^2 \tag{1}
$$

where $\widehat{\overline{Y}} = \widehat{Y}/\widehat{M}$. The factor $(1-f)$ is a finite population correction. If the user sets an fpc for the first stage, $f = m/\widehat{M}$ is used; otherwise, $f = 0$.

DEFT is estimated as described in Kish (1965)

$$
\text{DEFT} = \sqrt{\frac{\widehat{V}(\theta)}{\widehat{V}_{\text{srswr}}(\widetilde{\theta}_{\text{srs}})}}
$$

where $\widehat{V}_{\text{srswr}}(\widetilde{\theta}_{\text{srs}})$ is an estimate of the variance for an estimator $\widetilde{\theta}_{\text{srs}}$ obtained from a similar survey conducted using simple random sampling (srs) with replacement (wr). $\widehat{V}_{\text{srswr}}(\widetilde{\theta}_{\text{srs}})$ is computed using (1) with $f = 0$.

When computing estimates for a subpopulation S and the srssubpop option is *not* specified (i.e., the default), (1) is used with $w_{Sj} = I_S(j)\, w_j$ in place of w_j, where

$$
I_S(j) = \begin{cases} 1, & \text{if } j \in S \\ 0, & \text{otherwise} \end{cases}
$$

Note that the sums in (1) are still calculated over all elements in the sample, regardless of whether they belong to the subpopulation. This is because, by default, the simple random sampling is assumed to be done across the full population.

When the srssubpop option is specified, the simple random sampling is carried out within subpopulation S. In this case, (1) is used with the sums restricted to those elements belonging to the subpopulation; m is replaced with m_S, the number of sample elements from the subpopulation; $\widehat{M}$ is replaced with $\widehat{M}_S$, the sum of the weights from the subpopulation; and $\widehat{\overline{Y}}$ is replaced with $\widehat{\overline{Y}}_S = \widehat{Y}_S/\widehat{M}_S$, the weighted mean across the subpopulation.

Linear combinations

estat lceffects estimates $\eta = C\theta$, where θ is a $q \times 1$ vector of parameters (e.g., population means or population regression coefficients) and C is any $1 \times q$ vector of constants. The estimate of η is $\widehat{\eta} = C\widehat{\theta}$, and its variance estimate is

$$\widehat{V}(\widehat{\eta}) = C\widehat{V}(\widehat{\theta})C'$$

Similarly, the simple-random-sampling without replacement (srswor) variance estimator used in the computation of DEFF is

$$\widehat{V}_{\mathrm{srswor}}(\widetilde{\eta}_{\mathrm{srs}}) = C\widehat{V}_{\mathrm{srswor}}(\widehat{\theta}_{\mathrm{srs}})C'$$

and the simple-random-sampling with replacement (srswr) variance estimator used in the computation of DEFT is

$$\widehat{V}_{\mathrm{srswr}}(\widetilde{\eta}_{\mathrm{srs}}) = C\widehat{V}_{\mathrm{srswr}}(\widehat{\theta}_{\mathrm{srs}})C'$$

The variance estimator used in computing MEFF and MEFT is

$$\widehat{V}_{\mathrm{msp}}(\widetilde{\eta}_{\mathrm{msp}}) = C\widehat{V}_{\mathrm{msp}}(\widehat{\theta}_{\mathrm{msp}})C'$$

Misspecification effects

estat effects produces two estimators of misspecification effect, MEFF and MEFT.

$$\mathrm{MEFF} = \frac{\widehat{V}(\widehat{\theta})}{\widehat{V}_{\mathrm{msp}}(\widehat{\theta}_{\mathrm{msp}})}$$

$$\mathrm{MEFT} = \sqrt{\mathrm{MEFF}}$$

where $\widehat{V}(\widehat{\theta})$ is the design-based estimate of variance for a parameter θ, and $\widehat{V}_{\mathrm{msp}}(\widehat{\theta}_{\mathrm{msp}})$ is the variance estimate for $\widehat{\theta}_{\mathrm{msp}}$. These estimators, $\widehat{\theta}_{\mathrm{msp}}$ and $\widehat{V}_{\mathrm{msp}}(\widehat{\theta}_{\mathrm{msp}})$, are based on the incorrect assumption that the observations were obtained through simple random sampling with replacement—in other words, they are the estimators obtained by simply ignoring weights, stratification, and clustering. When θ is a total Y, the estimator and its variance estimate are computed using the standard formulas for an unweighted total:

$$\widehat{Y}_{\mathrm{msp}} = \widehat{M}\,\overline{y} = \frac{\widehat{M}}{m}\sum_{j=1}^{m} y_j$$

$$\widehat{V}_{\mathrm{msp}}(\widehat{Y}_{\mathrm{msp}}) = \frac{\widehat{M}^2}{m(m-1)}\sum_{j=1}^{m}(y_j - \overline{y})^2$$

When computing MEFF and MEFT for a subpopulation, sums are restricted to those elements belonging to the subpopulation, and $m_{\mathcal{S}}$ and $\widehat{M}_{\mathcal{S}}$ is used in place of m and $\widehat{M}$.

References

Eltinge, J. L. and W. M. Sribney. 1996a. Accounting for point-estimation bias in assessment of misspecification effects, confidence-set coverage rates and test sizes. Unpublished manuscript. Department of Statistics, Texas A&M University.

——. 1996b. svy5: Estimates of linear combinations and hypothesis tests for survey data. *Stata Technical Bulletin* 31: 31–42. Reprinted in *Stata Technical Bulletin Reprints*, vol. 6, pp. 246–259.

Kish, L. 1965. *Survey Sampling*. New York: Wiley.

McDowell, A., A. Engel, J. T. Massey, and K. Maurer. 1981. Plan and operation of the Second National Health and Nutrition Examination Survey, 1976–1980. *Vital and Health Statistics* 15(1). Hyattsville, MD: National Center for Health Statistics.

Also See

Complementary:	[SVY] **svy postestimation**
Background:	[SVY] **svy,**
	[SVY] **subpopulation estimation,**
	[SVY] **variance estimation**

Title

---
estimation options — Common options of estimation commands

Description

This entry describes the options common to most estimation commands. Not all the options documented below work with all estimation commands; see the documentation for the particular estimation command. If an option is listed there, it is applicable.

Options

┌─── Model ───

noconstant suppresses the constant term (intercept) from the model.

offset(*varname*) specifies that *varname* be included in the model with the coefficient constrained to be 1.

exposure(*varname*) specifies a variable that reflects the amount of exposure over which the *depvar* events were observed for each observation; ln(*varname*) with coefficient constrained to be 1 is entered into the linear predictor.

constraints(*clist* | *matname*) specifies the linear constraints to be applied during estimation. The default is to perform unconstrained estimation. constraints(*clist*) specifies the constraints by number after they have been defined using the constraint command; see [R] **constraint**. See [R] **reg3** for the use of constraints in multiple-equation contexts.

constraints(*matname*) specifies a matrix containing the constraints; see [P] **makecns**.

constraints(*clist*) is used by some estimation commands, such as mlogit, where *clist* has the form $\#\left[-\#\right]\left[,\#\left[-\#\right]\ \ldots\right]$.

┌─── Reporting ───

level(*#*) specifies the confidence level, as a percentage, for confidence intervals. The default is level(95) or as set by set level; see [U] **20.6 Specifying the width of confidence intervals**.

Also See

Background: [U] **20 Estimation and postestimation commands**

Title

jackknife_options — Additional options for jackknife variance estimation

Syntax

jackknife_options	description
SE	
mse	use MSE formula for variance estimation
nodots	suppress the replication dots
†saving(*filename*, ...)	save results to *filename*
†verbose	display the full table legend
†keep	keep pseudovalues
†noisily	display any output from *command*
†trace	trace the *command*
†title(*text*)	use *text* as the title for results
†reject(*exp*)	identify invalid results

†These options are not shown in the dialog boxes for estimation commands.

Description

svy accepts additional options when performing jackknife variance estimation.

Options

⌐SE⌐

mse indicates that svy compute the variance using deviations of the replicates from the observed value of the statistic based on the entire dataset. By default, svy computes the variance using deviations of the pseudovalues from their mean.

nodots suppresses display of the replication dots. By default, a single dot character is printed for each successful replication; however, 'x' is displayed if *command* returns with an error, 'e' is displayed if as least one of the values in the expression list is missing, and 'n' is printed if the sample size is not correct.

saving(), verbose, keep, noisily, trace, title(), reject(); see [SVY] **svy jackknife**.

Also See

Complementary: [SVY] **svy**, [SVY] **svy jackknife**

Title

ml for svy — Maximum pseudolikelihood estimation for survey data

Remarks

Stata's ml command can fit maximum-likelihood-based models for survey data. Many ml-based estimators can now be modified to handle one or more stages of clustering, stratification, sampling weights, finite population correction, poststratification, and subpopulation estimation. See [R] **ml** for details.

See [P] **program properties** for a discussion of the programming requirements for an estimation command to work with the svy prefix.

Also See

Complementary:	[P] **program properties**, [R] **maximize**, [R] **ml**
Background:	[SVY] **survey**

Title

> **poststratification** — Poststratification for survey data

Description

Poststratification is a method for adjusting the sampling weights, usually to account for underrepresented groups in the population. This entry discusses poststratification for survey data.

See [SVY] **direct standardization** for a similar method of adjustment that allows the comparison of rates that come from different frequency distributions.

Remarks

Poststratification involves adjusting the sampling weights so that they sum to the population sizes within each poststratum. This usually results in decreasing bias due to nonresponse and underrepresented groups in the population. Poststratification also tends to result in smaller variance estimates.

The svyset command has options to set variables for applying poststratification adjustments to the sampling weights. The poststrata() option takes a variable that contains poststratum identifiers, and the postweight() option takes a variable that contains the poststratum population sizes.

In the following example, we use an example from Levy and Lemeshow (1999) to show how poststratification affects the point estimates and their variance.

▷ Example 1: Poststratified mean

Levy and Lemeshow (1999, section 6.6) give an example of poststratification using simple survey data from a veterinarians client list. The data in poststrata.dta were collected using simple random sampling without replacement. The totexp variable contains the total expenses to the client, type identifies the cats and dots, postwgt contains the poststratum sizes (450 for cats and 850 for dogs), and fpc contains the total number of clients (850 + 450 = 1300).

```
. use http://www.stata-press.com/data/r9/poststrata
. svyset, poststrata(type) postweight(postwgt) fpc(fpc)
      pweight: <none>
          VCE: linearized
   Poststrata: type
   Postweight: postwgt
     Strata 1: <one>
         SU 1: <observations>
        FPC 1: fpc
. svy: mean totexp
(running mean on estimation sample)

Survey: Mean estimation

Number of strata =        1        Number of obs   =         50
Number of PSUs   =       50        Population size  =      1300
N. of poststrata =        2        Design df        =        49
```

		Linearized		
	Mean	Std. Err.	[95% Conf. Interval]	
totexp	40.11513	1.163498	37.77699	42.45327

The mean total expenses is \$40.12 with a standard error of \$1.16. In the following we omit the poststratification information from `svyset`, resulting in a mean total expenses of \$39.73 with standard error \$2.22. The difference between the mean estimates is explained by the fact that expenses tend to be larger for dogs than cats and that the dogs were very slightly underrepresented in the sample ($850/1300 \approx 0.65$ for the population, $32/50 = .64$ for the sample). This also explains why the variance estimate from the poststratified mean is smaller than the one that was not poststratified.

```
. svyset, fpc(fpc)

      pweight: <none>
          VCE: linearized
     Strata 1: <one>
         SU 1: <observations>
        FPC 1: fpc

. svy: mean totexp
(running mean on estimation sample)

Survey: Mean estimation

Number of strata =        1          Number of obs    =       50
Number of PSUs   =       50          Population size  =       50
                                     Design df        =       49
```

		Linearized		
	Mean	Std. Err.	[95% Conf. Interval]	
totexp	39.7254	2.221747	35.26063	44.19017

◁

Methods and Formulas

The following discussion assumes that you are already familiar with the topics discussed in [SVY] **variance estimation**.

Suppose that you used a complex survey design to sample m individuals from a population of size M. Let P_k be the set of individuals in the sample that belong to poststratum k and $I_{P_k}(j)$ indicate if the jth individual is in poststratum k

$$I_{P_k}(j) = \begin{cases} 1, \text{ if } j \in P_k \\ 0, \text{ otherwise} \end{cases}$$

Also let L_P be the number of poststrata and M_k be the population size for poststratum k.

If w_j is the unadjusted sampling weight for the jth sampled individual, the poststratification adjusted sampling weight is

$$w_j^* = \sum_{k=1}^{L_P} I_{P_k}(j) \frac{M_k}{\widehat{M_k}} w_j$$

where $\widehat{M_k}$ is

$$\widehat{M_k} = \sum_{j=1}^{m} I_{P_k}(j) w_j$$

The point estimates are computed using these adjusted weights. For example the poststratified total estimator is

$$\widehat{Y}^P = \sum_{j=1}^{m} w_j^* y_j$$

where y_j is an item from the jth sampled individual.

For replication based variance estimation, the BRR and jackknife replicate weight variables are similarly adjusted to produce the replicate values used in the respective variance formulas.

The score variable for the linearized variance estimator of a poststratified total is

$$z_j(\widehat{Y}^P) = \sum_{k=1}^{L_P} I_{P_k}(j) \frac{M_k}{\widehat{M}_k} \left(y_j - \frac{\widehat{Y}_k}{\widehat{M}_k} \right) \tag{P1}$$

where $\widehat{Y}_k$ is the total estimator for the kth poststratum

$$\widehat{Y}_k = \sum_{j=1}^{m} I_{P_k}(j) w_j y_j$$

For the poststratified ratio estimator, the score variable is

$$z_j(\widehat{R}^P) = \frac{\widehat{X}^P z_j(\widehat{Y}^P) - \widehat{Y}^P z_j(\widehat{X}^P)}{(\widehat{X}^P)^2} \tag{P2}$$

where $\widehat{X}^P$ is the poststratified total estimator for item x_j. For regression models, the equation-level scores are adjusted as in (P1). These score variables were derived using the method described in [SVY] **variance estimation** for the ratio estimator.

References

Cochran, W. G. 1977. *Sampling Techniques*. 3rd ed. New York: Wiley.

Demnati, A. and J. N. K. Rao. 2004. Linearization variance estimators for survey data. *Survey Methodology* 30: 17–26.

Deville, J.-C. 1999. Variance estimation for complex statistics and estimators: linearization and residual techniques. *Survey Methodology* 25: 193–203.

Levy, P. and S. Lemeshow. 1999. *Sampling of Populations*. 3rd ed. New York: Wiley.

Shah, B. V. 2004. Comment [on Demnati and Rao (2004)]. *Survey Methodology* 30: 29.

Also See

Complementary:	[SVY] **svy: mean**, [SVY] **svy: proportion**, [SVY] **svy: ratio**
Background:	[SVY] **svy**, [SVY] **svyset**, [SVY] **survey**

Title

---
subpopulation estimation — Subpopulation estimation for survey data
---

Description

Subpopulation estimation focuses on a subset of the population. This entry discusses subpopulation estimation and explains why you should not use the *if* and *in* options with survey data analysis.

Remarks

Subpopulation estimation involves computing point and variance estimates for a subset of the population. This is not the same as restricting the estimation sample to the collection of observations within the subpopulation because variance estimation for survey data measures sample-to-sample variability assuming the same survey design is used to collect the data; see the *Methods and Formulas* section for a detailed explanation.

The svy prefix command's subpop() option performs subpopulation estimation. The svy: mean, svy: proportion, svy: ratio, and svy: total commands also have the over() option to perform estimation for multiple subpopulations.

The following examples illustrate how to use the subpop() and over() options.

▷ Example 1

Suppose that we are interested in estimating the proportion of women in our population who have had a heart attack. In our NHANES II dataset, the female participants can be identified using the female variable, and the heartatk variable indicates if an individual has ever had a heart attack. In the following we use svy: mean with the heartatk variable to estimate the proportion of individuals who have had a heart attack and use subpop(female) to identify our subpopulation of interest.

```
. use http://www.stata-press.com/data/r9/nhanes2d
. svy, subpop(female): mean heartatk
(running mean on estimation sample)

Survey: Mean estimation

Number of strata =        31        Number of obs    =    10349
Number of PSUs   =        62        Population size  = 1.2e+08
                                  . Subpop. no. obs  =     5434
                                    Subpop. size     = 6.1e+07
                                    Design df        =       31
```

	Mean	Linearized Std. Err.	[95% Conf. Interval]	
heartatk	.0193276	.0017021	.0158562	.0227991

The subpop(*varname*) option takes a 0/1 variable, and the subpopulation of interest is defined by *varname* = 1. All other members of the sample not in the subpopulation are indicated by *varname* = 0.

If a person's subpopulation status is unknown, *varname* should be set to missing ('.'), so those observations will be omitted from the analysis. For instance, in the preceding analysis, if a person's sex was not recorded, female should be coded as missing rather than as male (female = 0).

◁

❑ Technical Note

Actually, the subpop(*varname*) option takes a zero/nonzero variable, and the subpopulation is defined by *varname* ≠ 0 and not missing. All other members of the sample not in the subpopulation are indicated by *varname* = 0, but 0, 1, and missing are typically the only values used for the subpop() variable.

Furthermore, you can specify an *if* option within subpop() to identify a subpopulation. The result is the same as generating a variable equal to the conditional expression and supplying it as the subpop() variable. If a *varname* and an *if* option are specified within the subpop() option, the subpopulation is identified by their logical conjunction (logical *and*) and observations with missing values in either are dropped from the estimation sample.

❑

▷ Example 2: Multiple subpopulation estimation

Means, proportions, ratios, and totals for multiple subpopulations can be estimated using the over() option with svy: mean, svy: proportion, svy: ratio, and svy: total; respectively. Here is an example using the NMIHS data, estimating mean birthweight over the categories of the race variable.

```
. use http://www.stata-press.com/data/r9/nmihs

. svy: mean birthwgt, over(race)
(running mean on estimation sample)

Survey: Mean estimation

Number of strata =        6          Number of obs    =     9946
Number of PSUs   =     9946          Population size  = 3.9e+06
                                     Design df        =     9940

         nonblack: race = nonblack
            black: race = black
```

Over	Mean	Linearized Std. Err.	[95% Conf. Interval]	
birthwgt				
nonblack	3402.32	7.609532	3387.404	3417.236
black	3127.834	6.529814	3115.035	3140.634

(*Continued on next page*)

More than one variable can be used in the over() option.

```
. svy: mean birthwgt, over(race marital)
(running mean on estimation sample)

Survey: Mean estimation

Number of strata =        6        Number of obs   =     9946
Number of PSUs   =     9946        Population size = 3.9e+06
                                   Design df       =     9940

             Over: race marital
        _subpop_1: nonblack single
        _subpop_2: nonblack married
        _subpop_3: black single
        _subpop_4: black married
```

		Linearized		
Over	Mean	Std. Err.	[95% Conf. Interval]	
birthwgt				
_subpop_1	3291.045	20.18795	3251.472	3330.617
_subpop_2	3426.407	8.379497	3409.982	3442.833
_subpop_3	3073.122	8.752553	3055.965	3090.279
_subpop_4	3221.616	12.42687	3197.257	3245.975

In this example, the variables race and marital have value labels. race has the value 0 labeled "nonblack" (i.e., white and other) and 1 labeled "black"; marital has the value 0 labeled "single" and 1 labeled "married". Value labels on the over() variables make for a more informative legend above the table of point estimates. See [U] **12.6.3 Value labels** for information on creating value labels.

We can also combine the subpop() option with the over() option.

```
. generate nonblack = (race == 0) if !missing(race)

. svy, subpop(nonblack): mean birthwgt, over(marital age20)
(running mean on estimation sample)

Survey: Mean estimation

Number of strata =        6        Number of obs   =     9946
Number of PSUs   =     9946        Population size = 3.9e+06
                                   Subpop. no. obs =     4724
                                   Subpop. size    = 3.2e+06
                                   Design df       =     9940

             Over: marital age20
        _subpop_1: single age20+
        _subpop_2: single age<20
        _subpop_3: married age20+
        _subpop_4: married age<20
```

		Linearized		
Over	Mean	Std. Err.	[95% Conf. Interval]	
birthwgt				
_subpop_1	3312.012	24.2869	3264.405	3359.619
_subpop_2	3244.709	36.85934	3172.457	3316.961
_subpop_3	3434.923	8.674633	3417.919	3451.927
_subpop_4	3287.301	34.15988	3220.341	3354.262

This time, we estimated means for the marital status and age (< 20 or ≥ 20) subpopulations for race == 0 (nonblack) only. Note that we carefully define nonblack so that it is missing when race is missing. If we omitted the `if !missing(race)` in our `generate` statement, `nonblack` would be 0 when `race` was missing. This would improperly assume that all individuals with a missing value for `race` were black and could cause our results to have incorrect standard errors. The standard errors could be incorrect because those observations for which `race` is missing would be counted as part of the estimation sample, potentially inflating the number of PSUs used in the formula for the variance estimator. For this reason, observations with missing values for any of the `over()` variables are omitted from the analysis.

◁

Methods and Formulas

The following discussion assumes that you are already familiar with the topics discussed in [SVY] **variance estimation**.

Cochran (1977, section 2.13) discusses a method by which you can derive estimates for subpopulation totals. This section uses this method to derive the formulas for a subpopulation total from a simple random sample (without replacement) in order to explain how the `subpop()` option works, shows why this method will often produce different results from those produced using an equivalent *if* (or *in*) option (outside the `subpop()` option), and discusses how this method applies to subpopulation means, proportions, ratios, and regression models.

Subpopulation totals

Let Y_j be a survey item for individual j in the population, where $j = 1, \ldots, N$ and N is the population size. Let S be a subset of individuals in the population and $I_S(j)$ indicate if the jth individual is in S

$$I_S(j) = \begin{cases} 1, \text{ if } j \in S \\ 0, \text{ otherwise} \end{cases}$$

The subpopulation total is

$$Y_S = \sum_{j=1}^{N} I_S(j) Y_j$$

and the subpopulation size is

$$N_S = \sum_{j=1}^{N} I_S(j)$$

Let y_j be the items for those individuals selected in the sample, where $j = 1, \ldots, n$ and n is the sample size. The number of individuals sampled from the subpopulation is

$$n_S = \sum_{j=1}^{n} I_S(j)$$

The estimator for the subpopulation total is

$$\widehat{Y}_S = \sum_{j=1}^{n} I_S(j) w_j y_j \tag{1}$$

where $w_j = N/n$ is the unadjusted sampling weight for this design. The estimator for N_S is

$$\widehat{N}_S = \sum_{j=1}^{n} I_S(j) w_j$$

The replicate values for the BRR and jackknife variance estimators are computed using the same method.

The linearized variance estimator for $\widehat{Y}_S$ is

$$\widehat{V}(\widehat{Y}_S) = \left(1 - \frac{n}{N}\right) \frac{n}{n-1} \sum_{j=1}^{n} \left\{ I_S(j) y_j - \frac{1}{n} \widehat{Y}_S \right\}^2 \tag{2}$$

The covariance estimator for the subpopulation totals $\widehat{Y}_S$ and $\widehat{X}_S$ (notation for X_S is defined similarly to that of Y_S) is

$$\widehat{\text{Cov}}(\widehat{Y}_S, \widehat{X}_S) = \left(1 - \frac{n}{N}\right) \frac{n}{n-1} \sum_{j=1}^{n} \left\{ I_S(j) y_j - \frac{1}{n} \widehat{Y}_S \right\} \left\{ I_S(j) x_j - \frac{1}{n} \widehat{X}_S \right\} \tag{3}$$

Note that (2) is not the same formula that results from restricting the estimation sample to the observations within S. The formula using this restricted sample (assuming a svyset with the respective FPC) is

$$\widetilde{V}(\widehat{Y}_S) = \left(1 - \frac{n_S}{\widehat{N}_S}\right) \frac{n_S}{n_S - 1} \sum_{j=1}^{n} I_S(j) \left\{ y_j - \frac{1}{n_S} \widehat{Y}_S \right\}^2 \tag{4}$$

These variance estimators (2) and (4) assume two very different survey designs. In (2), n individuals are sampled without replacement from the population comprised of the N_S values from the subpopulation with $N - N_S$ additional zeroes. In (4), n_S individuals are sampled without replacement from the subpopulation of N_S values. We discourage using (4) by warning against using the *if* and *in* options for subpopulation estimation because this variance estimator does not accurately measure the sample to sample variability of the subpopulation estimates for the survey design that was used to collect the data.

For survey data, there are only a few circumstances that necessitate the use of the *if* option. For example, if you suspected laboratory error for a certain set of measurements, then it might be proper to use the *if* option to omit these observations from the analysis.

Subpopulation estimates other than the total

To generalize the above results, note that the other point estimators—such as means, proportions, ratios, and regression coefficients—yield a linearized variance estimator based on one or more (equation-level) score variables. For example, the weighted sample estimation equations of a regression model for a given subpopulation (see (L1) from [SVY] **variance estimation**) is

$$\widehat{G}(\boldsymbol{\beta}_S) = \sum_{j=1}^{n} I_S(j) w_j S(\boldsymbol{\beta}_S; y_j, \mathbf{x}_j) = 0 \tag{5}$$

You can write $\widehat{G}(\boldsymbol{\beta}_S)$ as

$$\widehat{G}(\boldsymbol{\beta}_S) = \sum_{j=1}^{n} I_S(j) w_j \mathbf{d}_j$$

which is an estimator for the subpopulation total $G(\boldsymbol{\beta}_S)$, so its variance estimator can be computed using the design based variance estimator for a subpopulation total.

Subpopulation with replication methods

The above comparison between the variance estimator from the subpop() option and variance estimator from the *if* and *in* options is also true for the replication methods.

For the BRR method, the same number of replicates are produced with or without the subpop() option. The difference is how the replicate values are computed. Using the *if* and *in* options may cause an error since svy brr checks that there are two PSUs in every stratum within the restricted sample.

For the jackknife method, every PSU produces a replicate, even if it does not contain an observation within the subpopulation specified using the subpop() option. When the *if* and *in* options are used, only the PSUs that have a least one observation within the restricted sample will produce a replicate.

References

Cochran, W. G. 1977. *Sampling Techniques.* 3rd ed. New York: Wiley.

McDowell, A., A. Engel, J. T. Massey, and K. Maurer. 1981. Plan and operation of the Second National Health and Nutrition Examination Survey, 1976–1980. *Vital and Health Statistics* 15(1). Hyattsville, MD: National Center for Health Statistics.

Also See

Complementary:	[SVY] **svy: mean**, [SVY] **svy: ratio**, [SVY] **svy: total**
Background:	[SVY] **svy**, [SVY] **svyset**, [SVY] **survey**

Title

svy — The survey prefix command

Syntax

svy $\left[\text{vcetype} \right]$ $\left[, \text{svy\_options} \right]$: command

vcetype	description
SE	
linearized	Taylor linearized variance estimation
brr	BRR variance estimation; see [SVY] **svy brr**
jackknife	jackknife variance estimation; see [SVY] **svy jackknife**

Specifying a *vcetype* overrides the default from svyset.

svy_options	description
if/in	
subpop()	identify a subpopulation
SE	
brr_options	additional options allowed with BRR variance estimation; see [SVY] ***brr_options***
jackknife_options	additional options allowed with jackknife variance estimation; see [SVY] ***jackknife_options***
Reporting	
level(#)	set confidence level; default is level(95)
noheader	suppress the table header
nolegend	suppress the table legend
noadjust	do not adjust model Wald statistic
†noisily	display any output from *command*
†trace	trace the *command*

†noisily and trace are not shown in the dialog boxes for estimation commands.

svy requires that the survey-design variables be identified using svyset; see [SVY] **svyset**.

xi is allowed; see [R] **xi**.

See [U] **20 Estimation and postestimation commands** for additional capabilities of estimation commands.

Warning: Using *if* or *in* restrictions will not produce correct variance estimates for subpopulations in many cases. To compute estimates for a subpopulation, use the subpop() option. The full specification for subpop() is

subpop($\left[\text{varname} \right]$ $\left[\text{if} \right]$)

Description

svy fits statistical models for complex survey data. Typing

. svy: *command*

44

executes *command* while accounting for the survey settings identified by svyset.

command defines the estimation command to be executed. Not all estimation commands are supported by svy. See [SVY] **survey** for a list of Stata's estimation commands that are supported by svy. See [P] **program properties** for a discussion of what is required for svy to support an estimation command. The by prefix may not be part of *command*.

Options

_____⌐ if/in ⌐_____

subpop(*subpop*) specifies that estimates be computed for the single subpopulation identified by *subpop*, which is

$$\left[\,varname\,\right]\ \left[\,if\,\right]$$

Thus the subpopulation is defined by the observations for which *varname* $\neq 0$ that also meet the *if* conditions. Typically, *varname* $= 1$ defines the subpopulation, and *varname* $= 0$ indicates observations not belonging to the subpopulation. For observations whose subpopulation status is uncertain, *varname* should be set to a missing value; such observations are dropped from the estimation sample.

See [SVY] **subpopulation estimation** and [SVY] **estat**.

_____⌐ SE ⌐_____

brr_options are additional options that are allowed with BRR variance estimation specified by svy brr or as svyset using the vce(brr) option; see [SVY] ***brr_options***.

jackknife_options are additional options that are allowed with jackknife variance estimation specified by svy jackknife or as svyset using the vce(jackknife) option; see [SVY] ***jackknife_options***.

_____⌐ Reporting ⌐_____

level(*#*); see [SVY] **estimation options**.

noheader prevents the table header from being displayed. This option implies nolegend.

nolegend prevents the table legend identifying the subpopulations from being displayed.

noadjust specifies that the model Wald test be carried out as $W/k \sim F(k, d)$, where W is the Wald test statistic, k is the number of terms in the model excluding the constant term, $d =$ total number of sampled PSUs minus the total number of strata, and $F(k, d)$ is an F distribution with k numerator degrees of freedom and d denominator degrees of freedom. By default, an adjusted Wald test is conducted: $(d - k + 1)W/(kd) \sim F(k, d - k + 1)$.

See Korn and Graubard (1990) for a discussion of the Wald test and the adjustments thereof. Use of the noadjust option is not recommended.

The following option is usually available with svy for replaying estimation results but is not shown on all dialog boxes:

eform_option; see [SVY] ***eform_option***.

The following options are available with svy but are not shown on the dialog boxes:

noisily requests that any output from *command* be displayed.

trace causes a trace of the execution of *command* to be displayed.

Remarks

The svy prefix is designed for use with complex survey data. Typical survey-design characteristics include sampling weights, one or more stages of clustered sampling, and stratification. For a general discussion of various aspects of survey designs, including multistage designs, see [SVY] **svyset**.

Below we present an example of the effects of weights, clustering, and stratification. This is a typical case, but it is still dangerous to draw general rules from any single example. You could find particular analyses from other surveys that are counterexamples for each of the trends for standard errors exhibited here.

▷ Example 1: The effects of weights, clustering, and stratification

We use data from the Second National Health and Nutrition Examination Survey (NHANES II) (McDowell et al. 1981) as our example. This is a national survey, and the dataset has sampling weights, strata, and clustering. In this example, we will consider the estimation of the mean serum zinc level of all adults in the U.S.

First, consider a proper design-based analysis, which accounts for weighting, clustering, and stratification. Before we issue our svy estimation command, we set the weight, strata, and PSU identifier variables:

```
. use http://www.stata-press.com/data/r9/nhanes2f
. svyset psuid [pweight=finalwgt], strata(stratid)
      pweight: finalwgt
    Strata 1: stratid
       SU 1: psuid
      FPC 1: <zero>
```

We now estimate the mean using the proper design-based analysis:

```
. svy: mean zinc
(running mean on estimation sample)

Survey: Mean estimation

Number of strata =      31        Number of obs    =      9189
Number of PSUs   =      62        Population size  = 1.0e+08
                                  Design df        =        31
```

	Mean	Linearized Std. Err.	[95% Conf. Interval]	
zinc	87.18207	.4944827	86.17356	88.19057

If we ignore the survey design and use mean to estimate the mean, we get

```
. mean zinc

Mean estimation                   Number of obs    =      9189
```

	Mean	Std. Err.	[95% Conf. Interval]	
zinc	86.51518	.1510744	86.21904	86.81132

Note that the point estimate from the unweighted analysis is smaller by more than one standard error than the proper design-based estimate. In addition, note that design-based analysis produced a standard error that is 3.27 times larger than the standard error produced by our incorrect analysis.

◁

▷ Example 2: Halfway isn't enough–the importance of stratification and clustering

When some people analyze survey data, they say, "I know I have to use my survey weights, but I'll just ignore the stratification and clustering information." If we follow this strategy, we will obtain the proper design-based point estimates, but our standard errors, confidence intervals, and test statistics will usually be wrong.

To illustrate this, suppose that we used the svy: mean procedure with pweights only.

```
. svyset [pweight=finalwgt]

      pweight: finalwgt
          VCE: linearized
     Strata 1: <one>
        SU 1: <observations>
       FPC 1: <zero>

. svy: mean zinc
(running mean on estimation sample)

Survey: Mean estimation

Number of strata =        1        Number of obs    =     9189
Number of PSUs   =     9189        Population size  = 1.0e+08
                                   Design df        =     9188
```

		Linearized		
	Mean	Std. Err.	[95% Conf. Interval]	
zinc	87.18207	.1828747	86.82359	87.54054

This gives us the same point estimate as our design-based analysis, but the reported standard error is less than one-half the design-based standard error. If we only accounted for clustering and weights, and ignored stratification in NHANES II, we would obtain the following analysis:

```
. svyset psuid [pweight=finalwgt]

      pweight: finalwgt
          VCE: linearized
     Strata 1: <one>
        SU 1: psuid
       FPC 1: <zero>

. svy: mean zinc
(running mean on estimation sample)

Survey: Mean estimation

Number of strata =        1        Number of obs    =     9189
Number of PSUs   =        2        Population size  = 1.0e+08
                                   Design df        =        1
```

		Linearized		
	Mean	Std. Err.	[95% Conf. Interval]	
zinc	87.18207	.7426221	77.74616	96.61798

Here our standard error is about 50% larger than what we obtained in our proper design-based analysis.

◁

▷ Example 3

Let's look at a regression. We model zinc based on age, sex, race, and rural or urban residence. We compare a proper design-based analysis with an ordinary regression (which assumes i.i.d. error).

Here is our design-based analysis:

```
. svyset psuid [pweight=finalwgt], strata(stratid)
      pweight: finalwgt
          VCE: linearized
    Strata 1: stratid
       SU 1: psuid
      FPC 1: <zero>

. svy: regress zinc age age2 weight female black orace rural
(running regress on estimation sample)
Survey: Linear regression
```

Number of strata	=	31
Number of PSUs	=	62

Number of obs	= 9189
Population size	= 1.170e+08
Design df	= 31
F(7, 25)	= 62.50
Prob > F	= 0.0000
R-squared	= 0.0698

zinc	Coef.	Linearized Std. Err.	t	P>|t|	[95% Conf. Interval]	
age	-.1701161	.0844192	-2.02	0.053	-.3422901	.002058
age2	.0008744	.0008655	1.01	0.320	-.0008907	.0026396
weight	.0535225	.0139115	3.85	0.001	.0251499	.0818951
female	-6.134161	.4403625	-13.93	0.000	-7.032286	-5.236035
black	-2.881813	1.075958	-2.68	0.012	-5.076244	-.687381
orace	-4.118051	1.621121	-2.54	0.016	-7.424349	-.8117528
rural	-.5386327	.6171836	-0.87	0.390	-1.797387	.7201216
_cons	92.47495	2.228263	41.50	0.000	87.93038	97.01952

If we had improperly ignored our survey weights, stratification, and clustering (i.e., if we had used the usual Stata `regress` command), we would have obtained the following results:

```
. regress zinc age age2 weight female black orace rural
```

Source	SS	df	MS
Model	110417.827	7	15773.9753
Residual	1816535.3	9181	197.85811
Total	1926953.13	9188	209.724982

Number of obs	= 9189
F(7, 9181)	= 79.72
Prob > F	= 0.0000
R-squared	= 0.0573
Adj R-squared	= 0.0566
Root MSE	= 14.066

zinc	Coef.	Std. Err.	t	P>|t|	[95% Conf. Interval]	
age	-.090298	.0638452	-1.41	0.157	-.2154488	.0348528
age2	-.0000324	.0006788	-0.05	0.962	-.0013631	.0012983
weight	.0606481	.0105986	5.72	0.000	.0398725	.0814237
female	-5.021949	.3194705	-15.72	0.000	-5.648182	-4.395716
black	-2.311753	.5073536	-4.56	0.000	-3.306279	-1.317227
orace	-3.390879	1.060981	-3.20	0.001	-5.470637	-1.311121
rural	-.0966462	.3098948	-0.31	0.755	-.7041089	.5108166
_cons	89.49465	1.477528	60.57	0.000	86.59836	92.39093

The point estimates differ by 3–100%, and the standard errors for the proper designed-based analysis are 30–110% larger. The differences are not as dramatic as we saw with the estimation of the mean, but they are still substantial.

◁

Saved Results

svy saves in e():

Scalars

e(N)	number of observations	e(N_pop)	estimate of population size
e(N_sub)	subpopulation observations	e(N_subpop)	estimate of subpopulation size
e(N_strata)	number of strata	e(N_psu)	number of sampled PSUs
e(F)	model F statistic	e(k_eq)	number of equations
e(df_m)	model degrees of freedom	e(k_aux)	number of ancillary parameters
e(df_r)	variance degrees of freedom		

Macros

e(prefix)	svy	e(cmd)	same as e(cmdname) or e(vce)
e(cmdname)	command name from *command*	e(poststrata)	poststrata() variable
e(wtype)	weight type	e(postweight)	postweight() variable
e(wexp)	weight expression	e(vce)	*vcetype*
e(strata)	strata() variable	e(vcetype)	title for *vcetype*
e(psu)	psu() variable	e(mse)	mse or empty
e(fpc)	fpc() variable	e(subpop)	*subpop* from subpop()
e(title)	title in estimation output	e(adjust)	noadjust or empty

Matrices

e(b)	vector of estimates $\widehat{\beta}$
e(V)	variance estimates $\widehat{V}$
e(V_srs)	simple-random-sampling-without-replacement variance $\widehat{V}_{\mathrm{srswor}}$
e(V_srssub)	subpopulation simple-random-sampling-without-replacement variance $\widehat{V}_{\mathrm{srswor}}$ (only created when subpop() is specified)
e(V_srswr)	simple-random-sampling-with-replacement variance $\widehat{V}_{\mathrm{srswr}}$ (only created when fpc() option is svyset)
e(V_srssubwr)	subpopulation simple-random-sampling-with-replacement variance $\widehat{V}_{\mathrm{srswr}}$ (only created when subpop() is specified)
e(V_msp)	variance from misspecified model fit $\widehat{V}_{\mathrm{msp}}$

Functions

e(sample)	marks estimation sample

svy also carries forward most of the results already in e() from *command*, particularly e(predict).

Methods and Formulas

svy is implemented as an ado-file.

See [SVY] **variance estimation**, for all the details behind the point estimate and variance calculations made by svy.

Reference

McDowell, A., A. Engel, J. T. Massey, and K. Maurer. 1981. Plan and operation of the Second National Health and
Nutrition Examination Survey, 1976–1980. *Vital and Health Statistics* 15(1). Hyattsville, MD: National Center for
Health Statistics.

Also See

Complementary:	[SVY] **svy postestimation**,
	[SVY] **svy brr**, [SVY] **svy jackknife**, [SVY] **svyset**,
	[P] **_robust**
Background:	[U] **20 Estimation and postestimation commands**,
	[SVY] **estimation options**, [SVY] **poststratification**,
	[SVY] **subpopulation estimation**, [SVY] **variance estimation**,
	[P] **program properties**

Title

svy brr — Balanced repeated replication for survey data

Syntax

$$\left[\text{svy}\right] \text{ brr } \textit{exp\_list} \left[, \textit{ svy\_options brr\_options}\right] : \textit{command}$$

svy_options	description
if/in	
subpop()	identify a subpopulation
Reporting	
level(#)	set confidence level; default is level(95)
noheader	suppress the table header
nolegend	suppress the table legend
noadjust	do not adjust model Wald statistic

brr_options	description
Main	
hadamard(*matrix*)	Hadamard matrix
fay(#)	Fay's adjustment
Options	
saving(*filename*, ...)	save results to *filename*; save statistics in double precision; save results to *filename* every # replications
mse	use MSE formula for variance estimation
Reporting	
verbose	display the full table legend
nodots	suppress the replication dots
noisily	display any output from *command*
trace	trace the *command*
title(*text*)	use *text* as title for BRR results
Advanced	
nodrop	do not drop observations
reject(*exp*)	identify invalid results

weights are not allowed in *command*.

svy requires that the survey-design variables be identified using svyset; see [SVY] **svyset**.

xi is allowed; see [R] **xi**.

See [U] **20 Estimation and postestimation commands** for additional capabilities of estimation commands.

Warning: Using *if* or *in* restrictions will not produce correct variance estimates for subpopulations in many cases. To compute estimates for a subpopulation, use the subpop() option. The full specification for subpop() is

subpop($\left[\textit{varname}\right]$ $\left[\textit{if}\right]$)

exp_list contains	(*name*: *elist*)
	elist
	eexp
elist contains	*newvarname* = (*exp*)
	(*exp*)
eexp is	*specname*
	[*eqno*]*specname*
specname is	_b
	_b[]
	_se
	_se[]
eqno is	# #
	name

exp is a standard Stata expression; see [U] **13 Functions and expressions**.

Distinguish between [ ], which are to be typed, and [ ], which indicate optional arguments.

Description

svy brr performs balanced repeated replication (BRR) for complex survey data. Typing

. svy brr *exp_list*: *command*

executes *command* once for each replicate, using sampling weights that are adjusted according to the BRR methodology.

command defines the statistical command to be executed. Most Stata commands and user-written programs can be used with svy brr, as long as they follow standard Stata syntax, allow the *if* qualifier, and allow pweights and iweights; see [U] **11 Language syntax**. The by prefix may not be part of *command*.

exp_list specifies the statistics to be collected from the execution of *command*. *exp_list* is required unless *command* has the svyb program property, in which case *exp_list* defaults to _b; see [P] **program properties**.

Options

svy_options; see [SVY] **svy**.

___ Main _____

hadamard(*matrix*) specifies the Hadamard matrix to be used to determine which PSUs are chosen for each replicate.

fay(#) specifies Fay's adjustment. The sampling weight of the selected PSUs for a given replicate are multiplied by 2-#, where the sampling weight for the unselected PSUs is multiplied by #. fay(0) is the default and is equivalent to the original BRR method. fay(1) is not allowed.

saving(*filename*[, *suboptions*]) creates a Stata data file (.dta file) consisting of, for each statistic in *exp_list*, a variable containing the BRR replicates.

> double specifies that the results for each replication be stored as doubles, meaning 8-byte reals. By default, they are stored as floats, meaning 4-byte reals. This option may be used without the saving() option to compute the variance estimates using double precision.

> every(*#*) specifies that results be written to disk every #th replication. every() should only be specified in conjunction with saving() when *command* takes a long time for each replication. This will allow recovery of partial results should some other software crash your computer. See [P] **postfile**.

> replace indicates that *filename* be overwritten if it exists. This option is not shown on the dialog box.

mse indicates that svy brr compute the variance using deviations of the replicates from the observed value of the statistics based on the entire dataset. By default, svy brr computes the variance using deviations of the replicates from their mean.

verbose requests that the full table legend be displayed. By default, coefficients and standard errors are not displayed.

nodots suppresses display of the replication dots. By default, a single dot character is printed for each successful replication; however, 'x' is printed if *command* returns with an error, and 'e' is printed if one of the values in *exp_list* is missing.

noisily requests that any output from *command* be displayed. This option implies the nodots option.

trace causes a trace of the execution of *command* to be displayed. This option implies the noisily option.

title(*text*) specifies a title to be displayed above the table of BRR results; the default title is "BRR results".

nodrop prevents observations outside e(sample) and the *if* and *in* options from being dropped before the data are resampled.

reject(*exp*) identifies an expression that indicates when results should be rejected. When *exp* is true, the resulting values are reset to missing values.

Remarks

Balanced repeated replication (BRR) was first introduced by McCarthy (1966, 1969a, and 1969b) as a method of variance estimation for designs with two PSUs in every stratum. The BRR variance estimator tends to give more reasonable variance estimates for this design than the linearized variance estimator, which can result in large values and undesirably wide confidence intervals.

In BRR, the model is fitted multiple times, once for each of a balanced set of combinations where one PSU is dropped from each stratum. The variance is estimated using the resulting replicated point estimates. While the BRR method has since been generalized to include other designs, Stata's implementation of BRR requires two PSUs per stratum.

▷ Example 1: BRR replicate weight variables

The survey design for the NHANES II data (McDowell et al. 1981) is specifically suited to BRR; there are 2 PSUs in every stratum.

```
. use http://www.stata-press.com/data/r9/nhanes2
. svydes
      pweight: finalwgt
          VCE: linearized
    Strata 1: strata
       SU 1: psu
      FPC 1: <zero>
```

| | | | #Obs per PSU | | |
Strata strata	#PSUs	#Obs	min	mean	max
1	2	380	165	190.0	215
2	2	185	67	92.5	118
3	2	348	149	174.0	199
4	2	460	229	230.0	231
5	2	252	105	126.0	147
6	2	298	131	149.0	167
(output omitted)					
25	2	256	116	128.0	140
26	2	261	129	130.5	132
27	2	283	139	141.5	144
28	2	299	136	149.5	163
29	2	503	215	251.5	288
30	2	365	166	182.5	199
31	2	308	143	154.0	165
32	2	450	211	225.0	239
31	62	10351	67	167.0	288

In order to protect the privacy of survey participants, public survey datasets may contain replicate weight variables instead of variables that identify the PSUs and strata. These replicate weight variables are adjusted copies of the sampling weights. For BRR the sampling weights are adjusted for dropping one PSU from each stratum; see [SVY] **variance estimation** for more details.

Here is a privacy-conscious dataset equivalent to the one above; all the variable and values remain, except strata and psu are replaced with BRR replicate weight variables. Notice that the BRR replicate weight variables are already svyset, and the default method for variance estimation is vce(brr).

```
. use http://www.stata-press.com/data/r9/nhanes2brr
. svyset
      pweight: finalwgt
          VCE: brr
          MSE: off
    brrweight: brr_1 brr_2 brr_3 brr_4 brr_5 brr_6 brr_7 brr_8 brr_9 brr_10
               brr_11 brr_12 brr_13 brr_14 brr_15 brr_16 brr_17 brr_18 brr_19
               brr_20 brr_21 brr_22 brr_23 brr_24 brr_25 brr_26 brr_27 brr_28
               brr_29 brr_30 brr_31 brr_32
    Strata 1: <one>
       SU 1: <observations>
      FPC 1: <zero>
```

Suppose that we were interested in the population ratio of weight to height. Here we use total to estimate the population totals of weight and height and the svy brr prefix to estimate their ratio and variance; we use total instead of ratio (which is otherwise preferable in this case) to illustrate how to specify an *exp_list*.

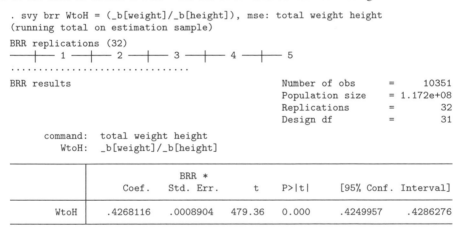

```
. svy brr WtoH = (_b[weight]/_b[height]): total weight height
(running total on estimation sample)

BRR replications (32)
———+— 1 ——+— 2 ——+— 3 ——+— 4 ——+— 5
...............................

BRR results                                Number of obs    =      10351
                                           Population size  = 1.172e+08
                                           Replications     =         32
                                           Design df        =         31

         command:  total weight height
            WtoH:  _b[weight]/_b[height]
```

		BRR				
	Coef.	Std. Err.	t	P>|t|	[95% Conf. Interval]	
WtoH	.4268116	.0008904	479.36	0.000	.4249957	.4286276

The mse option causes svy brr to use the MSE form of the BRR variance estimator. This variance estimator will tend to be larger than the previous due to the addition of the familiar squared bias term in the MSE; see [SVY] **varaince estimation** for further details. The header for the column of standard errors in the table of results is BRR * for the BRR variance estimator using the MSE formula.

```
. svy brr WtoH = (_b[weight]/_b[height]), mse: total weight height
(running total on estimation sample)

BRR replications (32)
———+— 1 ——+— 2 ——+— 3 ——+— 4 ——+— 5
...............................

BRR results                                Number of obs    =      10351
                                           Population size  = 1.172e+08
                                           Replications     =         32
                                           Design df        =         31

         command:  total weight height
            WtoH:  _b[weight]/_b[height]
```

		BRR *				
	Coef.	Std. Err.	t	P>|t|	[95% Conf. Interval]	
WtoH	.4268116	.0008904	479.36	0.000	.4249957	.4286276

The bias term is too small in this example to see any difference in the standard errors.

◁

▷ Example 2: Survey data without replicate weight variables

For survey data with the PSU and strata variables but no replication weights, svy brr can compute adjusted sampling weights within its replication loop. In this case, the hadamard() option must be supplied with the name of a Stata matrix that is a Hadamard matrix of appropriate order for the number of strata in your dataset (see the following technical note for a quick introduction to Hadamard matrices).

There are 31 strata in nhanes2.dta, so we need a Hadamard matrix of order 32 (or more) to use svy brr with this dataset. Here we use h32 (from the following technical note) to estimate the population ratio of weight to height using the BRR variance estimator.

```
. use http://www.stata-press.com/data/r9/nhanes2

. svy brr, hadamard(h32): ratio (WtoH: weight/height)
(running ratio on estimation sample)

BRR replications (32)
————+— 1 ——+— 2 ——+— 3 ——+— 4 ——+— 5
.............................

Survey: Ratio estimation

Number of strata =      31          Number of obs    =    10351
Number of PSUs   =      62          Population size  = 1.2e+08
                                    Replications     =       32
                                    Design df        =       31

        WtoH: weight/height
```

		BRR		
	Ratio	Std. Err.	[95% Conf. Interval]	
WtoH	.4268116	.0008904	.4249957	.4286276

◁

❑ Technical Note

A Hadamard matrix is a square matrix with r rows and columns that has the following property:

$$H'_r H_r = r I_r$$

where I_r is the identity matrix of order r. Generating a Hadamard matrix with order $r = 2^p$ is easily accomplished. Start with a Hadamard matrix of order 2 (H_2), and build your H_r by repeatedly applying Kronecker products with H_2. Here is the Stata code to generate the Hadamard matrix for the previous example.

```
matrix h2 = (-1, 1 \ 1, 1)
matrix h32 = h2
forvalues i = 1/4 {
        matrix h32 = h2 # h32
}
```

❑

Saved Results

svy brr saves in e(). In addition to the items documented in [SVY] **svy**, svy brr also saves the following:

Scalars
    e(N_reps)   number of replications

Macros
    e(cmdname)   command name from *command*
    e(cmd)   same as e(cmdname) or brr
    e(vce)   brr

Matrices
    e(brr_b)   BRR means
    e(V)   BRR variance estimates

When *exp_list* is _b, svy brr will also carry forward most of the results already in e() from *command*.

Methods and Formulas

svy brr is implemented as an ado-file.

See [SVY] **variance estimation** for details regarding BRR variance estimation.

References

Cochran, W. G. 1977. *Sampling Techniques*. 3rd ed. New York: Wiley.

Judkins, D. 1990. Fay's Method for Variance Estimation. *Journal of Official Statistics* 16: 25–45.

McCarthy, P. J. 1966. Replication: An Approach to the Analysis of Data from Complex Surveys. *Vital and Health Statistics* 2(14). Hyattsville, MD: National Center for Health Statistics.

——. 1969a. Pseudoreplication: Further Evaluation and Application of the Balanced Half-Sample Technique. *Vital and Health Statistics* 2(31). Hyattsville, MD: National Center for Health Statistics.

——. 1969b. Pseudoreplication: Half-Samples. *Review of the International Statistical Institute* 37: 239–264.

McDowell, A., A. Engel, J. T. Massey, and K. Maurer. 1981. Plan and operation of the Second National Health and Nutrition Examination Survey, 1976–1980. *Vital and Health Statistics* 15(1). Hyattsville, MD: National Center for Health Statistics.

Shao, J. and D. Tu 1995. *The Jackknife and Bootstrap*. New York: Springer.

Wolter, K. M. 1985. *Introduction to Variance Estimation*. New York: Springer.

Also See

Complementary:	[SVY] **svy postestimation**
Related:	[SVY] **svy jackknife**
Background:	[U] **20 Estimation and postestimation commands**,
	[SVY] **estimation options**, [SVY] **poststratification**,
	[SVY] **subpopulation estimation**, [SVY] **variance estimation**

Title

svy jackknife — Jackknife estimation for survey data

Syntax

svy jackknife *exp_list* [, *svy_options jackknife_options*] : *command*

svy_options	description
if/in	
subpop()	identify a subpopulation
Reporting	
level(#)	set confidence level; default is level(95)
noheader	suppress the table header
nolegend	suppress the table legend
noadjust	do not adjust model Wald statistic

jackknife_options	description
Main	
eclass	number of observations is in e(N)
rclass	number of observations is in r(N)
n(*exp*)	specify *exp* that evaluates to number of observations used
Options	
saving(*filename*, ...)	save results to *filename*; save statistics in double precision; save results to *filename* every # replications
keep	keep pseudovalues
mse	use MSE formula for variance estimation
Reporting	
verbose	display the full table legend
nodots	suppress the replication dots
noisily	display any output from *command*
trace	trace the *command*
title(*text*)	use *text* as title for jackknife results
Advanced	
nodrop	do not drop observations
reject(*exp*)	identify invalid results

weights are not allowed in *command*.

svy requires that the survey-design variables be identified using svyset; see [SVY] **svyset**.

xi is allowed; see [R] **xi**.

See [U] **20 Estimation and postestimation commands** for additional capabilities of estimation commands.

Warning: Using *if* or *in* restrictions will not produce correct variance estimates for subpopulations in many cases. To compute estimates for a subpopulation, use the subpop() option. The full specification for subpop() is

subpop([*varname*] [*if*])

58

exp_list contains	(*name*: *elist*)
	elist
	eexp
elist contains	*newvarname* = (*exp*)
	(*exp*)
eexp is	*specname*
	[*eqno*]*specname*
specname is	_b
	_b[]
	_se
	_se[]
eqno is	# #
	name

exp is a standard Stata expression; see [U] **13 Functions and expressions**.

Distinguish between [], which are to be typed, and [], which indicate optional arguments.

Description

svy jackknife performs jackknife estimation for complex survey data. Typing

    . svy jackknife *exp_list*: *command*

executes *command* once for each primary sampling unit (PSU) in the dataset, leaving the associated PSU out of the calculations that make up *exp_list*.

command defines the statistical command to be executed. Most Stata commands and user-written programs can be used with svy jackknife, as long as they follow standard Stata syntax, allow the *if* qualifier, and allow pweights and iweights; see [U] **11 Language syntax**. The by prefix may not be part of *command*.

exp_list specifies the statistics to be collected from the execution of *command*. *exp_list* is required unless *command* has the svyj program property, in which case *exp_list* defaults to _b; see [P] **program properties**.

Options

svy_options; see [SVY] **svy**.

┌─ Main ───

eclass, rclass, and n(*exp*) specify where *command* saves the number of observations on which it based the calculated results. We strongly advise you to specify one of these options.

  eclass specifies that *command* saves the number of observations in e(N).

  rclass specifies that *command* saves the number of observations in r(N).

  n(*exp*) allows you to specify an expression that evaluates to the number of observations used. Specifying n(r(N)) is equivalent to specifying option rclass. Specifying n(e(N)) is equivalent to specifying option eclass. If *command* saves the number of observations in r(N1), specify n(r(N1)).

If you don't specify any of these options, `svy jackknife` will assume `eclass` or `rclass` depending upon which of `e(N)` and `r(N)` is not missing (in that order). If both `e(N)` and `r(N)` are missing, `svy jackknife` assumes that all observations in the dataset contribute to the calculated result. If that assumption is incorrect, the reported standard errors will be incorrect. For instance, say that you specify

    . svy jackknife coef=_b[x2]: myreg y x1 x2 x3

where `myreg` uses `e(n)` instead of `e(N)` to identify the number of observations used in calculations. Further assume that observation 42 in the dataset has `x3` equal to missing. The 42nd observation plays no role in obtaining the estimates, but `svy jackknife` has no way of knowing that and will use the wrong N. If, on the other hand, you specify

    . svy jackknife coef=_b[x2], n(e(n)): myreg y x1 x2 x3

`svy jackknife` will notice that observation 42 plays no role. Option `n(e(n))` is specified because `myreg` is an estimation command, but it saves the number of observations used in `e(n)` (instead of the standard `e(N)`). When `svy jackknife` runs the regression omitting the 42nd observation, `svy jackknife` will observe that `e(n)` has the same value as when `svy jackknife` previously ran the regression using all the observations. Thus `svy jackknife` will know that `myreg` did not use the observation.

> ___ Options ___

saving(*filename*[, *suboptions*]) creates a Stata data file (.dta file) consisting of, for each statistic in *exp_list*, a variable containing the jackknife replicates.

   double specifies that the results for each replication be stored as `doubles`, meaning 8-byte reals. By default, they are stored as `floats`, meaning 4-byte reals. This option may be used without the `saving()` option to compute the variance estimates using double precision.

   every(*#*) specifies that results be written to disk every *#*th replication. `every()` should only be specified in conjunction with `saving()` when *command* takes a long time for each replication. This will allow recovery of partial results should some other software crash your computer. See [P] **postfile**.

   replace indicates that *filename* be overwritten if it exists. This option is not shown on the dialog box.

keep specifies that new variables be added to the dataset containing the pseudovalues of the requested statistics. For instance, if you typed

    . svy jackknife coef=_b[x2], eclass keep: regress y x1 x2 x3

new variable `coef` would be added to the dataset containing the pseudovalues for `_b[x2]`. Let b be defined as the value of `_b[x2]` when all observations are used to fit the model, and let $b(j)$ be the value when the jth observation is omitted. The pseudovalues are defined as

$$\text{pseudovalue}_j = N \times \{b - b(j)\} + b(j)$$

where N is the number of observations used to produce b.

mse specifies that `svy jackknife` compute the variance using deviations of the replicates from the observed value of the statistics based on the entire dataset. By default, `svy jackknife` computes the variance using deviations of the pseudovalues from their mean.

_____| More options |_____

verbose requests that the full table legend be displayed. By default, coefficients and standard errors are not displayed.

nodots suppresses display of the replication dots. By default, a single dot character is printed for each successful replication; however, 'x' is printed if *command* returns with an error, 'e' is printed if one of the values in *exp_list* is missing, and 'n' is printed if the sample size is not correct.

noisily requests that any output from *command* be displayed. This option implies the nodots option.

trace causes a trace of the execution of *command* to be displayed. This option implies the noisily option.

title(*text*) specifies a title to be displayed above the table of jackknife results; the default title is "Jackknife results".

_____| Advanced |_____

nodrop prevents observations outside e(sample) and the *if* and *in* options from being dropped before the data is resampled.

reject(*exp*) identifies an expression that indicates when results should be rejected. When *exp* is true, the resulting values are reset to missing values.

Remarks

The jackknife is

1. an alternative, first-order unbiased estimator for a statistic;

2. a data-dependent way to calculate the standard error of the statistic and to obtain significance levels and confidence intervals; and

3. a way of producing measures called pseudovalues for each observation, reflecting the observation's influence on the overall statistic.

The idea behind the simplest form of the jackknife—the one implemented in [R] **jackknife**—is to repeatedly calculate the statistic in question, each time omitting just one of the dataset's observations. Assume that our statistic of interest is the sample mean. Let y_j be the jth observation of our data on some measurement y, where $j = 1, \ldots, N$ and N is the sample size. If $\overline{y}$ is the sample mean of y using the entire dataset and $\overline{y}_{(j)}$ is the mean when the jth observation is omitted, then

$$\overline{y} = \frac{(N-1)\,\overline{y}_{(j)} + y_j}{N}$$

Solving for y_j, we obtain

$$y_j = N\,\overline{y} - (N-1)\,\overline{y}_{(j)}$$

These are the pseudovalues that svy: jackknife calculates. To move this discussion beyond the sample mean, let $\widehat{\theta}$ be the value of our statistic (not necessarily the sample mean) using the entire dataset, and let $\widehat{\theta}_{(j)}$ be the computed value of our statistic with the jth observation omitted. The pseudovalue for the jth observation is

$$\widehat{\theta}_j^* = N\,\widehat{\theta} - (N-1)\,\widehat{\theta}_{(j)}$$

The mean of the pseudovalues is the alternative, first-order unbiased estimator mentioned above, and the standard error of the mean of the pseudovalues is an estimator for the standard error of $\widehat{\theta}$ (Tukey 1958).

When the jackknife is applied to survey data, PSUs are omitted instead of observations, N is the number of PSUs instead of the sample size, and the sampling weights are adjusted due to omitting PSUs; see [SVY] **variance estimation** for further details.

Due to privacy concerns, many public survey datasets contains jackknife replication weight variables instead of variables containing information on the PSUs and strata. These replication weight variables are the adjusted sampling weights, and there is one replication weight variable for each omitted PSU.

▷ Example 1: Jackknife with information on PSUs and strata

Suppose that we were interested in a measure of association between the weight and height of individuals in our population. To measure the association, we will use the slope estimate from a linear regression of `weight` on `height`. We also use `svy jackknife` to estimate the variance of the slope.

```
. use http://www.stata-press.com/data/r9/nhanes2
. svyset
        pweight: finalwgt
            VCE: linearized
      Strata 1: strata
         SU 1: psu
        FPC 1: <zero>
. svy jackknife slope = _b[height]: regress weight height
(running regress on estimation sample)
Jackknife replications (62)
———+— 1 —+— 2 —+— 3 —+— 4 —+— 5
.................................................. 50
............
Linear regression
Number of strata    =      31       Number of obs       =      10351
Number of PSUs      =      62       Population size     = 1.172e+08
                                    Replications        =         62
                                    Design df           =         31

       command:  regress weight height
         slope:  _b[height]
          n():  e(N)
```

	Coef.	Jackknife Std. Err.	t	P>|t|	[95% Conf. Interval]
slope	.8014753	.0160281	50.00	0.000	.7687858 .8341648

◁

▷ Example 2: Jackknife replicate weight variables

The `nhanes2jknife.dta` dataset is a privacy-conscious equivalent to `nhanes2.dta`; all the variable and values remain, except `strata` and `psu` are replaced with jackknife replicate weight variables. Notice that the replicate weight variables are already `svyset`, and the default method for variance estimation is `vce(jackknife)`.

```
. use http://www.stata-press.com/data/r9/nhanes2jknife

. svyset
      pweight: finalwgt
          VCE: jackknife
          MSE: off
    jkrweight: jkw_1 jkw_2 jkw_3 jkw_4 jkw_5 jkw_6 jkw_7 jkw_8 jkw_9 jkw_10
               jkw_11 jkw_12 jkw_13 jkw_14 jkw_15 jkw_16 jkw_17 jkw_18 jkw_19
               jkw_20 jkw_21 jkw_22 jkw_23 jkw_24 jkw_25 jkw_26 jkw_27 jkw_28
               jkw_29 jkw_30 jkw_31 jkw_32 jkw_33 jkw_34 jkw_35 jkw_36 jkw_37
               jkw_38 jkw_39 jkw_40 jkw_41 jkw_42 jkw_43 jkw_44 jkw_45 jkw_46
               jkw_47 jkw_48 jkw_49 jkw_50 jkw_51 jkw_52 jkw_53 jkw_54 jkw_55
               jkw_56 jkw_57 jkw_58 jkw_59 jkw_60 jkw_61 jkw_62
    Strata 1: <one>
       SU 1: <observations>
      FPC 1: <zero>
```

Here we perform the same analysis as the previous example, using jackknife replication weights.

```
. svy jackknife slope = _b[height], nodots: regress weight height
Linear regression
Number of strata    =         31        Number of obs      =       10351
                                        Population size     = 1.172e+08
                                        Replications        =          62
                                        Design df           =          31

      command:  regress weight height
        slope:  _b[height]
```

		Jackknife			
	Coef.	Std. Err.	t	P>|t|	[95% Conf. Interval]
slope	.8014753	.0160281	50.00	0.000	.7687858 .8341648

The `mse` option causes `svy jackknife` to use the MSE form of the jackknife variance estimator. This variance estimator will tend to be larger than the previous due to the addition of the familiar squared bias term in the MSE; see [SVY] **varaince estimation** for further details. The header for the column of standard errors in the table of results is "Jknife *" for the jackknife variance estimator, which uses the MSE formula.

```
. svy jackknife slope = _b[height], mse nodots: regress weight height
Linear regression
Number of strata    =         31        Number of obs      =       10351
                                        Population size     = 1.172e+08
                                        Replications        =          62
                                        Design df           =          31

      command:  regress weight height
        slope:  _b[height]
```

		Jknife *			
	Coef.	Std. Err.	t	P>|t|	[95% Conf. Interval]
slope	.8014753	.0160284	50.00	0.000	.7687852 .8341654

◁

Saved Results

svy jackknife saves in e(). In addition to the items documented in [SVY] **svy**, svy jackknife also saves the following:

Scalars
    e(N_reps)   number of replications
Macros
    e(cmdname)   command name from *command*
    e(cmd)   same as e(cmdname) or jackknife
    e(vce)   jackknife
Matrices
    e(jk_b)   jackknife means
    e(V)   jackknife variance estimates

When *exp_list* is _b, svy jackknife will also carry forward most of the results already in e() from *command*.

Methods and Formulas

svy jackknife is implemented as an ado-file.

See [SVY] **variance estimation** for details on the jackknife variance estimator.

References

Cochran, W. G. 1977. *Sampling Techniques*. 3rd ed. New York: Wiley.

Shao, J. and D. Tu 1995. *The Jackknife and Bootstrap*. New York: Springer.

Tukey, J. W. 1958. Bias and confidence in not-quite large samples. Abstract in *Annals of Mathematical Statistics* 29: 614.

Wolter, K. M. 1985. *Introduction to Variance Estimation*. New York: Springer.

Also See

Complementary:	[SVY] **svy postestimation**
Related:	[R] **jackknife**;
	[SVY] **svy brr**
Background:	[U] **20 Estimation and postestimation commands**,
	[SVY] **estimation options**, [SVY] **poststratification**,
	[SVY] **subpopulation estimation**, [SVY] **variance estimation**

Title

svy postestimation — Postestimation tools for svy

Description

The following postestimation commands are available for svy:

command	description
estat	postestimation statistics for survey data
estimates	cataloging estimation results
lincom	point estimates, standard errors, testing, and inference for linear combinations of coefficients
mfx	marginal effects or elasticities
nlcom	point estimates, standard errors, testing, and inference for nonlinear combinations of coefficients
predict	predictions, residuals, influence statistics, and other diagnostic measures
predictnl	point estimates, standard errors, testing, and inference for generalized predictions
suest	seemingly unrelated estimation
test	Wald tests for simple and composite linear hypotheses
testnl	Wald tests of nonlinear hypotheses

See [SVY] **estat**.

See the corresponding entries in the *Stata Base Reference Manual* for details.

Syntax for predict

The syntax of `predict` (and even if `predict` is allowed) following `svy` depends upon the command used with `svy`. Specifically, `predict` is not allowed after `svy: mean`, `svy: proportion`, `svy: ratio`, `svy: tabulate`, or `svy: total`.

Remarks

▷ Example 1: Linear and nonlinear combinations

`lincom` will display an estimate of a linear combination of parameters, along with its standard error, a confidence interval, and a test that the linear combination is zero. `nlcom` will do likewise for nonlinear combinations of parameters.

`lincom` is commonly used to compute the differences of two subpopulation means. For example, suppose that we wish to estimate the difference of zinc levels in white males versus black males. First, we estimate the subpopulation means.

```
. use http://www.stata-press.com/data/r9/nhanes2
. generate male = (sex == 1)
```

```
. svy, subpop(male): mean zinc, over(race)
(running mean on estimation sample)

Survey: Mean estimation

Number of strata =        31          Number of obs    =      9202
Number of PSUs   =        62          Population size  = 1.0e+08
                                      Subpop. no. obs  =      4375
                                      Subpop. size     = 5.0e+07
                                      Design df        =        31

              White: race = White
              Black: race = Black
              Other: race = Other
```

	Over	Mean	Linearized Std. Err.	[95% Conf. Interval]	
zinc					
	White	91.15725	.541625	90.0526	92.2619
	Black	88.269	1.208336	85.80458	90.73342
	Other	85.54716	2.608974	80.22612	90.8682

Then we run `lincom`.

```
. lincom [zinc]White - [zinc]Black
 ( 1)  [zinc]White - [zinc]Black = 0
```

	Coef.	Std. Err.	t	P>|t|	[95% Conf. Interval]	
(1)	2.888249	1.103999	2.62	0.014	.6366288	5.139868

Note that the t statistic and its p-value give a survey analysis equivalent of a two-sample t test.

Suppose that we instead wanted to estimate the ratio of the means for white males and black males.

```
. nlcom ratio: [zinc]White / [zinc]Black
     ratio:  [zinc]White / [zinc]Black
```

	Coef.	Std. Err.	t	P>|t|	[95% Conf. Interval]	
ratio	1.032721	.0129093	80.00	0.000	1.006392	1.05905

`lincom` and `nlcom` can be used after any of the estimation commands described in [SVY] **survey**. `lincom` can, for example, display results as odds ratios after `svy: logit` and can be used to compute odds ratios for one covariate group relative to another. `nlcom` can display odds ratios, as well, and additionally allows more general nonlinear combinations of the parameters. See [R] **lincom** and [R] **nlcom** for full details.

Finally, note that `lincom` and `nlcom` operate on the estimated parameters only. To obtain estimates and inference for functions of the parameters and of the data, such as for an exponentiated linear predictor or a predicted probability of success from a logit model, we use `predictnl`; see [R] **predictnl**.

◁

▷ Example 2: Quadratic terms

The following is a linear regression of loglead (log of blood lead) on age, female (indicator), black (indicator), orace (indicator for "race = other"), and three of the four region indicators.

```
. use http://www.stata-press.com/data/r9/nhanes2e

. generate age2 = age*age

. svy: regress loglead age age2 female black orace region2-region4
(running regress on estimation sample)

Survey: Linear regression

Number of strata   =        31          Number of obs      =       4948
Number of PSUs     =        62          Population size    = 1.129e+08
                                        Design df          =         31
                                        F(  8,    24)      =     159.01
                                        Prob > F           =     0.0000
                                        R-squared          =     0.2380
```

loglead	Coef.	Linearized Std. Err.	t	P>|t|	[95% Conf. Interval]	
age	.0161682	.0027549	5.87	0.000	.0105495	.0217869
age2	-.00015	.0000295	-5.09	0.000	-.0002102	-.0000899
female	-.3638347	.0109888	-33.11	0.000	-.3862465	-.3414229
black	.1787038	.031122	5.74	0.000	.1152301	.2421775
orace	-.0515824	.0397199	-1.30	0.204	-.1325916	.0294268
region2	-.0234192	.0383221	-0.61	0.546	-.1015776	.0547392
region3	-.1658648	.0552766	-3.00	0.005	-.2786022	-.0531273
region4	-.0360316	.0381581	-0.94	0.352	-.1138555	.0417922
_cons	2.434106	.0620728	39.21	0.000	2.307508	2.560705

Since our model includes a quadratic in the age variable, the peak of loglead with respect to age will occur at -_b[age]/(2*_b[age2]), which we can estimate, along with its standard error, by using nlcom.

```
. nlcom peakloglead: -_b[age]/(2*_b[age2])
peakloglead:  -_b[age]/(2*_b[age2])
```

loglead	Coef.	Std. Err.	t	P>|t|	[95% Conf. Interval]	
peakloglead	53.87632	2.05564	26.21	0.000	49.68381	58.06882

We can use testnl to test that the peak of loglead in the population is 55 years.

```
. testnl -_b[age]/(2*_b[age2]) = 55
 (1)  -_b[age]/(2*_b[age2]) = 55
             F(1, 31) =        0.30
             Prob > F =        0.5885
```

These data do not reject our theory. Note that we could jointly test this hypothesis with others and testnl will adjust the degrees of freedom just as test does with survey results.

◁

▷ Example 3: Nonlinear predictions and their standard errors

Given that we modeled the natural log of the lead measurement, we can use `predictnl` to compute the exponentiated linear prediction (in the original units of the `lead` variable), along with its standard error.

```
. predictnl leadhat = exp(xb()), se(leadhat_se)
. list lead leadhat leadhat_se age age2 in 1/10, abbrev(10)
```

	lead	leadhat	leadhat_se	age	age2
1.	13	10.12563	.6622425	41	1681
2.	20	10.22228	1.147574	64	4096
3.	13	10.11586	1.208863	67	4489
4.	17	17.33201	2.100061	68	4624
5.	20	12.34221	1.256082	60	3600
6.	13	9.079463	.5203859	24	576
7.	29	16.62117	.8260598	32	1024
8.	22	10.15426	1.188794	66	4356
9.	10	9.826402	1.320044	73	5329
10.	15	14.61032	1.699342	66	4356

◁

▷ Example 4: Multiple-hypothesis testing

Joint-hypothesis tests can be performed after `svy` estimation commands using the `test` command. Here we perform a linear regression of `loglead` (log of blood lead).

```
. use http://www.stata-press.com/data/r9/nhanes2e
. svy: regress loglead age female black orace region2-region4
(running regress on estimation sample)
```

Survey: Linear regression

Number of strata	=	31	Number of obs	=	4948
Number of PSUs	=	62	Population size	=	1.129e+08
			Design df	=	31
			F(7, 25)	=	186.18
			Prob > F	=	0.0000
			R-squared	=	0.2321

loglead	Coef.	Linearized Std. Err.	t	P>|t|	[95% Conf. Interval]	
age	.0027842	.0004318	6.45	0.000	.0019036	.0036649
female	-.3645445	.0110947	-32.86	0.000	-.3871724	-.3419167
black	.1783735	.0321995	5.54	0.000	.1127022	.2440447
orace	-.0473781	.0383677	-1.23	0.226	-.1256295	.0308733
region2	-.0242082	.0384767	-0.63	0.534	-.1026819	.0542655
region3	-.1646067	.0549628	-2.99	0.005	-.276704	-.0525094
region4	-.0361289	.0377054	-0.96	0.345	-.1130296	.0407717
_cons	2.696084	.0236895	113.81	0.000	2.647769	2.744399

We can use `test` to test the joint significance of the region dummies: `region1` is the Northeast, `region2` is the Midwest, `region3` is the South, and `region4` is the West. We test the hypothesis that `region2` = 0, `region3` = 0, and `region4` = 0.

```
. test region2 region3 region4
```

Adjusted Wald test

```
( 1)  region2 = 0
( 2)  region3 = 0
( 3)  region4 = 0

      F(  3,    29) =    2.97
           Prob > F =    0.0480
```

The `nosvyadjust` option on `test` produces an unadjusted Wald test.

```
. test region2 region3 region4, nosvyadjust
```

Unadjusted Wald test

```
( 1)  region2 = 0
( 2)  region3 = 0
( 3)  region4 = 0

      F(  3,    31) =    3.18
           Prob > F =    0.0377
```

Note that for one-dimensional tests, the adjusted and unadjusted F statistics are identical, but they differ for higher dimensional tests. Using the `nosvyadjust` option is not recommended since the unadjusted F statistic can produce extremely anticonservative p-values (i.e., p-values that are too small) when the variance degrees of freedom (equal to the number of sampled PSUs minus the number of strata) are not large relative to the dimension of the test.

Bonferroni-adjusted p-values can also be computed:

```
. test region2 region3 region4, mtest(bonferroni)
```

Adjusted Wald test

```
( 1)  region2 = 0
( 2)  region3 = 0
( 3)  region4 = 0
```

	F(df,29)	df	p
(1)	0.40	1	1.0000 #
(2)	8.97	1	0.0161 #
(3)	0.92	1	1.0000 #
all	2.97	3	0.0480

 # Bonferroni adjusted p-values

See Korn and Graubard (1990) for a discussion of these three different procedures for conducting joint-hypothesis tests.

◁

References

Beale, E. M. L. 1960. Confidence regions in nonlinear estimation. *Journal of the Royal Statistical Society*, Series B 22: 41–88.

Cochran, W. G. 1977. *Sampling Techniques*. 3rd ed. New York: Wiley.

Eltinge, J. L. and W. M. Sribney. 1996. svy5: Estimates of linear combinations and hypothesis tests for survey data. *Stata Technical Bulletin* 31: 31–42. Reprinted in *Stata Technical Bulletin Reprints*, vol. 6, pp. 246–259.

Gourieroux, C. and A. Monfort. 1995/1998. *Statistics and Econometric Models*. 2 Volumes. Cambridge: Cambridge University Press.

Holm, C. 1979. A simple sequentially rejective multiple test procedure. *Scandinavian Journal of Statistics* 6: 65–70.

Judge, G. G., W. E. Griffiths, R. C., Hill, H. Lütkepohl, and T.-C. Lee. 1985. *The Theory and Practice of Econometrics.* 2nd ed. New York: Wiley.

Korn, E. L., and B. I. Graubard. 1990. Simultaneous testing of regression coefficients with complex survey data: Use of Bonferroni *t* statistics. *The American Statistician* 44: 270–276.

Weesie, J. 1999. sg100: Two-stage linear constrained estimation. *Stata Technical Bulletin* 47: 24–30. Reprinted in *Stata Technical Bulletin Reprints*, vol. 8, pp. 217–225.

Also See

Complementary:	[SVY] **svy**, [SVY] **svy brr**, [SVY] **svy jackknife**, [SVY] **estat**,
	[R] **estimates**, [R] **lincom**, [R] **mfx**, [R] **nlcom**, [R] **predict**,
	[R] **predictnl**, [R] **suest**, [R] **test**, [R] **testnl**
Background:	[U] **13.5 Accessing coefficients and standard errors**,
	[U] **20 Estimation and postestimation commands**

Title

svy: heckman — Heckman selection model for survey data

Syntax

Basic syntax

svy: heckman *depvar* [*indepvars*] , **sel**ect([$depvar_s$ =] $varlist_s$)

Full syntax

svy [*vcetype*] [, *svy_options*] : **heckman** *depvar* [*indepvars*] [*if*] [*in*] ,

select([$depvar_s$ =] $varlist_s$ [, **off**set(*varname*) **noc**onstant]) [*options*]

vcetype	description
SE	
linearized	Taylor linearized variance estimation
brr	BRR variance estimation; see [SVY] **svy brr**
jackknife	jackknife variance estimation; see [SVY] **svy jackknife**

Specifying a *vcetype* overrides the default from svyset.

svy_options	description
if/in	
subpop()	identify a subpopulation
SE	
brr_options	additional options allowed with BRR variance estimation; see [SVY] ***brr_options***
jackknife_options	additional options allowed with jackknife variance estimation; see [SVY] ***jackknife_options***
Reporting	
level(#)	set confidence level; default is level(95)
noheader	suppress the table header
nolegend	suppress the table legend
noadjust	do not adjust model Wald statistic

svy requires that the survey-design variables be identified using svyset; see [SVY] **svyset**.

xi is allowed; see [R] **xi**.

See [U] **20 Estimation and postestimation commands** for additional capabilities of estimation commands.

Warning: Using *if* or *in* restrictions will not produce correct variance estimates for subpopulations in many cases. To compute estimates for a subpopulation, use the subpop() option. The full specification for subpop() is

subpop([*varname*] [*if*])

options	description
Model	
*`select()`**	specify selection equation dependent and independent variables; whether to have constant term and offset variable
`noconstant`	suppress the constant term
`offset(varname)`	include *varname* in model with coefficient constrained to 1
`constraints(constraints)`	apply specified linear constraints
Reporting	
`nshazard(newvar)`	generate nonselection hazard variable
`mills(newvar)`	synonym for `nshazard()`
Max options	
maximize_options	control the maximization process; seldom used

*`select()` is required. The full specification is
  `select( [ depvar`s` = ] varlist`s` [ , offset(varname) noconstant ] )`

Description

`svy: heckman` fits regression models with selection for complex survey data; see [R] **heckman** for a description of this model involving nonsurvey data and [SVY] **svy: heckprob** for probit regression with selection for survey data.

Options

svy_options; see [SVY] **svy**.

  Model

`select(...)` specifies the variables and options for the selection equation. It is an integral part of specifying a selection model and is required. The selection equation should contain at least one variable that is not in the outcome equation.

If *depvar*`s` is specified, it should be coded as 0 or 1, 0 indicating an observation not selected and 1 indicating a selected observation. If *depvar*`s` is not specified, observations for which *depvar* is not missing are assumed to be selected, and those for which *depvar* is missing are assumed to be not selected.

`noconstant`, `offset(varname)`, `constraints(constraints)`; see [SVY] **estimation options**.

  Reporting

`nshazard(newvar)` and `mills(newvar)` are synonyms; either will create a new variable containing the nonselection hazard—what Heckman (1979) refers to as the inverse of the Mills' ratio—from the selection equation. The nonselection hazard is computed from the estimated parameters of the selection equation.

___| Max options |_____

maximize_options: <u>dif</u>ficult, <u>techni</u>que(*algorithm_spec*), <u>iter</u>ate(*#*), [<u>no</u>]<u>log</u>, <u>tr</u>ace, <u>grad</u>ient, <u>showstep</u>, <u>hess</u>ian, <u>shownr</u>tolerance, <u>tol</u>erance(*#*), <u>ltol</u>erance(*#*), <u>gtol</u>erance(*#*), <u>nrtol</u>erance(*#*), <u>nonrtol</u>erance, <u>from</u>(*init_specs*); see [R] **maximize**. These options are seldom used. If the maximization is taking a long time, you may wish to specify the log option to view the iteration log. The log option implies svy's noisily option; see [SVY] **svy**.

Remarks

The Heckman selection model (Gronau 1974, Lewis 1974, Heckman 1976) assumes that there exists an underlying regression relationship

$$y_j = \mathbf{x}_j \boldsymbol{\beta} + u_{1j} \qquad\qquad regression \ equation$$

The dependent variable, however, is not always observed. Rather, the dependent variable for observation j is observed if

$$\mathbf{z}_j \boldsymbol{\gamma} + u_{2j} > 0 \qquad\qquad selection \ equation$$

where

$$u_1 \sim N(0, \sigma)$$
$$u_2 \sim N(0, 1)$$
$$\mathrm{corr}(u_1, u_2) = \rho$$

When $\rho \neq 0$, standard regression techniques applied to the first equation yield biased results. heckman provides consistent, asymptotically efficient estimates for all the parameters in such models.

In one classic example, the first equation describes the wages of women. Women choose whether to work, and thus, from our point of view as researchers, whether we observe their wages in our data. If women made this decision randomly, we could ignore the fact that not all wages are observed and use ordinary regression to fit a wage model. Such an assumption of random participation, however, is unlikely to be true; women who would have low wages may be unlikely to choose to work, and thus the sample of observed wages is biased upward. In the jargon of economics, women choose not to work when their personal reservation wage is greater than the wage offered by employers. Thus women who choose not to work might have even higher offer wages than those who do work—they may have high offer wages, but they have even higher reservation wages. We could tell a story that competency is related to wages, but competency is rewarded more at home than in the labor force.

In any case, in this problem—which is the paradigm for most such problems—a solution can be found if there are some variables that strongly affect the chances for observation (the reservation wage) but not the outcome under study (the offer wage). Such a variable might be the number of children in the home. (Theoretically, we do not need such identifying variables, but without them, we depend on functional form to identify the model. It would be difficult for anyone to take such results seriously since the functional-form assumptions have no firm basis in theory.)

▷ Example 1

Use svy: heckman to fit the Heckman selection model for survey data just as you would use heckman for nonsurvey data. To illustrate, we fit a Heckman model using a stratified SRS version of the (fictional) dataset from [R] **heckman**. We assume that the hourly wage is a function of education and age, and the chance of working (the chance of the wage being observed) is a function of marital status, number of children at home, and (implicitly) the wage (via the inclusion of age and education, which we think determine the wage):

```
. use http://www.stata-press.com/data/r9/svywomenwk
. svyset
      pweight: sampwgt
          VCE: linearized
    Strata 1: strid
        SU 1: <observations>
       FPC 1: strsize
. svy: heckman wage educ age, select(married children educ age)
(running heckman on estimation sample)
```

Survey: Heckman selection model
(regression model with sample selection)

Number of strata	=	20		Number of obs	=	2000
Number of PSUs	=	2000		Population size	=	385286
				Design df	=	1980
				F(2, 1979)	=	274.40
				Prob > F	=	0.0000

	Coef.	Linearized Std. Err.	t	P>|t|	[95% Conf.	Interval]
wage						
education	1.00327	.0514924	19.48	0.000	.9022849	1.104255
age	.2140314	.0203281	10.53	0.000	.1741647	.2538982
_cons	.2460718	1.063382	0.23	0.817	-1.839394	2.331537
select						
married	.4380077	.0453573	9.66	0.000	.3490547	.5269607
children	.4360262	.0166384	26.21	0.000	.4033956	.4686569
education	.0587589	.0065437	8.98	0.000	.0459257	.0715922
age	.0362149	.0025498	14.20	0.000	.0312143	.0412155
_cons	-2.507642	.1175987	-21.32	0.000	-2.738273	-2.277012
/athrho	.8881946	.1050786	8.45	0.000	.6821183	1.094271
/lnsigma	1.801681	.0287921	62.58	0.000	1.745215	1.858147
rho	.7105009	.0520337			.5928948	.7984317
sigma	6.059825	.1744752			5.727132	6.411844
lambda	4.305511	.415245			3.491148	5.119874

◁

Saved Results

svy: heckman saves in e(). In addition to the items documented in [SVY] **svy**, svy: heckman also saves the following:

Scalars

e(N_cens)	number of censored observations
e(sigma)	σ
e(rho)	ρ
e(lambda)	$\lambda = \rho\sigma$

Macros

e(cmd)	heckman
e(depvar)	name of dependent variable
e(offset#)	offset for equation #
e(crittype)	log pseudolikelihood
e(predict)	program used to implement predict

Methods and Formulas

svy: heckman is implemented as an ado-file.

Regression estimates using the nonselection hazard (Heckman 1979) provide starting values for maximum likelihood estimation. For this model, nonselection refers to a choice made by the sampled individual; this is separate from the sampling performed by the survey design.

The regression equation is

$$y_j = \mathbf{x}_j\boldsymbol{\beta} + \text{offset}_j^{\beta} + u_{1j}$$

The selection equation is

$$\mathbf{z}_j\boldsymbol{\gamma} + \text{offset}_j^{\gamma} + u_{2j} > 0$$

where

$$u_1 \sim N(0, \sigma)$$
$$u_2 \sim N(0, 1)$$
$$\text{corr}(u_1, u_2) = \rho$$

The log pseudolikelihood is

$$\ln L = \sum_{j \in S} w_j \ln \Phi \left\{ \frac{\mathbf{z}_j\boldsymbol{\gamma} + \text{offset}_j^{\gamma} + (y_j - \mathbf{x}_j\boldsymbol{\beta} - \text{offset}_j^{\beta})\rho/\sigma}{\sqrt{1 - \rho^2}} \right\}$$
$$- \sum_{j \in S} \frac{w_j}{2} \left\{ \left(\frac{y_j - \mathbf{x}_j\boldsymbol{\beta} - \text{offset}_j^{\beta}}{\sigma} \right)^2 + \ln(2\pi\sigma^2) \right\}$$
$$+ \sum_{j \notin S} w_j \ln \Phi(-\mathbf{z}_j\boldsymbol{\gamma} - \text{offset}_j^{\gamma})$$

where S is the set of observations for which y_j is observed, $\Phi()$ is the standard cumulative normal, and w_j is a sampling weight. The equation-level scores used in the linearized variance estimator are derived by taking partial derivatives of the log pseudolikelihood; see [SVY] **variance estimation**.

In the maximum pseudolikelihood estimation, $\ln \sigma$ and atanh ρ are directly estimated instead of σ and ρ, where

$$\text{atanh } \rho = \frac{1}{2} \ln\left(\frac{1+\rho}{1-\rho}\right)$$

References

Greene, W. H. 2003. *Econometric Analysis*. 5th ed. Upper Saddle River, NJ: Prentice Hall.

Gronau, R. 1974. Wage comparisons: A selectivity bias. *Journal of Political Economy* 82: 1119–1155.

Heckman, J. 1976. The common structure of statistical models of truncation, sample selection, and limited dependent variables and a simple estimator for such models. *The Annals of Economic and Social Measurement* 5: 475–492.

——. 1979. Sample selection bias as a specification error. *Econometrica* 47: 153–161.

Johnston, J. and J. DiNardo. 1997. *Econometric Methods*. 4th ed. New York: McGraw–Hill.

Lewis, H. 1974. Comments on selectivity biases in wage comparisons. *Journal of Political Economy* 82: 1119–1155.

Also See

Title

svy: heckman postestimation — Postestimation tools for svy: heckman

Description

The following postestimation commands are available for svy: heckman:

command	description
estat	postestimation statistics for survey data
estimates	cataloging estimation results
lincom	point estimates, standard errors, testing, and inference for linear combinations of coefficients
mfx	marginal effects or elasticities
nlcom	point estimates, standard errors, testing, and inference for nonlinear combinations of coefficients
predict	predictions, residuals, influence statistics, and other diagnostic measures
predictnl	point estimates, standard errors, testing, and inference for generalized predictions
suest	seemingly unrelated estimation
test	Wald tests for simple and composite linear hypotheses
testnl	Wald tests of nonlinear hypotheses

See [SVY] **estat**.

See the corresponding entries in the *Stata Base Reference Manual* for details.

(*Continued on next page*)

Syntax for predict

predict [*type*] *newvarname* [*if*] [*in*] [, *statistic* <u>nooff</u>set]

predict [*type*] { *stub** | *newvar*_{reg} *newvar*_{sel} *newvar*_{athrho} *newvar*_{lnsigma} }

    [*if*] [*in*] , <u>sc</u>ores

statistic	description
xb	fitted values for regression equation, $\mathbf{x}_j\beta$; the default
stdp	standard error of the linear prediction
<u>xbsel</u>	linear prediction for selection equation, $\mathbf{z}_j\gamma$
<u>stdpsel</u>	standard error of the linear prediction for selection equation
<u>pr</u>(*a,b*)	$P(y_j \mid a < y_j < b)$
e(*a,b*)	$E(y_j \mid a < y_j < b)$
<u>ystar</u>(*a,b*)	$E(y_j^*)$, $y_j^* = \max\{a, \min(y_j, b)\}$
<u>yc</u>ond	$E(y_j \mid y_j \text{ observed})$
<u>yexp</u>ected	$E(y_j^*)$, y_j taken to be 0 where unobserved
<u>nsh</u>azard	nonselection hazard (also called the inverse of Mills' ratio)
<u>mill</u>s	synonym for nshazard
<u>psel</u>	$P(y_j \text{ observed})$

These statistics are available both in and out of sample; type predict ... if e(sample) ... if wanted only for the estimation sample.

where *a* and *b* may be numbers of variables; *a* missing ($a \geq .$) means $-\infty$, and *b* missing ($b \geq .$) means $+\infty$; see [U] **12.2.1 Missing values.**

Options for predict

xb, the default, calculates the linear prediction $\mathbf{x}_j\beta$.

stdp calculates the standard error of the prediction. It can be thought of as the standard error of the predicted expected value or mean for the observation's covariate pattern. This is also referred to as the standard error of the fitted value.

xbsel calculates the linear prediction for the selection equation.

stdpsel calculates the standard error of the linear prediction for the selection equation.

pr(*a,b*) calculates $\Pr(a < \mathbf{x}_j\beta + u_1 < b)$, the probability that $y_j \mid \mathbf{x}_j$ would be observed in the interval (a, b).

    a and *b* may be specified as numbers or variable names; *lb* and *ub* are variable names; pr(20,30) calculates $\Pr(20 < \mathbf{x}_j\beta + u_1 < 30)$; pr(*lb,ub*) calculates $\Pr(lb < \mathbf{x}_j\beta + u_1 < ub)$; and pr(20,*ub*) calculates $\Pr(20 < \mathbf{x}_j\beta + u_1 < ub)$.

    a missing ($a \geq .$) means $-\infty$; pr(.,30) calculates $\Pr(-\infty < \mathbf{x}_j\beta + u_j < 30)$; pr(*lb*,30) calculates $\Pr(-\infty < \mathbf{x}_j\beta + u_j < 30)$ in observations for which $lb \geq .$ and calculates $\Pr(lb < \mathbf{x}_j\beta + u_j < 30)$ elsewhere.

    b missing ($b \geq .$) means $+\infty$; pr(20,.) calculates $\Pr(+\infty > \mathbf{x}_j\beta + u_j > 20)$; pr(20,*ub*) calculates $\Pr(+\infty > \mathbf{x}_j\beta + u_j > 20)$ in observations for which $ub \geq .$ and calculates $\Pr(20 < \mathbf{x}_j\beta + u_j < ub)$ elsewhere.

e(a,b) calculates $E(\mathbf{x}_j\boldsymbol{\beta} + u_1 \mid a < \mathbf{x}_j\boldsymbol{\beta} + u_1 < b)$, the expected value of $y_j|\mathbf{x}_j$ conditional on $y_j|\mathbf{x}_j$ being in the interval (a, b), meaning that $y_j|\mathbf{x}_j$ is censored. a and b are specified as they are for pr().

ystar(a,b) calculates $E(y_j^*)$, where $y_j^* = a$ if $\mathbf{x}_j\boldsymbol{\beta} + u_j \leq a$, $y_j^* = b$ if $\mathbf{x}_j\boldsymbol{\beta} + u_j \geq b$, and $y_j^* = \mathbf{x}_j\boldsymbol{\beta} + u_j$ otherwise, meaning that y_j^* is truncated. a and b are specified as they are for pr().

ycond calculates the expected value of the dependent variable conditional on the dependent variable being observed, i.e., selected; $E(y_j \mid y_j$ observed$)$.

yexpected calculates the expected value of the dependent variable (y_j^*), where that value is taken to be 0 when it is expected to be unobserved; $y_j^* = \Pr(y_j$ observed$)E(y_j \mid y_j$ observed$)$.

The assumption of 0 is valid for many cases where nonselection implies nonparticipation (e.g., unobserved wage levels, insurance claims from those who are uninsured, etc.) but may be inappropriate for some problems (e.g., unobserved disease incidence).

nshazard and mills are synonyms; either calculates the nonselection hazard—what Heckman (1979) refers to as the inverse of the Mills' ratio—from the selection equation.

psel calculates the probability of selection (or being observed):
$$P(y_j \text{ observed}) = \Pr(\mathbf{z}_j\boldsymbol{\gamma} + u_{2j} > 0).$$

nooffset is relevant if you specified offset() when you fitted the model. It modifies the calculations made by predict so that they ignore the offset variable; the linear prediction is treated as $\mathbf{x}_j\boldsymbol{\beta}$ rather than as $\mathbf{x}_j\boldsymbol{\beta} + \text{offset}_j$.

scores calculates equation-level score variables.

The first new variable will contain $\partial \ln L / \partial (\mathbf{x}_j\boldsymbol{\beta})$.

The second new variable will contain $\partial \ln L / \partial (\mathbf{z}_j\boldsymbol{\gamma})$.

The third new variable will contain $\partial \ln L / \partial (\operatorname{atanh} \rho)$.

The fourth new variable will contain $\partial \ln L / \partial (\ln \sigma)$.

Remarks

▷ Example 1

Continuing with our example from [SVY] **svy: heckman**, we use predict to compute the Mills' ratio for each observation and save the values in the new variable mills.

```
. predict mills, mills
```

(Continued on next page)

Here we use `estat effects` to report the table of design effects for the estimated coefficients.

```
. estat effects
```

wage	Coef.	Linearized Std. Err.	Deff	Deft
wage				
education	1.00327	.0514924	1.01761	1.00614
age	.2140314	.0203281	1.00698	1.00088
_cons	.2460718	1.063382	1.005	.999893
select				
married	.4380077	.0453573	.981616	.988191
children	.4360262	.0166384	1.01108	1.00291
education	.0587589	.0065437	.998364	.996585
age	.0362149	.0025498	.935353	.964623
_cons	-2.507642	.1175987	.852307	.920805
/athrho	.8881946	.1050786	1.02171	1.00817
/lnsigma	1.801681	.0287921	1.04238	1.01832

Note: Weights must represent population totals for deff to be correct when using an FPC; however, deft is invariant to the scale of weights.

◁

Methods and Formulas

All postestimation commands listed above are implemented as ado-files.

Also See

Complementary:	[SVY] **svy: heckman**, [SVY] **estat**;
	[R] **estimates**, [R] **lincom**, [R] **mfx**, [R] **nlcom**, [R] **predict**,
	[R] **predictnl**, [R] **suest**, [R] **test**, [R] **testnl**
Background:	[U] **13.5 Accessing coefficients and standard errors**,
	[U] **20 Estimation and postestimation commands**

Title

svy: heckprob — Probit regression with selection for survey data

Syntax

Basic syntax

svy: heckprob *depvar* [*indepvars*] , <u>sel</u>ect([*depvar_s* =] *varlist_s*)

svy: heckprob *depvar* $\left[\textit{indepvars}\right]$, <u>sel</u>ect($\left[\textit{depvar}_s =\right]$ *varlist$_s$*)

Full syntax

svy $\left[\textit{vcetype}\right]$ $\left[$, *svy_options* $\right]$: heckprob *depvar* $\left[\textit{indepvars}\right]$ $\left[\textit{if}\right]$ $\left[\textit{in}\right]$,

      <u>sel</u>ect($\left[\textit{depvar}_s =\right]$ *varlist$_s$* $\left[$, <u>off</u>set(*varname*) <u>noc</u>onstant $\right]$) $\left[\textit{options}\right]$

vcetype	description
SE	
<u>linea</u>rized	Taylor linearized variance estimation
brr	BRR variance estimation; see [SVY] **svy brr**
<u>jackknife</u>	jackknife variance estimation; see [SVY] **svy jackknife**

Specifying a *vcetype* overrides the default from svyset.

svy_options	description
if/in	
<u>subp</u>op()	identify a subpopulation
SE	
brr_options	additional options allowed with BRR variance estimation; see [SVY] *brr_options*
jackknife_options	additional options allowed with jackknife variance estimation; see [SVY] *jackknife_options*
Reporting	
<u>level</u>(#)	set confidence level; default is level(95)
<u>nohe</u>ader	suppress the table header
<u>nole</u>gend	suppress the table legend
<u>noadj</u>ust	do not adjust model Wald statistic

svy requires that the survey-design variables be identified using svyset; see [SVY] **svyset**.

xi is allowed; see [R] **xi**.

See [U] **20 Estimation and postestimation commands** for additional capabilities of estimation commands.

Warning: Using *if* or *in* restrictions will not produce correct variance estimates for subpopulations in many cases. To compute estimates for a subpopulation, use the subpop() option. The full specification for subpop() is

      <u>subp</u>op($\left[\textit{varname}\right]$ $\left[\textit{if}\right]$)

options	description
Model	
<u>sel</u>ect()	specify selection equation dependent and independent variables; whether to have constant term and offset variable
<u>nocon</u>stant	suppress the constant term
<u>off</u>set(*varname*)	include *varname* in model with coefficient constrained to 1
<u>constr</u>aints(*constraints*)	apply specified linear constraints
Max options	
maximize_options	control the maximization process; seldom used

*<u>sel</u>ect() is required. The full specification is

    <u>sel</u>ect([*depvar$_s$* =] *varlist$_s$* [, <u>off</u>set(*varname*) <u>noc</u>onstant])

Description

svy: heckprob fits probit models with selection for complex survey data; see [R] **heckprob** for a description of this model involving nonsurvey data and [SVY] **svy: heckman** for regression models with selection for complex survey data.

Options

svy_options; see [SVY] **svy**.

    ⌐ Model ⌐

select(...) specifies the variables and options for the selection equation. It is an integral part of specifying a selection model and is required. The selection equation should contain at least one variable that is not in the outcome equation.

If *depvar$_s$* is specified, it should be coded as 0 or 1, 0 indicating an observation not selected and 1 indicating a selected observation. If *depvar$_s$* is not specified, observations for which *depvar* is not missing are assumed to be selected, and those for which *depvar* is missing are assumed to be not selected.

noconstant, offset(*varname*), constraints(*constraints*); see [SVY] **estimation options**.

    ⌐ Max options ⌐

maximize_options: <u>diff</u>icult, <u>tech</u>nique(*algorithm_spec*), <u>iter</u>ate(*#*), [<u>no</u>]<u>log</u>, <u>tr</u>ace, gradient, showstep, <u>hess</u>ian, shownrtolerance, <u>tol</u>erance(*#*), <u>ltol</u>erance(*#*), <u>gtol</u>erance(*#*), <u>nrtol</u>erance(*#*), nonrtolerance, from(*init_specs*); see [R] **maximize**. These options are seldom used. If the maximization is taking a long time, you may wish to specify the log option to view the iteration log. The log option implies svy's noisily option; see [SVY] **svy**.

Remarks

The probit model with sample selection (Van de Ven and Van Pragg 1981) assumes that there exists an underlying relationship

$$y_j^* = \mathbf{x}_j \boldsymbol{\beta} + u_{1j} \qquad\qquad latent\ \ equation$$

such that we observe only the binary outcome

$$y_j^{\text{probit}} = (y_j^* > 0) \qquad\qquad probit\ \ equation$$

The dependent variable, however, is not always observed. Rather, the dependent variable for observation j is observed if

$$y_j^{\text{select}} = (\mathbf{z}_j \boldsymbol{\gamma} + u_{2j} > 0) \qquad\qquad selection\ \ equation$$

where

$$u_1 \sim N(0,1)$$
$$u_2 \sim N(0,1)$$
$$\text{corr}(u_1, u_2) = \rho$$

When $\rho \neq 0$, standard probit techniques applied to the first equation yield biased results. heckprob provides consistent, asymptotically efficient estimates for all the parameters in such models.

In order for the model to be well-identified, the selection equation should have at least one variable that is not in the probit equation. Otherwise, the model is identified only by functional form, and the coefficients have no structural interpretation.

▷ Example 1

Using the data from Pindyck and Rubinfeld (1998), we fit the same model as in [R] **heckprob** but use svy jackknife: heckprob to get jackknife standard errors for survey data. Note that we first use svyset to specify an SRS design. Note also that, without sampling weights, the estimated population size equals the sample size.

```
. use http://www.stata-press.com/data/r9/school
. svyset _n
      pweight: <none>
          VCE: linearized
    Strata 1: <one>
        SU 1: <observations>
       FPC 1: <zero>
```

(Continued on next page)

```
. svy jackknife, nodots: heckprob private years logptax, select(vote=years
> loginc logptax)

Survey: Probit model with sample selection

Number of strata   =        1          Number of obs      =        95
Number of PSUs     =       95          Population size    =        95
                                       Replications       =        95
                                       Design df          =        94
                                       F(   2,      93)    =      0.84
                                       Prob > F           =    0.4331
```

		Jackknife				
	Coef.	Std. Err.	t	P>|t|	[95% Conf. Interval]	
private						
years	-.1142597	.1160176	-0.98	0.327	-.3446154	.1160961
logptax	.3516098	1.059409	0.33	0.741	-1.751872	2.455091
_cons	-2.780665	6.887293	-0.40	0.687	-16.45555	10.89422
vote						
years	-.0167511	.0202698	-0.83	0.411	-.0569973	.0234951
loginc	.9923024	.4594099	2.16	0.033	.0801333	1.904471
logptax	-1.278783	.5726627	-2.23	0.028	-2.415818	-.1417478
_cons	-.545821	5.159821	-0.11	0.916	-10.79077	9.699125
/athrho	-.8663156	2.963252	-0.29	0.771	-6.749921	5.01729

◁

Saved Results

svy: heckprob saves in e(). In addition to the items documented in [SVY] **svy**, svy: heckprob also saves the following:

Scalars
    e(N_cens)   number of censored observations
    e(rho) ρ

Macros
    e(cmd)   heckprob
    e(depvar)   name of dependent variable
    e(offset#)   offset for equation #
    e(crittype)   log pseudolikelihood
    e(predict)   program used to implement predict

Methods and Formulas

svy: heckprob is implemented as an ado-file.

The probit equation is

$$y_j = (\mathbf{x}_j \boldsymbol{\beta} + \text{offset}_j^{\beta} + u_{1j} > 0)$$

The selection equation is

$$\mathbf{z}_j \boldsymbol{\gamma} + \text{offset}_j^{\gamma} + u_{2j} > 0$$

where

$$u_1 \sim N(0,1)$$
$$u_2 \sim N(0,1)$$
$$\text{corr}(u_1, u_2) = \rho$$

The log pseudolikelihood is

$$\ln L = \sum_{\substack{j \in S \\ y_j \neq 0}} w_j \ln \left\{ \Phi_2 \left(\mathbf{x}_j \boldsymbol{\beta} + \text{offset}_j^{\beta}, \mathbf{z}_j \boldsymbol{\gamma} + \text{offset}_j^{\gamma}, \rho \right) \right\}$$

$$+ \sum_{\substack{j \in S \\ y_j = 0}} w_j \ln \left\{ \Phi_2 \left(-\mathbf{x}_j \boldsymbol{\beta} + \text{offset}_j^{\beta}, \mathbf{z}_j \boldsymbol{\gamma} + \text{offset}_j^{\gamma}, -\rho \right) \right\}$$

$$+ \sum_{j \notin S} w_j \ln \left\{ 1 - \Phi \left(\mathbf{z}_j \boldsymbol{\gamma} + \text{offset}_j^{\gamma} \right) \right\}$$

where S is the set of observations for which y_j is observed, $\Phi_2(a, b; \rho) = \Pr(x \leq a, y \leq b)$ where (x, y) is bivariate normal with mean vector $\mathbf{0}$ and correlation matrix

$$\begin{pmatrix} 1 & \rho \\ \rho & 1 \end{pmatrix}$$

$\Phi()$ is the standard cumulative normal, and w_j is a sampling weight. The equation-level scores used in the linearized variance estimator are derived by taking partial derivatives of the log pseudolikelihood; see [SVY] **variance estimation**.

In the maximum pseudolikelihood estimation, atanh ρ is directly estimated instead of ρ.

$$\text{atanh}\, \rho = \frac{1}{2} \ln \left(\frac{1 + \rho}{1 - \rho} \right)$$

References

Greene, W. H. 2003. *Econometric Analysis*. 5th ed. Upper Saddle River, NJ: Prentice Hall.

Heckman, J. 1979. Sample selection bias as a specification error. *Econometrica* 47: 153–161.

Pindyck, R. and D. Rubinfeld. 1998. *Econometric Models and Economic Forecasts*. 4th ed. New York: McGraw–Hill.

Van de Ven, W. P. M. M. and B. M. S. Van Pragg. 1981. The demand for deductibles in private health insurance: A probit model with sample selection. *Journal of Econometrics* 17: 229–252.

Also See

Complementary:	[SVY] **svy: heckprob postestimation**
Related:	[R] **heckprob**;
	[SVY] **svy: heckman**, [SVY] **svy: probit**
Background:	[U] **20 Estimation and postestimation commands**,
	[SVY] **estimation options**, [SVY] **poststratification**,
	[SVY] **subpopulation estimation**, [SVY] **svy**, [SVY] **variance estimation**,
	[R] **maximize**

Title

svy: heckprob postestimation — Postestimation tools for svy: heckprob

Description

The following postestimation commands are available for `svy: heckprob`:

command	description
estat	postestimation statistics for survey data
estimates	cataloging estimation results
lincom	point estimates, standard errors, testing, and inference for linear combinations of coefficients
mfx	marginal effects or elasticities
nlcom	point estimates, standard errors, testing, and inference for nonlinear combinations of coefficients
predict	predictions, residuals, influence statistics, and other diagnostic measures
predictnl	point estimates, standard errors, testing, and inference for generalized predictions
suest	seemingly unrelated estimation
test	Wald tests for simple and composite linear hypotheses
testnl	Wald tests of nonlinear hypotheses

See [SVY] **estat**.

See the corresponding entries in the *Stata Base Reference Manual* for details.

(*Continued on next page*)

Syntax for predict

> predict [*type*] *newvarname* [*if*] [*in*] [, *statistic* <u>nooff</u>set]

> predict [*type*] { *stub** | *newvar*$_{reg}$ *newvar*$_{sel}$ *newvar*$_{athrho}$ } [*if*] [*in*] , <u>sc</u>ores

statistic	description
<u>pmargin</u>	$\Phi(\mathbf{x}_j\boldsymbol{\beta})$, success probability; the default
p11	$\Phi_2(\mathbf{x}_j\boldsymbol{\beta}, \mathbf{z}_j\boldsymbol{\gamma}, \rho)$, predicted probability $\Pr(y_j^{\text{probit}} = 1, y_j^{\text{select}} = 1)$
p10	$\Phi_2(\mathbf{x}_j\boldsymbol{\beta}, -\mathbf{z}_j\boldsymbol{\gamma}, -\rho)$, predicted probability $\Pr(y_j^{\text{probit}} = 1, y_j^{\text{select}} = 0)$
p01	$\Phi_2(-\mathbf{x}_j\boldsymbol{\beta}, \mathbf{z}_j\boldsymbol{\gamma}, -\rho)$, predicted probability $\Pr(y_j^{\text{probit}} = 0, y_j^{\text{select}} = 1)$
p00	$\Phi_2(-\mathbf{x}_j\boldsymbol{\beta}, -\mathbf{z}_j\boldsymbol{\gamma}, \rho)$, predicted probability $\Pr(y_j^{\text{probit}} = 0, y_j^{\text{select}} = 0)$
<u>psel</u>	$\Phi(\mathbf{z}_j\boldsymbol{\gamma})$, selection probability
<u>pcond</u>	$\Phi_2(\mathbf{x}_j\boldsymbol{\beta}, \mathbf{z}_j\boldsymbol{\gamma}, \rho)/\Phi(\mathbf{z}_j\boldsymbol{\gamma})$, probability of success conditional on selection
xb	linear prediction, $\mathbf{x}_j\boldsymbol{\beta}$
stdp	standard error of the linear prediction
<u>xbsel</u>	linear prediction for selection equation, $\mathbf{z}_j\boldsymbol{\gamma}$
stdpsel	standard error of the linear prediction for selection equation

These statistics are available both in and out of sample; type predict ... if e(sample) ... if wanted only for the estimation sample.

where $\Phi()$ is the standard normal distribution function and $\Phi_2()$ is the bivariate normal distribution function.

Options for predict

pmargin, the default, calculates the univariate (marginal) predicted probability of success $\Pr(y_j^{\text{probit}} = 1)$.

p11 calculates the bivariate predicted probability $\Pr(y_j^{\text{probit}} = 1, y_j^{\text{select}} = 1)$.

p10 calculates the bivariate predicted probability $\Pr(y_j^{\text{probit}} = 1, y_j^{\text{select}} = 0)$.

p01 calculates the bivariate predicted probability $\Pr(y_j^{\text{probit}} = 0, y_j^{\text{select}} = 1)$.

p00 calculates the bivariate predicted probability $\Pr(y_j^{\text{probit}} = 0, y_j^{\text{select}} = 0)$.

psel calculates the univariate (marginal) predicted probability of selection $\Pr(y_j^{\text{select}} = 1)$.

pcond calculates the conditional (on selection) predicted probability of success $\Pr(y_j^{\text{probit}} = 1, y_j^{\text{select}} = 1)/\Pr(y_j^{\text{select}} = 1)$.

xb calculates the probit linear prediction $\mathbf{x}_j\boldsymbol{\beta}$.

stdp calculates the standard error of the prediction. It can be thought of as the standard error of the predicted expected value or mean for the observation's covariate pattern. This is also referred to as the standard error of the fitted value.

xbsel calculates the linear prediction $\mathbf{z}_j\boldsymbol{\gamma}$ for the selection equation.

stdpsel calculates the standard error of the linear prediction for the selection equation.

nooffset is relevant if you specified offset() when you fitted the model. It modifies the calculations made by predict so that they ignore the offset variable; the linear prediction is treated as $\mathbf{x}_j\boldsymbol{\beta}$ rather than as $\mathbf{x}_j\boldsymbol{\beta} + \text{offset}_j$.

scores calculates equation-level score variables.

The first new variable will contain $\partial \ln L / \partial(\mathbf{x}_j\boldsymbol{\beta})$.

The second new variable will contain $\partial \ln L / \partial(\mathbf{z}_j\boldsymbol{\gamma})$.

The third new variable will contain $\partial \ln L / \partial(\text{atanh}\,\rho)$.

Remarks

▷ Example 1

Continuing with our example from [SVY] **svy: heckprob**, we use predict to compute the marginal probability that a child will attend a private school for each covariate pattern in the dataset and save the values in the new variable p_private.

```
predict p_private, pmargin
```

◁

Methods and Formulas

All postestimation commands listed above are implemented as ado-files.

Also See

Complementary:	[SVY] **svy: heckprob**, [SVY] **estat**;
	[R] **estimates**, [R] **lincom**, [R] **mfx**, [R] **nlcom**, [R] **predict**,
	[R] **predictnl**, [R] **suest**, [R] **test**, [R] **testnl**
Background:	[U] **13.5 Accessing coefficients and standard errors**,
	[U] **20 Estimation and postestimation commands**

Title

svy: intreg — Interval regression for survey data

Syntax

svy [*vcetype*] [, *svy_options*] : intreg *depvar*$_1$ *depvar*$_2$ [*indepvars*] [*if*] [*in*] [, *options*]

vcetype	description
SE	
<u>linear</u>ized	Taylor linearized variance estimation
brr	BRR variance estimation; see [SVY] **svy brr**
<u>jack</u>knife	jackknife variance estimation; see [SVY] **svy jackknife**

Specifying a *vcetype* overrides the default from svyset.

svy_options	description
if/in	
<u>subpop</u>()	identify a subpopulation
SE	
brr_options	additional options allowed with BRR variance estimation; see [SVY] *brr_options*
jackknife_options	additional options allowed with jackknife variance estimation; see [SVY] *jackknife_options*
Reporting	
<u>level</u>(#)	set confidence level; default is level(95)
<u>nohe</u>ader	suppress the table header
<u>nole</u>gend	suppress the table legend
<u>noadj</u>ust	do not adjust model Wald statistic

svy requires that the survey-design variables be identified using svyset; see [SVY] **svyset**.

xi is allowed; see [R] **xi**.

See [U] **20 Estimation and postestimation commands** for additional capabilities of estimation commands.

Warning: Using *if* or *in* restrictions will not produce correct variance estimates for subpopulations in many cases. To compute estimates for a subpopulation, use the subpop() option. The full specification for subpop() is

<u>subpop</u>([*varname*] [*if*])

(Continued on next page)

options	description
Model	
<u>noc</u>onstant	suppress the constant term
<u>het</u>(*varlist*[, <u>noconst</u>ant])	independent variables to model the variance; use noconstant to suppress constant term
<u>off</u>set(*varname*)	include *varname* in model with coefficient constrained to 1
<u>constr</u>aints(*constraints*)	apply specified linear constraints
Max options	
maximize_options	control the maximization process; seldom used

Description

svy: intreg fits interval and censored linear models for complex survey data; see [R] **intreg** for a description of this model involving nonsurvey data, [SVY] **svy: regress** for linear regression (uncensored) for survey data.

depvar$_1$ and *depvar*$_2$ should have the following form:

type of data		*depvar*$_1$	*depvar*$_2$
point data	$a = [a, a]$	a	a
interval data	$[a, b]$	a	b
left-censored data	$(-\infty, b]$	.	b
right-censored data	$[a, +\infty)$	a	.

Hence, svy: intreg can be used to fit tobit models or models with more general types of censoring for complex survey data. See [R] **intreg** for more information.

Options

svy_options; see [SVY] **svy**.

⌐ **Model** ⌐

noconstant; see [SVY] **estimation options**.

het(*varlist* [, noconstant]) specifies that *varlist* be included in the specification of the conditional variance. This *varlist* enters the variance specification collectively as multiplicative heteroskedasticity.

offset(*varname*), constraints(*constraints*); see [SVY] **estimation options**.

⌐ **Max options** ⌐

maximize_options: <u>diff</u>icult, <u>tech</u>nique(*algorithm_spec*), <u>iter</u>ate(*#*), [<u>no</u>]<u>log</u>, <u>trace</u>, <u>grad</u>ient, <u>show</u>step, <u>hess</u>ian, <u>shownr</u>tolerance, <u>tol</u>erance(*#*), <u>ltol</u>erance(*#*), <u>gtol</u>erance(*#*), <u>nrtol</u>erance(*#*), <u>nonr</u>tolerance, from(*init_specs*); see [R] **maximize**. These options are seldom used. If the maximization is taking a long time, you may wish to specify the log option to view the iteration log. The log option implies svy's noisily option; see [SVY] **svy**.

Remarks

svy: intreg can fit models for data where each observation represents interval data, left-censored data, right-censored data, or point data. Regardless of the type of observation, the data should be stored in the dataset as interval data; that is, two dependent variables, *depvar*$_1$ and *depvar*$_2$, are used to hold the endpoints of the interval. If the data are left-censored, the lower endpoint is $-\infty$ and is represented by a missing value '.' or an extended missing value '.a, .b, ..., .z' in *depvar*$_1$. If the data are right-censored, the upper endpoint is $+\infty$ and is represented by a missing value '.' (or an extended missing value) in *depvar*$_2$. Point data are represented by the two endpoints being equal.

type of data		*depvar*$_1$	*depvar*$_2$
point data	$a = [a, a]$	a	a
interval data	$[a, b]$	a	b
left-censored data	$(-\infty, b]$	.	b
right-censored data	$[a, +\infty)$	a	.

Note: Truly missing values of the dependent variable must be represented by missing values in both *depvar*$_1$ and *depvar*$_2$.

Interval data arise naturally in many contexts, such as education level. Often you only know that, for example, a person made it to high school but did not graduate. Below we give an example using education level as the dependent variable and show how to set up *depvar*$_1$ and *depvar*$_2$.

▷ Example 1

We will use the sample adult dataset from the NHIS 2003 survey. In this dataset, the PSU, strata, and sampling weight variables are respectively psu, stratum, and wtfa_sa.

```
. use http://www.stata-press.com/data/r9/nhis03adult
. svyset psu [pweight=wtfa_sa], strata(stratum)
      pweight: wtfa_sa
         VCE: linearized
    Strata 1: stratum
       SU 1: psu
      FPC 1: <zero>
. svydes
Survey: Describing stage 1 sampling units
      pweight: wtfa_sa
         VCE: linearized
    Strata 1: stratum
       SU 1: psu
      FPC 1: <zero>
```

(Continued on next page)

Stratum	#Units	#Obs	#Obs per Unit		
			min	mean	max
1	2	106	50	53.0	56
2	2	103	51	51.5	52
3	2	40	8	20.0	32
4	2	85	25	42.5	60
5	2	72	26	36.0	46
(output omitted)					
335	2	63	26	31.5	37
336	2	133	64	66.5	69
337	2	65	22	32.5	43
338	2	26	8	13.0	18
339	2	59	28	29.5	31
339	678	30852	3	45.5	113

Suppose that we were interested in estimating the average number of years of education for adults in the population. While this dataset does not have a variable that measures the exact number of years of education for each sampled adult, the educ variable does contain enough information for us to construct a rough estimate.

```
. describe educ
```

variable name	storage type	display format	value label	variable label
educ	byte	%43.0g	sap020x	Highest level of school completed

```
. label list sap020x
sap020x:
            0 00 Never attended/ kindergarten only
           12 12 12th grade, no diploma
           13 13 HIGH SCHOOL GRADUATE
           14 14 GED or equivalent
           15 15 Some college, no degree
           16 16 AA degree: technical or vocational
           17 17 AA degree: academic program
           18 18 Bachelor's degree (BA, AB, BS, BBA)
           19 19 Master's degree (MA, MS, MEng, MEd, MBA)
           20 20 Professional degree (MD, DDS, DVM, JD)
           21 21 Doctoral degree (PhD, EdD)
           96 96 Child under 5 years old
           97 97 Refused
           98 98 Not Ascertained
           99 99 Don't know
```

In the following example, we construct two variables, leduc and ueduc, that bound the number of years of education for each sampled adult based on the coded values in educ. Values of educ that are less than 12 are assumed to be the true number of years of education. For individuals who reached their senior year of high school but did not graduate, we set a range of 11 to 12 years of education. For high school graduates, we assume 12 years of education (although we could argue that a range of 10 to 14 years). For individuals who got their GED or equivalent, we set a maximum of 12 years of education but leave the lower bound missing. For individuals with an associate's degrees, we set a range of 13 to 15 years. For individuals with a bachelor's degree, we set a range of 15 to 17 years. For individuals with a master's degree, we set a range of 17 to 19 years. For individuals with a professional or doctoral degree, we set a range of 17 to 20 years. Category 96 was not observed since this dataset consists of sampled adults. For the remaining categories, we set the lower bound to 0 and leave the upper bound missing.

```
. gen byte leduc = educ if educ < 12
(25583 missing values generated)
. gen byte ueduc = educ if educ < 12
(25583 missing values generated)
. replace leduc = 11 if educ == 12
(681 real changes made)
. replace ueduc = 12 if educ == 12
(681 real changes made)
. replace leduc = 12 if educ == 13
(7904 real changes made)
. replace ueduc = 12 if educ == 13
(7904 real changes made)
. replace leduc = .  if educ == 14
(0 real changes made)
. replace ueduc = 12 if educ == 14
(854 real changes made)
. replace leduc = 12 if educ == 15
(6000 real changes made)
. replace ueduc = 16 if educ == 15
(6000 real changes made)
. replace leduc = 13 if inlist(educ,16,17)
(2691 real changes made)
. replace ueduc = 15 if inlist(educ,16,17)
(2691 real changes made)
. replace leduc = 15 if educ == 18
(4614 real changes made)
. replace ueduc = 17 if educ == 18
(4614 real changes made)
. replace leduc = 17 if educ == 19
(1729 real changes made)
. replace ueduc = 19 if educ == 19
(1729 real changes made)
. replace leduc = 17 if inlist(educ,20,21)
(669 real changes made)
. replace ueduc = 20 if inlist(educ,20,21)
(669 real changes made)
. replace leduc = 0  if inlist(educ,97,98,99)
(441 real changes made)
. replace ueduc = .  if inlist(educ,97,98,99)
(0 real changes made)
. label var leduc "Lower bound (years) for education level"
. label var ueduc "Upper bound (years) for education level"
```

We can now use svy: intreg with these new lower- and upper-bound variables to estimate the mean number of years of education for the population of adults. This results in a mean of 13 years with a population standard deviation of about 3 years (sigma = 2.99).

(*Continued on next page*)

```
. svy: intreg leduc ueduc
(running intreg on estimation sample)
Survey: Interval regression
Number of strata    =       339                Number of obs     =       30852
Number of PSUs      =       678                Population size    = 2.130e+08
                                               Design df         =         339
                                               F(   0,    339)   =           .
                                               Prob > F          =           .
```

	Coef.	Linearized Std. Err.	t	P>|t|	[95% Conf. Interval]
_cons	13.05521	.0278957	468.00	0.000	13.00034 13.11008
/lnsigma	1.096257	.0075512	145.18	0.000	1.081404 1.111111
sigma	2.992944	.0226005			2.948818 3.03773

```
Observation summary:       854  left-censored  observations
                         13173       uncensored  observations
                           441 right-censored  observations
                         16384        interval  observations
```

◁

Saved Results

svy: intreg saves in e(). In addition to the items documented in [SVY] **svy**, svy: intreg also saves the following:

Scalars
    e(N_unc)   number of uncensored observations
    e(N_lc)   number of left-censored observations
    e(N_rc)   number of right-censored observations
    e(N_int)   number of interval observations
    e(sigma)   sigma

Macros
    e(cmd)   intreg
    e(depvar)   name of dependent variable
    e(offset)   offset
    e(crittype)   log pseudolikelihood
    e(predict)   program used to implement predict

Methods and Formulas

svy: intreg is implemented as an ado-file.

Let $\mathbf{y} = \mathbf{X}\boldsymbol{\beta} + \boldsymbol{\epsilon}$ be the model. $\mathbf{y}$ represents continuous outcomes—either observed or not observed. Our model assumes $\boldsymbol{\epsilon} \sim N(\mathbf{0}, \sigma^2\mathbf{I})$.

For observations $j \in \mathcal{C}$, we observe y_j, i.e., point data. Observations $j \in \mathcal{L}$ are left-censored; we know only that the unobserved y_j is less than or equal to $y_{\mathcal{L}j}$, a censoring value that we do know. Similarly, observations $j \in \mathcal{R}$ are right-censored; we know only that the unobserved y_j is greater than or equal to $y_{\mathcal{R}j}$. Observations $j \in \mathcal{I}$ are intervals; we know only that the unobserved y_j is in the interval $[y_{1j}, y_{2j}]$.

The log pseudolikelihood is

$$\ln L = - \sum_{j \in \mathcal{C}} \frac{w_j}{2} \left\{ \left(\frac{y_j - \mathbf{x}\boldsymbol{\beta}}{\sigma} \right)^2 + \log(2\pi\sigma^2) \right\}$$
$$+ \sum_{j \in \mathcal{L}} w_j \log \Phi \left(\frac{y_{\mathcal{L}j} - \mathbf{x}\boldsymbol{\beta}}{\sigma} \right)$$
$$+ \sum_{j \in \mathcal{R}} w_j \log \left\{ 1 - \Phi \left(\frac{y_{\mathcal{R}j} - \mathbf{x}\boldsymbol{\beta}}{\sigma} \right) \right\}$$
$$+ \sum_{j \in \mathcal{I}} w_j \log \left\{ \Phi \left(\frac{y_{2j} - \mathbf{x}\boldsymbol{\beta}}{\sigma} \right) - \Phi \left(\frac{y_{1j} - \mathbf{x}\boldsymbol{\beta}}{\sigma} \right) \right\}$$

where $\Phi()$ is the standard cumulative normal and w_j is a sampling weight. The equation-level scores used in the linearized variance estimator are derived by taking partial derivatives of the log pseudolikelihood; see [SVY] **variance estimation**.

References

Amemiya, T. 1973. Regression analysis when the dependent variable is truncated Normal. *Econometrica* 41: 997–1016.

Hurd, M. 1979. Estimation in truncated samples when there is heteroscedasticity. *Journal of Econometrics* 11: 247–258.

Johnston, J. and J. DiNardo. 1997. *Econometric Methods*. 4th ed. New York: McGraw–Hill.

Kendall, M. G. and A Stuart. 1973. *The Advanced Theory of Statistics*, vol. 2. New York: Hafner.

Long, J. S. 1997. *Regression Models for Categorical and Limited Dependent Variables*. Thousand Oaks, CA: Sage.

Also See

Complementary: [SVY] **svy: intreg postestimation**,

Related: [R] **intreg**;
     [SVY] **svy: regress**

Background: [U] **20 Estimation and postestimation commands**,
     [SVY] **estimation options**, [SVY] **poststratification**,
     [SVY] **subpopulation estimation**, [SVY] **svy**, [SVY] **variance estimation**,
     [R] **maximize**

Title

svy: intreg postestimation — Postestimation tools for svy: intreg

Description

The following postestimation commands are available for svy: intreg:

command	description
estat	postestimation statistics for survey data
estimates	cataloging estimation results
lincom	point estimates, standard errors, testing, and inference for linear combinations of coefficients
mfx	marginal effects or elasticities
nlcom	point estimates, standard errors, testing, and inference for nonlinear combinations of coefficients
predict	predictions, residuals, influence statistics, and other diagnostic measures
predictnl	point estimates, standard errors, testing, and inference for generalized predictions
suest	seemingly unrelated estimation
test	Wald tests for simple and composite linear hypotheses
testnl	Wald tests of nonlinear hypotheses

See [SVY] **estat**.

See the corresponding entries in the *Stata Base Reference Manual* for details.

Syntax for predict

> predict [*type*] *newvarname* [*if*] [*in*] [, *statistic* <u>nooff</u>set]
>
> predict [*type*] { *stub** | *newvar*$_{\text{reg}}$ *newvar*$_{\text{lnsigma}}$ } [*if*] [*in*] , <u>sc</u>ores

statistic	description
xb	linear prediction, $\mathbf{x}_j\boldsymbol{\beta}$; the default
stdp	standard error of the linear prediction
<u>pr</u>(a,b)	$\Pr(a < y_j < b)$
e(a,b)	$E(y_j \mid a < y_j < b)$
<u>y</u>star(a,b)	$E(y_j^*), \; y_j^* = \max\{a, \min(y_j, b)\}$

These statistics are available both in and out of sample; type predict ... if e(sample) ... if wanted only for the estimation sample.

where a and b may be numbers of variables; a missing ($a \geq .$) means $-\infty$, and b missing ($b \geq .$) means $+\infty$; see [U] **12.2.1 Missing values**.

Options for predict

xb, the default, calculates the linear prediction $\mathbf{x}_j\beta$.

pr(a,b) calculates $\Pr(a < \mathbf{x}_j\beta + u_j < b)$, the probability that $y_j|\mathbf{x}_j$ would be observed in the interval (a, b).

a and b may be specified as numbers or variable names; lb and ub are variable names;
pr(20,30) calculates $\Pr(20 < \mathbf{x}_j\beta + u_j < 30)$;
pr(lb,ub) calculates $\Pr(lb < \mathbf{x}_j\beta + u_j < ub)$; and
pr(20,ub) calculates $\Pr(20 < \mathbf{x}_j\beta + u_j < ub)$.

a missing ($a \geq .$) means $-\infty$; pr(.,30) calculates $\Pr(-\infty < \mathbf{x}_j\beta + u_j < 30)$;
pr(lb,30) calculates $\Pr(-\infty < \mathbf{x}_j\beta + u_j < 30)$ in observations for which $lb \geq .$
and calculates $\Pr(lb < \mathbf{x}_j\beta + u_j < 30)$ elsewhere.

b missing ($b \geq .$) means $+\infty$; pr(20,.) calculates $\Pr(+\infty > \mathbf{x}_j\beta + u_j > 20)$;
pr(20,ub) calculates $\Pr(+\infty > \mathbf{x}_j\beta + u_j > 20)$ in observations for which $ub \geq .$
and calculates $\Pr(20 < \mathbf{x}_j\beta + u_j < ub)$ elsewhere.

e(a,b) calculates $E(\mathbf{x}_j\beta + u_j \mid a < \mathbf{x}_j\mathbf{b} + u_j < b)$, the expected value of $y_j|\mathbf{x}_j$ conditional on $y_j|\mathbf{x}_j$ being in the interval (a, b), meaning that $y_j|\mathbf{x}_j$ is censored.
a and b are specified as they are for pr().

ystar(a,b) calculates $E(y_j^*)$, where $y_j^* = a$ if $\mathbf{x}_j\mathbf{b} + u_j \leq a$, $y_j^* = b$ if $\mathbf{x}_j\mathbf{b} + u_j \geq b$, and $y_j^* = \mathbf{x}_j\mathbf{b} + u_j$ otherwise, meaning that y_j^* is truncated. a and b are specified as they are for pr().

stdp calculates the standard error of the prediction. It can be thought of as the standard error of the predicted expected value or mean for the observation's covariate pattern. This is also referred to as the standard error of the fitted value.

nooffset is relevant if you specified offset(*varname*) when you fitted the model. It modifies the calculations made by predict so that they ignore the offset variable; the linear prediction is treated as $\mathbf{x}_j\mathbf{b}$ rather than as $\mathbf{x}_j\mathbf{b} + \text{offset}_j$.

scores calculates equation-level score variables.

The first new variable will contain $\partial \ln L / \partial(\mathbf{x}_j\beta)$.

The second new variable will contain $\partial \ln L / \partial \ln \sigma$.

Remarks

▷ Example 1

Continuing with the example from [SVY] **svy: intreg**, we use predict to compute the probability that a person will have 15 to 17 years of education for each covariate pattern in the data and save the values in the new variable p_college.

```
. predict p_college, pr(15,17)
```

◁

Methods and Formulas

All postestimation commands listed above are implemented as ado-files.

Also See

Complementary: [SVY] **svy: intreg**, [SVY] **estat**;

                        [R] **estimates**, [R] **lincom**, [R] **mfx**, [R] **nlcom**, [R] **predict**,

                        [R] **predictnl**, [R] **suest**, [R] **test**, [R] **testnl**

Background: [U] **13.5 Accessing coefficients and standard errors**,

                        [U] **20 Estimation and postestimation commands**

Title

svy: ivreg — Instrumental variables regression for survey data

Syntax

svy [*vcetype*] [, *svy_options*] : ivreg *depvar* [*varlist*$_1$] (*varlist*$_2$ = *varlist*$_{iv}$)

[*if*] [*in*] [, *options*]

vcetype	description
SE	
linearized	Taylor linearized variance estimation
brr	BRR variance estimation; see [SVY] **svy brr**
jackknife	jackknife variance estimation; see [SVY] **svy jackknife**

Specifying a *vcetype* overrides the default from svyset.

svy_options	description
if/in	
subpop()	identify a subpopulation
SE	
brr_options	additional options allowed with BRR variance estimation; see [SVY] *brr_options*
jackknife_options	additional options allowed with jackknife variance estimation; see [SVY] *jackknife_options*
Reporting	
level(#)	set confidence level; default is level(95)
noheader	suppress the table header
nolegend	suppress the table legend
noadjust	do not adjust model Wald statistic

svy requires that the survey-design variables be identified using svyset; see [SVY] **svyset**.

xi is allowed; see [R] **xi**.

See [U] **20 Estimation and postestimation commands** for additional capabilities of estimation commands.

Warning: Using *if* or *in* restrictions will not produce correct variance estimates for subpopulations in many cases. To compute estimates for a subpopulation, use the subpop() option. The full specification for subpop() is

subpop([*varname*] [*if*])

options	description
Model	
noconstant	suppress the constant term
Reporting	
first	report first-stage estimates

Description

svy: ivreg fits instrumental variables regression for complex survey data; see [R] **ivreg** for a description of this model involving nonsurvey data, and see [SVY] **svy: regress** for linear regression for survey data.

Specifically, ivreg fits a linear regression model using instrumental variables (or two-stage least squares) of *depvar* on *varlist*$_1$ and *varlist*$_2$, using *varlist*$_{iv}$ (along with *varlist*$_1$) as instruments for *varlist*$_2$.

In the language of two-stage least squares, *varlist*$_1$ and *varlist*$_{iv}$ are the exogenous variables, and *varlist*$_2$ are the endogenous variables.

Options

svy_options; see [SVY] **svy**.

___ Model ___

noconstant; see [SVY] **estimation options**.

___ Reporting ___

first requests that the first-stage regression results be displayed.

Remarks

svy: ivreg performs instrumental variables regression (or two-stage least squares) and weighted instrumental variables regression for survey data. For a general discussion of two-stage least squares, see Johnston and DiNardo (1997), Kmenta (1997), and Wooldridge (2002a, 2002b). Davidson and MacKinnon (1993, 209–224) present their computationally identical discussion using instrumental variables terminology. Some of the earliest work on simultaneous systems can be found in Cowles Commission monographs—Koopmans and Marschak (1950) and Koopmans and Hood (1953)—with the first development of two-stage least squares appearing in Theil (1953) and Basmann (1957). However, Stock and Watson (2003, 334–337) present an example of the method of instrumental variables that was first published in 1928 by Philip Wright.

The syntax for svy: ivreg assumes that you want to estimate a single equation from a system of equations, or an equation for which you do not want to specify the functional form of the remaining system. An advantage of ivreg is that you can estimate a single equation of a multiple-equation system without specifying the functional form of the remaining equations.

▷ Example 1

Let us assume that we wish to estimate

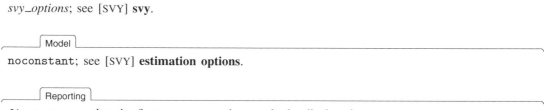

$$\texttt{hsngval} = \alpha_0 + \alpha_1 \texttt{faminc} + \alpha_2 \texttt{reg2} + \alpha_3 \texttt{reg3} + \alpha_4 \texttt{reg4} + \epsilon$$

$$\texttt{rent} = \beta_0 + \beta_1 \texttt{hsngval} + \beta_2 \texttt{pcturban} + \nu$$

We have state data from the 1980 US census. hsngval is the median dollar value of owner-occupied housing, and rent is the median monthly gross rent. We postulate that hsngval is a function of family income (faminc) and region of the country (reg2 through reg4). We also postulate that rent is a function of hsngval and the percentage of the population living in urban areas (pcturban).

If you are familiar with multiple-equation models, you have probably already noted the triangular (recursive) structure of our model. This structure is not required, In fact, and if we were to assume that ϵ and ν were uncorrelated, either of the equations could be consistently estimated by ordinary least squares. This is strictly a characteristic of triangular systems and would not hold if `hsngval` were assumed to also depend on `rent`, regardless of assumptions about ϵ and ν. For a more detailed discussion of triangular systems, see Kmenta (1997, 719–720).

We tell Stata to estimate the `rent` equation by specifying the structural equation and the additional exogenous variables in a specific form. The dependent variable appears first and is followed by the exogenous variables in the structural model for `rent`. These are followed by a group of variables in parentheses separated by an equal sign. The variables to the left of the equal sign are the endogenous regressors in the structural model for `rent`, and those to the right are the additional exogenous variables that will instrument for the endogenous variables. Only the additional exogenous variables must be specified to the right of the equal sign; those already in the structural model are automatically included as instruments.

As the following shows, this is more difficult to describe than to perform. In this example, `rent` is the endogenous dependent variable, `hsngval` is an endogenous regressor, and `faminc`, `reg2`, `reg3`, `reg4`, and `pcturban` are the exogenous variables.

```
. use http://www.stata-press.com/data/r9/hsng2
(1980 Census housing data)

. svyset _n
      pweight: <none>
          VCE: linearized
    Strata 1: <one>
        SU 1: <observations>
       FPC 1: <zero>

. svy: ivreg rent pcturban (hsngval = faminc reg2-reg4)
(running ivreg on estimation sample)

Survey: Instrumental variables (2SLS) regression

Number of strata   =        1          Number of obs      =         50
Number of PSUs     =       50          Population size    =         50
                                       Design df          =         49
                                       F(  2,     48)     =      21.59
                                       Prob > F           =     0.0000
                                       R-squared          =     0.5989
```

rent	Coef.	Linearized Std. Err.	t	P>|t|	[95% Conf. Interval]	
hsngval	.0022398	.0006788	3.30	0.002	.0008757	.003604
pcturban	.081516	.4491076	0.18	0.857	-.8209996	.9840315
_cons	120.7065	15.41034	7.83	0.000	89.73828	151.6748

```
Instrumented:  hsngval
Instruments:   pcturban faminc reg2 reg3 reg4
```

◁

Saved Results

`svy: ivreg` saves in `e()`. In addition to the items documented in [SVY] **svy**, `svy: ivreg` also saves the following:

Macros

e(r2)	R-squared
e(rmse)	root mean square error
e(mss)	model sum of squares
e(rss)	residual sum of squares

Macros

e(cmd)	ivreg
e(version)	version number of ivreg
e(depvar)	name of dependent variable
e(instd)	instrumented variables
e(insts)	instruments
e(model)	iv
e(predict)	program used to implement predict

Methods and Formulas

svy: ivreg is implemented as an ado-file.

For a discussion of robust (linearized) variance estimates in the context of regression and regression models with instrumental variables, see [R] **regress**, *Methods and Formulas*. Also see [SVY] **variance estimation** for details regarding multistage survey designs.

References

Baltagi, B. H. 1998. *Econometrics*. New York: Springer.

Basmann, R. L. 1957. A generalized classical method of linear estimation of coefficients in a structural equation. *Econometrica* 25: 77–83.

Davidson, R. and J. G. MacKinnon. 1993. *Estimation and Inference in Econometrics*. New York: Oxford University Press.

Johnston, J. and J. DiNardo. 1997. *Econometric Methods*. 4th ed. New York: McGraw–Hill.

Kmenta, J. 1997. *Elements of Econometrics*. 2nd ed. Ann Arbor: University of Michigan Press.

Koopmans, T. C. and W. C. Hood. 1953. *Studies in Econometric Method*. New York: Wiley.

Koopmans, T. C. and J. Marschak. 1950. *Statistical Inference in Dynamic Economic Models*. New York: Wiley.

Stock, J. H. and M. W. Watson. 2003. *Introduction to Econometrics*. Boston: Addison–Wesley.

Theil, H. 1953. *Repeated Least Squares Applied to Complete Equation Systems*. Mimeograph from the Central Planning Bureau, The Hague.

Wooldridge, J. M. 2002a. *Introductory Econometrics: A Modern Approach*. 2nd ed. Cincinnati, OH: South-Western.

——. 2002b. *Econometric Analysis of Cross Section and Panel Data*. Cambridge, MA: MIT Press.

Also See

Complementary:	[SVY] **svy: ivreg postestimation**
Related:	[R] **ivreg**;
	[SVY] **svy: regress**
Background:	[U] **20 Estimation and postestimation commands**,
	[SVY] **estimation options**, [SVY] **poststratification**,
	[SVY] **subpopulation estimation**, [SVY] **svy**, [SVY] **variance estimation**

Title

svy: ivreg postestimation — Postestimation tools for svy: ivreg

Description

The following postestimation commands are available for svy: ivreg:

command	description
estat	postestimation statistics for survey data
estimates	cataloging estimation results
lincom	point estimates, standard errors, testing, and inference for linear combinations of coefficients
mfx	marginal effects or elasticities
nlcom	point estimates, standard errors, testing, and inference for nonlinear combinations of coefficients
predict	predictions, residuals, influence statistics, and other diagnostic measures
predictnl	point estimates, standard errors, testing, and inference for generalized predictions
suest	seemingly unrelated estimation
test	Wald tests for simple and composite linear hypotheses
testnl	Wald tests of nonlinear hypotheses

See [SVY] **estat**.

See the corresponding entries in the *Stata Base Reference Manual* for details.

Syntax for predict

predict [*type*] *newvarname* [*if*] [*in*] [, *statistic*]

statistic	description
xb	linear prediction, $x_j\beta$; the default
<u>r</u>esiduals	residuals
<u>sc</u>ore	score; equivalent to residuals
stdp	standard error of the linear prediction

These statistics are available both in and out of sample; type predict ... if e(sample) ... if wanted only for the estimation sample.

Options for predict

xb, the default, calculates the linear prediction $x_j\beta$.

residuals calculates the residuals, i.e., the value of the dependent variable minus the predicted value of the dependent variable.

score is a synonym for residuals.

stdp calculates the standard error of the prediction.

Remarks

▷ Example 1

Continuing with our example from [SVY] **svy: ivreg**, we use `predict` to compute the linear prediction for each observation in the dataset and save the values in the new variable `xb`.

```
. predict xb
```

◁

Methods and Formulas

All postestimation commands listed above are implemented as ado-files.

Also See

Complementary:	[SVY] **svy: ivreg**, [SVY] **estat**;
	[R] **estimates**, [R] **lincom**, [R] **mfx**, [R] **nlcom**, [R] **predict**,
	[R] **predictnl**, [R] **suest**, [R] **test**, [R] **testnl**
Background:	[U] **13.5 Accessing coefficients and standard errors**,
	[U] **20 Estimation and postestimation commands**

Title

> **svy: logistic** — Logistic regression, reporting odds ratios, for survey data

Syntax

svy [*vcetype*] [, *svy_options*] : logistic *depvar* [*indepvars*] [*if*] [*in*] [, *options*]

vcetype	description
SE	
linearized	Taylor linearized variance estimation
brr	BRR variance estimation; see [SVY] **svy brr**
jackknife	jackknife variance estimation; see [SVY] **svy jackknife**

Specifying a *vcetype* overrides the default from svyset.

svy_options	description
if/in	
subpop()	identify a subpopulation
SE	
brr_options	additional options allowed with BRR variance estimation; see [SVY] *brr_options*
jackknife_options	additional options allowed with jackknife variance estimation; see [SVY] *jackknife options*
Reporting	
level(#)	set confidence level; default is level(95)
noheader	suppress the table header
nolegend	suppress the table legend
noadjust	do not adjust model Wald statistic

svy requires that the survey-design variables be identified using svyset; see [SVY] **svyset**.

xi is allowed; see [R] **xi**.

See [U] **20 Estimation and postestimation commands** for additional capabilities of estimation commands.

Warning: Using *if* or *in* restrictions will not produce correct variance estimates for subpopulations in many cases. To compute estimates for a subpopulation, use the subpop() option. The full specification for subpop() is

subpop([*varname*] [*if*])

(Continued on next page)

105

options	description
Model	
<u>nocon</u>stant	suppress the constant term
<u>off</u>set(*varname*)	include *varname* in model with coefficient constrained to 1
asis	retain perfect predictor variables
Reporting	
coef	report estimated coefficients
Max options	
maximize_options	control the maximization process; seldom used

Description

svy: logistic fits logistic regression models for complex survey data. In the logistic regression model, *depvar* is a 0/1 variable (or, more precisely, a 0/non-0 variable).

See [R] **logistic** for a description of this model involving nonsurvey data, [SVY] **svy: logit** for logistic regression reporting coefficients, [SVY] **svy: probit** for probit regression, [SVY] **svy: mlogit** for multinomial logistic regression, [SVY] **svy: ologit** for ordered logistic regression, and [SVY] **svy: oprobit** for ordered probit regression for survey data.

Options

svy_options; see [SVY] **svy**.

⌐‾‾‾| Model |‾‾

noconstant, offset(*varname*); see [SVY] **estimation options**.

asis forces retention of perfect predictor variables and their associated perfectly predicted observations and may produce instabilities in maximization; see [R] **probit** (sic).

⌐‾‾‾| Reporting |‾‾‾

coef causes svy: logistic to report the estimated coefficients rather than the odds ratios (exponentiated coefficients). coef may be specified when the model is fitted or used later to redisplay results. coef affects only how the results are displayed and not how they are estimated.

⌐‾‾‾| Max options |‾‾‾

maximize_options: <u>iter</u>ate(*#*), [<u>no</u>]<u>log</u>, <u>trace</u>, <u>tol</u>erance(*#*), <u>ltol</u>erance(*#*); see [R] **maximize**. These options are seldom used. If the maximization is taking a long time, you may wish to specify the log option to view the iteration log. The log option implies svy's noisily option; see [SVY] **svy**.

Remarks

svy: logistic provides an alternative and preferred way to fit logistic regression models, the other choice being svy: logit.

First, let us dispose of some confusing terminology. We use the words logit and logistic to mean the same thing: maximum pseudolikelihood estimation. To some, one or the other of these words connotes transforming the dependent variable and using weighted least squares to fit the model, but that is not how we use either word here. Thus the svy: logit and svy: logistic commands produce the same results.

The svy: logistic command is generally preferred to svy: logit because svy: logistic presents the estimates in terms of odds ratios rather than coefficients. To a few people, this may seem a disadvantage, but you can type svy: logit without arguments after svy: logistic to see the underlying coefficients.

For an introduction to logistic regression, see Lemeshow and Hosmer (1998), Pagano and Gauvreau (2000, 470–487), or Pampel (2000); for a complete but nonmathematical treatment, see Kleinbaum and Klein (2002); and for a thorough discussion, see Hosmer and Lemeshow (2000). See Gould (2000) for a discussion of the interpretation of logistic regression. See Dupont (2002) for a discussion of logistic regression with examples using Stata.

▷ Example 1

We begin by using svydes to verify the design characteristics. For example, there are 2 PSUs in each of the 31 strata (stratum 19 is missing) in the NHANES II dataset.

```
. use http://www.stata-press.com/data/r9/nhanes2d
. svydes
Survey: Describing stage 1 sampling units

        pweight: finalwgt
            VCE: linearized
      Strata 1: strata
          SU 1: psu
         FPC 1: <zero>
```

| | | | #Obs per Unit | | |
Stratum	#Units	#Obs	min	mean	max
1	2	380	165	190.0	215
2	2	185	67	92.5	118
3	2	348	149	174.0	199
4	2	460	229	230.0	231
(output omitted)					
29	2	503	215	251.5	288
30	2	365	166	182.5	199
31	2	308	143	154.0	165
32	2	450	211	225.0	239
31	62	10351	67	167.0	288

Using the above information, we generate a Hadamard matrix of order 32 and then fit a logistic regression with BRR standard errors using svy brr: logistic. See the technical note in [SVY] **svy brr** for a discussion of Hadamard matrices.

```
. matrix h2 = (1, -1 \ 1, 1)
. matrix h32 = h2 # h2 # h2 # h2 # h2
```

```
. svy brr, hadamard(h32) nodots: logistic highbp height weight age age2
> female black
```

Survey: Logistic regression

Number of strata	=	31		Number of obs	=	10351
Number of PSUs	=	62		Population size	=	1.172e+08
				Replications	=	32
				Design df	=	31
				F(6, 26)	=	98.50
				Prob > F	=	0.0000

highbp	Odds Ratio	BRR Std. Err.	t	P>|t|	[95% Conf. Interval]	
height	.967926	.0057121	-5.52	0.000	.956346	.9796462
weight	1.050298	.0033842	15.23	0.000	1.043419	1.057223
age	1.166625	.0245042	7.34	0.000	1.117704	1.217688
age2	.998926	.0002035	-5.27	0.000	.9985109	.9993412
female	.7001246	.0615036	-4.06	0.000	.5852821	.8375012
black	1.40907	.1940341	2.49	0.018	1.064049	1.865965

The odds ratio for the `female` predictor is 0.7, and is significantly less than 1. This implies that females have a lower incidence of high blood pressure than males.

◁

Saved Results

`svy: logistic` saves in `e()`. In addition to the items documented in [SVY] **svy**, `svy: logistic` also saves the following:

Macros
e(cmd)	logistic
e(depvar)	name of dependent variable
e(offset)	offset
e(crittype)	log pseudolikelihood
e(predict)	program used to implement predict

Methods and Formulas

`svy: logistic` is implemented as an ado-file.

The log pseudolikelihood is

$$\ln L = \sum_{j \in S} w_j \ln F(\mathbf{x}_j \boldsymbol{\beta}) + \sum_{j \notin S} w_j \ln \left\{ 1 - F(\mathbf{x}_j \boldsymbol{\beta}) \right\}$$

where S is the set of all observations such that $y_j \neq 0$, $F(z) = e^z / (1 + e^z)$, and w_j is a sampling weight. The equation-level scores used in the linearized variance estimator are derived by taking partial derivatives of the log pseudolikelihood; see [SVY] **variance estimation**.

References

Aldrich, J. H. and F. D. Nelson. 1984. *Linear Probability, Logit, and Probit Models.* Newbury Park, CA: Sage.

Cramer, J. S. 2003. *Logit Models from Economics and Other Fields.* Cambridge: Cambridge University Press.

Dupont, W. D. 2002. *Statistical Modeling for Biomedical Researchers.* Cambridge: Cambridge University Press.

Eltinge, J. L. and W. M. Sribney. 1996. svy4: Linear, logistic, and probit regressions for survey data. *Stata Technical Bulletin* 31: 26–31. Reprinted in *Stata Technical Bulletin Reprints*, vol. 6, pp. 239–245.

Gould, W. W. 2000. sg124: Interpreting logistic regression in all its forms. *Stata Technical Bulletin* 53: 19–29. Reprinted in *Stata Technical Bulletin Reprints*, vol. 9, pp. 257–270.

Hosmer, D. W., Jr., and S. Lemeshow. 2000. *Applied Logistic Regression.* 2nd ed. New York: Wiley.

Kleinbaum, D. G. and M. Klein. 2002. *Logistic Regression: A Self-Learning Text.* 2nd ed. New York: Springer.

Lemeshow, S. and D. W. Hosmer, Jr. 1998. Logistic regression. In *Encyclopedia of Biostatistics*, ed. P. Armitage and T. Colton, 2316–2327. New York: Wiley.

Long, J. S. 1997. *Regression Models for Categorical and Limited Dependent Variables.* Thousand Oaks, CA: Sage.

Long, J. S. and J. Freese. 2003. *Regression Models for Categorical Dependent Variables Using Stata.* rev. ed. College Station, TX: Stata Press.

Pagano, M. and K. Gauvreau. 2000. *Principles of Biostatistics.* 2nd ed. Pacific Grove, CA: Brooks/Cole.

Pampel, F. C. 2000. *Logistic Regression: A Primer.* Thousand Oaks, CA: Sage.

Powers, D. A. and Y. Xie. 2000. *Statistical Methods for Categorical Data Analysis.* San Diego, CA: Academic Press.

Also See

Complementary: [SVY] **svy: logistic postestimation**

Related: [R] **logistic**;
[SVY] **svy: logit**, [SVY] **svy: mlogit**, [SVY] **svy: probit**,
[SVY] **svy: ologit**, [SVY] **svy: oprobit**

Background: [U] **20 Estimation and postestimation commands**,
[SVY] **estimation options**, [SVY] **poststratification**,
[SVY] **subpopulation estimation**, [SVY] **svy**, [SVY] **variance estimation**,
[R] **maximize**

Title

> **svy: logistic postestimation** — Postestimation tools for svy: logistic

Description

The following postestimation commands are available for svy: logistic:

command	description
estat	postestimation statistics for survey data
estimates	cataloging estimation results
lincom	point estimates, standard errors, testing, and inference for linear combinations of coefficients
mfx	marginal effects or elasticities
nlcom	point estimates, standard errors, testing, and inference for nonlinear combinations of coefficients
predict	predictions, residuals, influence statistics, and other diagnostic measures
predictnl	point estimates, standard errors, testing, and inference for generalized predictions
suest	seemingly unrelated estimation
test	Wald tests for simple and composite linear hypotheses
testnl	Wald tests of nonlinear hypotheses

See [SVY] **estat**.

See the corresponding entries in the *Stata Base Reference Manual* for details.

Syntax for predict

predict [*type*] *newvarname* [*if*] [*in*] [, *statistic* <u>nooff</u>set]

statistic	description
<u>pr</u>	probability of a positive outcome; the default
xb	linear prediction, $x_j\beta$
stdp	standard error of the prediction
<u>sc</u>ore	first derivative of the log pseudolikelihood with respect to $x_j\beta$

These statistics are available both in and out of sample; type predict ... if e(sample) ... if wanted only for the estimation sample.

Options for predict

pr, the default, calculates the probability of a positive outcome.

xb calculates the linear prediction $x_j\beta$.

stdp calculates the standard error of the linear prediction.

score calculates the equation-level score, $\partial \ln L / \partial(x_j\beta)$.

nooffset is relevant if you specified offset() when you fitted the model. It modifies the calculations made by predict so that they ignore the offset variable; the linear prediction is treated as $\mathbf{x}_j\boldsymbol{\beta}$ rather than as $\mathbf{x}_j\boldsymbol{\beta} + \text{offset}_j$.

Remarks

▷ Example 1

Continuing with our example from [SVY] **svy: logistic**, we use predict to compute the probability of high blood pressure for each covariate pattern in the dataset and save the values in the new variable p_highbp.

```
. predict p_highbp, pr
```

◁

Methods and Formulas

All postestimation commands listed above are implemented as ado-files.

Also See

Complementary:	[SVY] **svy: logistic**, [SVY] **estat**;
	[R] **estimates**, [R] **lincom**, [R] **mfx**, [R] **nlcom**, [R] **predict**,
	[R] **predictnl**, [R] **suest**, [R] **test**, [R] **testnl**
Background:	[U] **13.5 Accessing coefficients and standard errors**,
	[U] **20 Estimation and postestimation commands**

Title

svy: logit — Logistic regression, reporting coefficients, for survey data

Syntax

svy [*vcetype*] [, *svy_options*] : <u>logit</u> *depvar* [*indepvars*] [*if*] [*in*] [, *options*]

vcetype	description
SE	
<u>linearized</u>	Taylor linearized variance estimation
brr	BRR variance estimation; see [SVY] **svy brr**
<u>jackknife</u>	jackknife variance estimation; see [SVY] **svy jackknife**

Specifying a *vcetype* overrides the default from svyset.

svy_options	description
if/in	
<u>subpop</u>()	identify a subpopulation
SE	
brr_options	additional options allowed with BRR variance estimation; see [SVY] ***brr_options***
jackknife_options	additional options allowed with jackknife variance estimation; see [SVY] ***jackknife_options***
Reporting	
<u>level</u>(#)	set confidence level; default is level(95)
<u>no</u>header	suppress the table header
<u>no</u>legend	suppress the table legend
<u>noadjust</u>	do not adjust model Wald statistic

svy requires that the survey-design variables be identified using svyset; see [SVY] **svyset**.

xi is allowed; see [R] **xi**.

See [U] **20 Estimation and postestimation commands** for additional capabilities of estimation commands.

Warning: Using *if* or *in* restrictions will not produce correct variance estimates for subpopulations in many cases. To compute estimates for a subpopulation, use the subpop() option. The full specification for subpop() is

<u>subpop</u>([*varname*] [*if*])

options	description
Model	
<u>nocon</u>stant	suppress the constant term
<u>off</u>set(*varname*)	include *varname* in model with coefficient constrained to 1
asis	retain perfect predictor variables
Reporting	
or	report odds ratios
Max options	
maximize_options	control the maximization process; seldom used

Description

svy: logit fits logistic regression models for complex survey data. In the logistic regression model, *depvar* is a 0/1 variable (or, more precisely, a 0/non-0 variable).

See [R] **logit** for a description of this model involving nonsurvey data, [SVY] **svy: logistic** for logistic regression reporting odds ratios, [SVY] **svy: probit** for probit regression, [SVY] **svy: mlogit** for multinomial logistic regression, [SVY] **svy: ologit** for ordered logistic regression, and [SVY] **svy: oprobit** for ordered probit regression for survey data.

Options

svy_options; see [SVY] **svy**.

___ Model _____

noconstant, offset(*varname*); see [SVY] **estimation options**.

asis forces retention of perfect predictor variables and their associated perfectly predicted observations and may produce instabilities in maximization; see [R] **probit** (sic).

___ Reporting _____

or; see [SVY] *eform_option*.

___ Max options _____

maximize_options: <u>iter</u>ate(*#*), [<u>no</u>]<u>log</u>, <u>trace</u>, <u>tol</u>erance(*#*), <u>ltol</u>erance(*#*); see [R] **maximize**. These options are seldom used. If the maximization is taking a long time, you may wish to specify the log option to view the iteration log. The log option implies svy's noisily option; see [SVY] **svy**.

Remarks

Use svy: logit or svy: logistic to fit regression models with a binary dependent variable. svy: logit reports the estimated coefficients, svy: logistic reports the estimated odds ratios. These two commands are equivalent in every way except how the results are displayed.

▷ Example 1

In [SVY] **svy: logistic**, we mentioned that there are 2 PSUs in each of the 31 strata (stratum 19 is missing) in the NHANES II dataset, and then we fitted a logistic regression using BRR variance estimation. Here we use svy jackknife: logit to fit a logistic regression with the jackknife method for variance estimation. We model whether a person has high blood pressure as a function of age, race, gender, height, and weight.

```
. use http://www.stata-press.com/data/r9/nhanes2d
. svy jackknife, nodots: logit highbp height weight age age2 female black
Survey: Logistic regression
```

Number of strata	=	31	Number of obs	=	10351
Number of PSUs	=	62	Population size	=	1.172e+08
			Replications	=	62
			Design df	=	31
			F(6, 26)	=	87.62
			Prob > F	=	0.0000

highbp	Coef.	Jackknife Std. Err.	t	P>|t|	[95% Conf. Interval]	
height	-.0325996	.0058749	-5.55	0.000	-.0445815	-.0206177
weight	.049074	.0031973	15.35	0.000	.0425531	.055595
age	.1541151	.0208772	7.38	0.000	.1115357	.1966944
age2	-.0010746	.0002026	-5.30	0.000	-.0014878	-.0006615
female	-.356497	.0885785	-4.02	0.000	-.537154	-.17584
black	.3429301	.1413975	2.43	0.021	.054548	.6313121
_cons	-4.89574	1.159628	-4.22	0.000	-7.260817	-2.530664

Our results show that females are less likely than males to have high blood pressure and that blacks are more likely than people of other races to have high blood pressure.

◁

Saved Results

svy: logit saves in e(). In addition to the items documented in [SVY] **svy**, svy: logit also saves the following:

Macros
    e(cmd)   logit
    e(depvar)   name of dependent variable
    e(offset)   offset
    e(crittype) log pseudolikelihood
    e(predict)   program used to implement predict

Methods and Formulas

`svy: logit` is implemented as an ado-file.

The log pseudolikelihood is

$$\ln L = \sum_{j \in S} w_j \ln F(\mathbf{x}_j \boldsymbol{\beta}) + \sum_{j \notin S} w_j \ln\{1 - F(\mathbf{x}_j \boldsymbol{\beta})\}$$

where S is the set of all observations such that $y_j \neq 0$, $F(z) = e^z / (1 + e^z)$ and w_j is a sampling weight. The equation-level scores used in the linearized variance estimator are derived by taking partial derivatives of the log pseudolikelihood; see [SVY] **variance estimation**.

References

Aldrich, J. H. and F. D. Nelson. 1984. *Linear Probability, Logit, and Probit Models*. Newbury Park, CA: Sage.

Cramer, J. S. 2003. *Logit Models from Economics and Other Fields*. Cambridge: Cambridge University Press.

Eltinge, J. L. and W. M. Sribney. 1996. svy4: Linear, logistic, and probit regressions for survey data. *Stata Technical Bulletin* 31: 26–31. Reprinted in *Stata Technical Bulletin Reprints*, vol. 6, pp. 239–245.

Hosmer, D. W., Jr., and S. Lemeshow. 2000. *Applied Logistic Regression*. 2nd ed. New York: Wiley.

Long, J. S. 1997. *Regression Models for Categorical and Limited Dependent Variables*. Thousand Oaks, CA: Sage.

Long, J. S. and J. Freese. 2003. *Regression Models for Categorical Dependent Variables Using Stata*. rev. ed. College Station, TX: Stata Press.

Powers, D. A. and Y. Xie. 2000. *Statistical Methods for Categorical Data Analysis*. San Diego, CA: Academic Press.

Also See

Complementary:	[SVY] **svy: logit postestimation**
Related:	[R] **logit**;
	[SVY] **svy: logistic**, [SVY] **svy: probit**, [SVY] **svy: mlogit**,
	[SVY] **svy: ologit**, [SVY] **svy: oprobit**
Background:	[U] **20 Estimation and postestimation commands**,
	[SVY] **estimation options**, [SVY] **poststratification**,
	[SVY] **subpopulation estimation**, [SVY] **svy**, [SVY] **variance estimation**,
	[R] **maximize**

Title

> **svy: logit postestimation** — Postestimation tools for svy: logit

Description

The following postestimation commands are available for svy: logit:

command	description
estat	postestimation statistics for survey data
estimates	cataloging estimation results
lincom	point estimates, standard errors, testing, and inference for linear combinations of coefficients
mfx	marginal effects or elasticities
nlcom	point estimates, standard errors, testing, and inference for nonlinear combinations of coefficients
predict	predictions, residuals, influence statistics, and other diagnostic measures
predictnl	point estimates, standard errors, testing, and inference for generalized predictions
suest	seemingly unrelated estimation
test	Wald tests for simple and composite linear hypotheses
testnl	Wald tests of nonlinear hypotheses

See [SVY] **estat**.

See the corresponding entries in the *Stata Base Reference Manual* for details.

Syntax for predict

predict [*type*] *newvarname* [*if*] [*in*] [, *statistic* <u>nooff</u>set]

statistic	description
<u>p</u>r	probability of a positive outcome; the default
xb	linear prediction, $x_j\beta$
stdp	standard error of the prediction
<u>sco</u>re	first derivative of the log pseudolikelihood with respect to $x_j\beta$

These statistics are available both in and out of sample; type predict ... if e(sample) ... if wanted only for the estimation sample.

Options for predict

pr, the default, calculates the probability of a positive outcome.

xb calculates the linear prediction $x_j\beta$.

stdp calculates the standard error of the linear prediction.

score calculates the equation-level score, $\partial \ln L / \partial (x_j\beta)$.

nooffset is relevant if you specified offset() when you fitted the model. It modifies the calculations made by predict so that they ignore the offset variable; the linear prediction is treated as $\mathbf{x}_j\beta$ rather than as $\mathbf{x}_j\beta + \text{offset}_j$.

Remarks

▷ Example 1

Continuing with our example from [SVY] **svy: logit**, we use predict to compute the linear prediction for each observation in the dataset and save the values in the new variable xb.

```
. predict xb, xb
```

◁

Methods and Formulas

All postestimation commands listed above are implemented as ado-files.

Also See

Complementary:	[SVY] **svy: logit**, [SVY] **estat**;
	[R] **estimates**, [R] **lincom**, [R] **mfx**, [R] **nlcom**, [R] **predict**,
	[R] **predictnl**, [R] **suest**, [R] **test**, [R] **testnl**
Background:	[U] **13.5 Accessing coefficients and standard errors**,
	[U] **20 Estimation and postestimation commands**

Title

> **svy: mean** — Estimate means for survey data

Syntax

svy [*vcetype*] [, *svy_options*] : mean *varlist* [*if*] [*in*] [, *options*]

vcetype	description
SE	
linearized	Taylor linearized variance estimation
brr	BRR variance estimation; see [SVY] **svy brr**
jackknife	jackknife variance estimation; see [SVY] **svy jackknife**

Specifying a *vcetype* overrides the default from svyset.

svy_options	description
if/in/over	
subpop()	identify a subpopulation
SE	
brr_options	additional options allowed with BRR variance estimation; see [SVY] *brr_options*
jackknife_options	additional options allowed with jackknife variance estimation; see [SVY] *jackknife_options*
Reporting	
level(#)	set confidence level; default is level(95)
noheader	suppress the table header
nolegend	suppress the table legend

svy requires that the survey-design variables be identified using svyset; see [SVY] **svyset**.

See [U] **20 Estimation and postestimation commands** for additional capabilities of estimation commands.

Warning: Using *if* or *in* restrictions will not produce correct variance estimates for subpopulations in many cases. To compute estimates for a subpopulation, use the subpop() option. The full specification for subpop() is

subpop([*varname*] [*if*])

options	description
Model	
stdize(*varname*)	variable identifying strata for standardization
stdweight(*varname*)	weight variable for standardization
nostdrescale	do not rescale the standard weight variable
if/in/over	
over(*varlist* [, nolabel])	identify multiple subpopulations

Description

svy: mean produces estimates of finite-population means from survey data; see [R] **mean** for a description of sample means from nonsurvey data.

Options

svy_options; see [SVY] **svy**.

_____ Model _____

stdize(*varname*) specifies that the point estimates be adjusted by direct standardization across the strata identified by *varname*. This option requires the stdweight() option.

stdweight(*varname*) specifies the weight variable associated with the standard strata identified in the stdize() option. The standardization weights must be constant within the standard strata.

nostdrescale prevents the standardization weights from being rescaled within the over() groups. This option requires stdize() but is ignored if the over() option is not specified.

_____ if/in/over _____

over(*varlist* [, nolabel]) specifies that estimates be computed for multiple subpopulations.

The subpopulations are identified by the different values of the variables in *varlist*.

When over() is supplied with a single variable name, such as over(*varname*), the value labels of *varname* are used to identify the subpopulations. If *varname* does not have labeled values (or there are unlabeled values), the values themselves are used, provided that they are non-negative integers. Non-integer values, negative values, and labels that are not valid Stata names will be substituted with a default identifier.

When supplied with multiple variable names, a subpopulation index (starting at 1) is used to identify subpopulations. In this case, the index is listed with the values that identify the subpopulations.

nolabel requests that value labels attached to the variables identifying the subpopulations be ignored.

Remarks

svy: mean will produce finite-population means for one or more variables and over multiple subpopulations. svy: mean also produces a full covariance matrix, enabling the use of postestimation commands to draw inferences and make comparisons of means (and functions of means) between variables and subpopulations.

▷ Example 1

For the following examples, we use data from the National Maternal and Infant Health Survey (NMIHS) (Gonzalez, Krauss, and Scott 1992, Johnson 1995). This dataset has a stratification variable, stratan. Primary sampling units are mothers; i.e., PSUs are individual observations—there is no separate PSU variable. The sampling weights are given by the variable finwgt. We do not include a finite-population correction for this analysis.

We use the svyset command to set the stratification variable and the pweight variable.

```
. use http://www.stata-press.com/data/r9/nmihs
. svyset [pweight=finwgt], strata(stratan)
      pweight: finwgt
          VCE: linearized
     Strata 1: stratan
         SU 1: <observations>
        FPC 1: <zero>
```

We can now use svy: mean to estimate the average birthweight for the population under study.

```
. svy: mean birthwgt
(running mean on estimation sample)

Survey: Mean estimation

Number of strata =        6          Number of obs    =    9946
Number of PSUs   =     9946          Population size  = 3.9e+06
                                     Design df        =    9940
```

		Linearized		
	Mean	Std. Err.	[95% Conf. Interval]	
birthwgt	3355.452	6.402741	3342.902	3368.003

◁

▷ Example 2: Multiple subpopulations

We can estimate mean birthweight for two or more subpopulations using the over() option. The variable race identifies black and nonblack mothers that participated in NMIHS.

```
. svy: mean birthwgt, over(race)
(running mean on estimation sample)

Survey: Mean estimation

Number of strata =        6          Number of obs    =    9946
Number of PSUs   =     9946          Population size  = 3.9e+06
                                     Design df        =    9940

        nonblack: race = nonblack
           black: race = black
```

		Linearized		
Over	Mean	Std. Err.	[95% Conf. Interval]	
birthwgt				
nonblack	3402.32	7.609532	3387.404	3417.236
black	3127.834	6.529814	3115.035	3140.634

See example 1 in [SVY] **svy: mean postestimation** where we use test, lincom, and estat lceffects to compare the estimated mean birthweights between the subpopulations defined by the race variable.

◁

▷ Example 3: Multiple subpopulations over multiple variables

When there are two or more over() variables, each subpopulation is identified by a standard label. For example, married and single mothers are identified by the marital variable, so we could look at the subpopulations of mothers over race and marital status.

```
. svy: mean birthwgt, over(race marital)
(running mean on estimation sample)

Survey: Mean estimation

Number of strata =        6        Number of obs    =      9946
Number of PSUs   =     9946        Population size  = 3.9e+06
                                   Design df        =      9940

            Over: race marital
      _subpop_1: nonblack single
      _subpop_2: nonblack married
      _subpop_3: black single
      _subpop_4: black married
```

Over	Mean	Linearized Std. Err.	[95% Conf. Interval]	
birthwgt				
_subpop_1	3291.045	20.18795	3251.472	3330.617
_subpop_2	3426.407	8.379497	3409.982	3442.833
_subpop_3	3073.122	8.752553	3055.965	3090.279
_subpop_4	3221.616	12.42687	3197.257	3245.975

◁

▷ Example 4: Restricting attention to specific subpopulations

Suppose that we were interested in a comparison of mean birthweight between single and married black mothers. We can use the subpop() option to restrict our attention to the subpopulation of black mothers and use the over() option to get the mean estimates between single and married mothers.

```
. svy, subpop(if race == "black":race) nolegend: mean birthwgt, over(marital)
(running mean on estimation sample)

Survey: Mean estimation

Number of strata =        6        Number of obs    =      9946
Number of PSUs   =     9946        Population size  = 3.9e+06
                                   Subpop. no. obs  =      5222
                                   Subpop. size     =    665159
                                   Design df        =      9940
```

Over	Mean	Linearized Std. Err.	[95% Conf. Interval]	
birthwgt				
single	3073.122	8.752553	3055.965	3090.279
married	3221.616	12.42687	3197.257	3245.975

◁

Leslie Kish (1910–2000) was born in Poprad, Hungary, and entered the United States with his family in 1926. He worked as a lab assistant at the Rockefeller Institute for Medical Research and studied at the College of the City of New York, fighting in the Spanish Civil War before receiving his first degree in mathematics. Kish worked for the Bureau of the Census, the Department of Agriculture, the Army Air Corps, and finally the University of Michigan. He carried out pioneering work in the theory and practice of survey sampling, including design effects, balanced repeated replication, response errors, rolling samples and censuses, controlled selection, multipurpose designs, and small-area estimation.

Saved Results

svy: mean saves in e(). In addition to the items documented in [SVY] **svy**, svy: mean also saves the following:

Scalars
    e(N_over)   number of subpopulations

Macros

e(cmd)	mean	e(varlist)	*varlist*
e(over)	*varlist* from over()	e(stdize)	*varname* from stdize()
e(over_labels)	labels from over() variables	e(stdweight)	*varname* from stdweight()
e(over_namelist)	names from e(over_labels)		

Matrices
    e(_N)   vector of sample sizes
    e(_N_subp)   vector of subpopulation size estimates

Methods and Formulas

svy: mean is implemented as an ado-file.

See [SVY] **variance estimation**, [SVY] **direct standardization**, and [SVY] **poststratification** for discussions that provide background information for the following formulas. Note that the following formulas are derived from the fact that the mean is a special case of the ratio estimator where the denominator variable is one, $x_j = 1$.

The mean estimator

Let Y_j be a survey item for the jth individual in the population, where $j = 1, \ldots, M$ and M is the size of the population. The associated population mean for the item of interest is $\overline{Y} = Y/M$ where

$$Y = \sum_{j=1}^{M} Y_j$$

Let y_j be the survey item for the jth sampled individual from the population, where $j = 1, \ldots, m$ and m is the number of observations in the sample.

The estimator for the mean is $\overline{y} = \widehat{Y}/\widehat{M}$, where

$$\widehat{Y} = \sum_{j=1}^{m} w_j y_j \quad \text{and} \quad \widehat{M} = \sum_{j-1}^{m} w_j$$

and w_j is a sampling weight. The score variable for the mean estimator is

$$z_j(\overline{y}) = \frac{y_j - \overline{y}}{\widehat{M}} = \frac{\widehat{M}y_j - \widehat{Y}}{\widehat{M}^2}$$

The standardized mean estimator

Let D_g denote the set of sampled observations that belong to the gth standard stratum and define $I_{D_g}(j)$ to indicate if the jth observation is a member of the gth standard stratum; where $g = 1$, ..., L_D and L_D is the number of standard strata. Also let π_g denote the fraction of the population that belongs to the gth standard stratum, thus $\pi_1 + \cdots + \pi_{L_D} = 1$. Note that π_g is derived from the stdweight() option.

The estimator for the standardized mean is

$$\overline{y}^D = \sum_{g=1}^{L_D} \pi_g \frac{\widehat{Y}_g}{\widehat{M}_g}$$

where

$$\widehat{Y}_g = \sum_{j=1}^{m} I_{D_g}(j)\, w_j y_j \qquad \text{and} \qquad \widehat{M}_g = \sum_{j=1}^{m} I_{D_g}(j)\, w_j$$

The score variable for the standardized mean is

$$z_j(\overline{y}^D) = \sum_{g=1}^{L_D} \pi_g I_{D_g}(j) \frac{\widehat{M}_g y_j - \widehat{Y}_g}{\widehat{M}_g^2}$$

The poststratified mean estimator

Let P_k denote the set of sampled observations that belong to poststratum k and define $I_{P_k}(j)$ to indicate if the jth observation is a member of poststratum k; where $k = 1, \ldots, L_P$ and L_P is the number of poststrata. Also let M_k denote the population size for poststratum k. P_k and M_k are identified by specifying the poststrata() and postweight() options on svyset.

The estimator for the poststratified mean is

$$\overline{y}^P = \frac{\widehat{Y}^P}{\widehat{M}^P} = \frac{\widehat{Y}^P}{M}$$

where

$$\widehat{Y}^P = \sum_{k=1}^{L_P} \frac{M_k}{\widehat{M}_k}\widehat{Y}_k = \sum_{k=1}^{L_P} \frac{M_k}{\widehat{M}_k} \sum_{j=1}^{m} I_{P_k}(j)\, w_j y_j$$

and

$$\widehat{M}^P = \sum_{k=1}^{L_P} \frac{M_k}{\widehat{M}_k}\widehat{M}_k = \sum_{k=1}^{L_P} M_k = M$$

The score variable for the poststratified mean is

$$z_j(\overline{y}^P) = \frac{z_j(\widehat{Y}^P)}{M} = \frac{1}{M}\sum_{k=1}^{L_P} I_{P_k}(j) \frac{M_k}{\widehat{M}_k}\left(y_j - \frac{\widehat{Y}_k}{\widehat{M}_k}\right)$$

The standardized poststratified mean estimator

The estimator for the standardized poststratified mean is

$$
\overline{y}^{DP} = \sum_{g=1}^{L_D} \pi_g \frac{\widehat{Y}_g^P}{\widehat{M}_g^P}
$$

where

$$
\widehat{Y}_g^P = \sum_{k=1}^{L_p} \frac{M_k}{\widehat{M}_k} \widehat{Y}_{g,k} = \sum_{k=1}^{L_p} \frac{M_k}{\widehat{M}_k} \sum_{j=1}^{m} I_{D_g}(j) I_{P_k}(j) \, w_j y_j
$$

and

$$
\widehat{M}_g^P = \sum_{k=1}^{L_p} \frac{M_k}{\widehat{M}_k} \widehat{M}_{g,k} = \sum_{k=1}^{L_p} \frac{M_k}{\widehat{M}_k} \sum_{j=1}^{m} I_{D_g}(j) I_{P_k}(j) \, w_j
$$

The score variable for the standardized poststratified mean is

$$
z_j(\overline{y}^{DP}) = \sum_{g=1}^{L_D} \pi_g \frac{\widehat{M}_g^P z_j(\widehat{Y}_g^P) - \widehat{Y}_g^P z_j(\widehat{M}_g^P)}{(\widehat{M}_g^P)^2}
$$

where

$$
z_j(\widehat{Y}_g^P) = \sum_{k=1}^{L_P} I_{P_k}(j) \frac{M_k}{\widehat{M}_k} \left\{ I_{D_g}(j) y_j - \frac{\widehat{Y}_{g,k}}{\widehat{M}_k} \right\}
$$

and

$$
z_j(\widehat{M}_g^P) = \sum_{k=1}^{L_P} I_{P_k}(j) \frac{M_k}{\widehat{M}_k} \left\{ I_{D_g}(j) - \frac{\widehat{M}_{g,k}}{\widehat{M}_k} \right\}
$$

Subpopulation estimation

Let S denote the set of sampled observations that belong to the subpopulation of interest, and define $I_S(j)$ to indicate if the jth observation falls within the subpopulation.

The estimator for the subpopulation mean is $\overline{y}^S = \widehat{Y}^S / \widehat{M}^S$, where

$$
\widehat{Y}^S = \sum_{j=1}^{m} I_S(j) \, w_j y_j \qquad \text{and} \qquad \widehat{M}^S = \sum_{j=1}^{m} I_S(j) \, w_j
$$

Its score variable is

$$
z_j(\overline{y}^S) = I_S(j) \frac{y_j - \overline{y}^S}{\widehat{M}^S} = I_S(j) \frac{\widehat{M}^S y_j - \widehat{Y}^S}{(\widehat{M}^S)^2}
$$

The estimator for the standardized subpopulation mean is

$$
\overline{y}^{DS} = \sum_{g=1}^{L_D} \pi_g \frac{\widehat{Y}_g^S}{\widehat{M}_g^S}
$$

where

$$\widehat{Y}_g^S = \sum_{j=1}^m I_{D_g}(j) I_S(j)\, w_j y_j \qquad \text{and} \qquad \widehat{M}_g^S = \sum_{j=1}^m I_{D_g}(j) I_S(j)\, w_j$$

Its score variable is

$$z_j(\overline{y}^{DS}) = \sum_{g=1}^{L_D} \pi_g I_{D_g}(j) I_S(j) \frac{\widehat{M}_g^S y_j - \widehat{Y}_g^S}{(\widehat{M}_g^S)^2}$$

The estimator for the poststratified subpopulation mean is

$$\overline{y}^{PS} = \frac{\widehat{Y}^{PS}}{\widehat{M}^{PS}}$$

where

$$\widehat{Y}^{PS} = \sum_{k=1}^{L_P} \frac{M_k}{\widehat{M}_k} \widehat{Y}_k^S = \sum_{k=1}^{L_P} \frac{M_k}{\widehat{M}_k} \sum_{j=1}^m I_{P_k}(j) I_S(j)\, w_j y_j$$

and

$$\widehat{M}^{PS} = \sum_{k=1}^{L_P} \frac{M_k}{\widehat{M}_k} \widehat{M}_k^S = \sum_{k=1}^{L_P} \frac{M_k}{\widehat{M}_k} \sum_{j=1}^m I_{P_k}(j) I_S(j)\, w_j$$

Its score variable is

$$z_j(\overline{y}^{PS}) = \frac{\widehat{M}^{PS} z_j(\widehat{Y}^{PS}) - \widehat{Y}^{PS} z_j(\widehat{M}^{PS})}{(\widehat{M}^{PS})^2}$$

where

$$z_j(\widehat{Y}^{PS}) = \sum_{k=1}^{L_P} I_{P_k}(j) \frac{M_k}{\widehat{M}_k} \left\{ I_S(j) y_j - \frac{\widehat{Y}_k^S}{\widehat{M}_k} \right\}$$

and

$$z_j(\widehat{M}^{PS}) = \sum_{k=1}^{L_P} I_{P_k}(j) \frac{M_k}{\widehat{M}_k} \left\{ I_S(j) - \frac{\widehat{M}_k^S}{\widehat{M}_k} \right\}$$

The estimator for the standardized poststratified subpopulation mean is

$$\overline{y}^{DPS} = \sum_{g=1}^{L_D} \pi_g \frac{\widehat{Y}_g^{PS}}{\widehat{M}_g^{PS}}$$

where

$$\widehat{Y}_g^{PS} = \sum_{k=1}^{L_p} \frac{M_k}{\widehat{M}_k} \widehat{Y}_{g,k}^S = \sum_{k=1}^{L_p} \frac{M_k}{\widehat{M}_k} \sum_{j=1}^m I_{D_g}(j) I_{P_k}(j) I_S(j)\, w_j y_j$$

and

$$\widehat{M}_g^{PS} = \sum_{k=1}^{L_p} \frac{M_k}{\widehat{M}_k} \widehat{M}_{g,k}^S = \sum_{k=1}^{L_p} \frac{M_k}{\widehat{M}_k} \sum_{j=1}^m I_{D_g}(j) I_{P_k}(j) I_S(j)\, w_j$$

Its score variable is

$$z_j(\overline{y}^{DPS}) = \sum_{g=1}^{L_D} \pi_g \frac{\widehat{M}_g^{PS} z_j(\widehat{Y}_g^{PS}) - \widehat{Y}_g^{PS} z_j(\widehat{M}_g^{PS})}{(\widehat{M}_g^{PS})^2}$$

where

$$z_j(\widehat{Y}_g^{PS}) = \sum_{k=1}^{L_P} I_{P_k}(j) \frac{M_k}{\widehat{M}_k} \left\{ I_{D_g}(j) I_S(j)\, y_j - \frac{\widehat{Y}_{g,k}^S}{\widehat{M}_k} \right\}$$

and

$$z_j(\widehat{M}_g^{PS}) = \sum_{k=1}^{L_P} I_{P_k}(j) \frac{M_k}{\widehat{M}_k} \left\{ I_{D_g}(j) I_S(j) - \frac{\widehat{M}_{g,k}^S}{\widehat{M}_k} \right\}$$

References

Cochran, W. G. 1977. *Sampling Techniques.* 3rd ed. New York: Wiley.

Eltinge, J. L. and W. M. Sribney. 1996. svy2: Estimation of means, totals, ratios, and proportions for survey data. *Stata Technical Bulletin* 31: 6–23. Reprinted in *Stata Technical Bulletin Reprints*, vol. 6, pp. 213–235.

Frankel, M. and B. King. 1996. A conversation with Leslie Kish. *Statistical Science* 11: 65–87.

Gonzalez J. F., Jr., N. Krauss, and C. Scott. 1992. Estimation in the 1988 National Maternal and Infant Health Survey. In *Proceedings of the Section on Statistics Education, American Statistical Association*, 343–348.

Johnson, W. 1995. Variance estimation for the NMIHS. Technical document. Hyattsville, MD: National Center for Health Statistics.

Kish, L. 1965. *Survey Sampling.* New York: Wiley.

Wolter, K. M. 1985. *Introduction to Variance Estimation.* New York: Springer.

Also See

Complementary:	[SVY] **svy: mean postestimation**
Related:	[R] **mean**;
	[SVY] **svy: proportion**, [SVY] **svy: ratio**, [SVY] **svy: total**
Background:	[U] **20 Estimation and postestimation commands**,
	[SVY] **estimation options**, [SVY] **direct standardization**,
	[SVY] **poststratification**, [SVY] **subpopulation estimation**,
	[SVY] **svy**, [SVY] **variance estimation**

Title

svy: mean postestimation — Postestimation tools for svy: mean

Description

The following postestimation commands are available for svy: mean:

command	description
estat	postestimation statistics for survey data
estimates	cataloging estimation results
lincom	point estimates, standard errors, testing, and inference for linear combinations of descriptive statistics
nlcom	point estimates, standard errors, testing, and inference for nonlinear combinations of descriptive statistics
test	Wald tests for simple and composite linear hypotheses
testnl	Wald tests of nonlinear hypotheses

See [SVY] **estat**.

See the corresponding entries in the *Stata Base Reference Manual* for details on the other postestimation commands.

predict is not allowed after svy: mean.

Remarks

▷ Example 1: Multiple subpopulations

Continuing with example 2 from [SVY] **svy: mean**, we can perform a test of equality of the means between the two subpopulations.

```
. test [birthwgt]nonblack = [birthwgt]black
Adjusted Wald test
 ( 1)  [birthwgt]nonblack - [birthwgt]black = 0
        F(  1,   9940) =   749.35
              Prob > F =     0.0000
```

Instead of testing equality, we can use lincom to estimate the difference.

```
. lincom [birthwgt]nonblack - [birthwgt]black
 ( 1)  [birthwgt]nonblack - [birthwgt]black = 0
```

	Coef.	Std. Err.	t	P>|t|	[95% Conf. Interval]	
(1)	274.4858	10.02714	27.37	0.000	254.8306	294.1411

We can also use `estat lceffects` to report the design and misspecification effects for this difference.

```
. estat lceffects [birthwgt]nonblack - [birthwgt]black, deff deft meff meft
 ( 1)  [birthwgt]nonblack - [birthwgt]black = 0
```

	Coef.	Std. Err.	Deff	Deft	Meff	Meft
(1)	274.4858	10.02714	.349174	.59091	.2582	.508134

◁

Methods and Formulas

All postestimation commands listed above are implemented as ado-files.

Also See

Complementary:	[SVY] **svy: mean**, [SVY] **estat**;
	[R] **estimates**, [R] **lincom**, [R] **nlcom**, [R] **test**, [R] **testnl**
Background:	[U] **13.5 Accessing coefficients and standard errors**,
	[U] **20 Estimation and postestimation commands**

Title

svy: mlogit — Multinomial logistic regression for survey data

Syntax

svy [vcetype] [, svy_options] : mlogit depvar [indepvars] [if] [in] [, options]

vcetype	description
SE	
linearized	Taylor linearized variance estimation
brr	BRR variance estimation; see [SVY] **svy brr**
jackknife	jackknife variance estimation; see [SVY] **svy jackknife**

Specifying a *vcetype* overrides the default from svyset.

svy_options	description
if/in	
subpop()	identify a subpopulation
SE	
brr_options	additional options allowed with BRR variance estimation; see [SVY] *brr_options*
jackknife_options	additional options allowed with jackknife variance estimation; see [SVY] *jackknife_options*
Reporting	
level(#)	set confidence level; default is level(95)
noheader	suppress the table header
nolegend	suppress the table legend
noadjust	do not adjust model Wald statistic

svy requires that the survey-design variables be identified using svyset; see [SVY] svyset.

xi is allowed; see [R] **xi**.

See [U] **20 Estimation and postestimation commands** for additional capabilities of estimation commands.

Warning: Using *if* or *in* restrictions will not produce correct variance estimates for subpopulations in many cases. To compute estimates for a subpopulation, use the subpop() option. The full specification for subpop() is

subpop([varname] [if])

(Continued on next page)

options	description
Model	
<u>nocon</u>stant	suppress the constant term
<u>base</u>category(*#*)	identify the base category
<u>const</u>raints(*clist*)	apply specified linear constraints
Reporting	
<u>rrr</u>	report relative-risk ratios
Max options	
maximize_options	control the maximization process; seldom used

Description

svy: mlogit fits multinomial logistic regression models for complex survey data. In the multinomial logistic regression model, *depvar* is a discrete variable that takes on two or more outcomes that have no natural ordering.

See [R] **mlogit** for a description of this model involving nonsurvey data, [SVY] **svy: logistic** for logistic regression reporting odds ratios, [SVY] **svy: logit** for logistic regression, [SVY] **svy: probit** for probit regression, [SVY] **svy: ologit** for ordered logistic regression, and [SVY] **svy: oprobit** for ordered probit regression for survey data.

Options

svy_options; see [SVY] **svy**.

___Model|_____

noconstant; see [SVY] **estimation options**.

basecategory(*#*) specifies the value of the dependent variable that is to be treated as the base category. The default is to choose the most-frequent category.

constraints(*clist*); see [SVY] **estimation options**.

___Reporting|_____

rrr; see [SVY] *eform_option*.

___Max options|_____

maximize_options: <u>iter</u>ate(*#*), [<u>no</u>]<u>log</u>, <u>trace</u>, <u>tol</u>erance(*#*), <u>ltol</u>erance(*#*); see [R] **maximize**. These options are seldom used. If the maximization is taking a long time, you may wish to specify the log option to view the iteration log. The log option implies svy's noisily option; see [SVY] **svy**.

Remarks

svy: mlogit fits multinomial logistic regression models where the dependent variable takes on two or more outcomes and the outcomes have no natural ordering. If the dependent variable takes on only two outcomes, estimates are identical to those produced by svy: logistic or svy: logit. If the outcomes are ordered, see [SVY] **svy: ologit**.

For an introduction to multinomial logit models, see Aldrich and Nelson (1984, 73–77), Greene (2003, chapter 21), Hosmer and Lemeshow (2000, 260–287), Long (1997, chapter 6), and Long and Freese (2003, chapter 6). For a description emphasizing the difference in assumptions and data requirements for conditional and multinomial logit, see Judge et al. (1985, 768–772).

Consider the outcomes 1, 2, 3, ..., m recorded in y, and the explanatory variables X. Assume that there are $m = 3$ outcomes: "pet is a dog", "pet is a cat", and "pet is a fish". The values of y are then said to be "unordered". Even though the outcomes are coded 1, 2, and 3, the numerical values are arbitrary because $1 < 2 < 3$ does not imply that outcome 1 (pet is a dog) is less than outcome 2 (pet is a cat) is less than outcome 3 (pet is a fish). This unordered categorical property of y distinguishes the use of svy: mlogit from svy: regress (which is appropriate for a continuous dependent variable), from svy: ologit (which is appropriate for ordered categorical data), and from svy: logit (which is appropriate for two outcomes, which can be thought of as ordered).

In the multinomial logit model, you estimate a set of coefficients, $\beta^{(1)}$, $\beta^{(2)}$, and $\beta^{(3)}$, corresponding to each outcome:

$$\Pr(y = 1) = \frac{e^{X\beta^{(1)}}}{e^{X\beta^{(1)}} + e^{X\beta^{(2)}} + e^{X\beta^{(3)}}}$$

$$\Pr(y = 2) = \frac{e^{X\beta^{(2)}}}{e^{X\beta^{(1)}} + e^{X\beta^{(2)}} + e^{X\beta^{(3)}}}$$

$$\Pr(y = 3) = \frac{e^{X\beta^{(3)}}}{e^{X\beta^{(1)}} + e^{X\beta^{(2)}} + e^{X\beta^{(3)}}}$$

The model, however, is unidentified in the sense that there is more than one solution to $\beta^{(1)}$, $\beta^{(2)}$, and $\beta^{(3)}$ that leads to the same probabilities for $y = 1$, $y = 2$, and $y = 3$. To identify the model, you arbitrarily set one of $\beta^{(1)}$, $\beta^{(2)}$, or $\beta^{(3)}$ to 0—it does not matter which. That is, if you arbitrarily set $\beta^{(1)} = 0$, the remaining coefficients $\beta^{(2)}$ and $\beta^{(3)}$ will measure the change relative to the $y = 1$ alternative. If you instead set $\beta^{(2)} = 0$, the remaining coefficients $\beta^{(1)}$ and $\beta^{(3)}$ will measure the change relative to the $y = 2$ alternative. The coefficients will differ because they have different interpretations, but the predicted probabilities for $y = 1$, 2, and 3 will still be the same. Thus either parameterization will be a solution to the same underlying model.

Setting $\beta^{(1)} = 0$, the equations become

$$\Pr(y = 1) = \frac{1}{1 + e^{X\beta^{(2)}} + e^{X\beta^{(3)}}}$$

$$\Pr(y = 2) = \frac{e^{X\beta^{(2)}}}{1 + e^{X\beta^{(2)}} + e^{X\beta^{(3)}}}$$

$$\Pr(y = 3) = \frac{e^{X\beta^{(3)}}}{1 + e^{X\beta^{(2)}} + e^{X\beta^{(3)}}}$$

The relative probability of $y = 2$ to the base outcome is

$$\frac{\Pr(y = 2)}{\Pr(y = 1)} = e^{X\beta^{(2)}}$$

Let us call this ratio the relative risk, and let us further assume that X and $\beta_k^{(2)}$ are vectors equal to $(x_1, x_2, \ldots, x_k)$ and $(\beta_1^{(2)}, \beta_2^{(2)}, \ldots, \beta_k^{(2)})'$, respectively. The ratio of the relative risk for a one-unit change in x_i is then

$$\frac{e^{\beta_1^{(2)} x_1 + \cdots + \beta_i^{(2)}(x_i + 1) + \cdots + \beta_k^{(2)} x_k}}{e^{\beta_1^{(2)} x_1 + \cdots + \beta_i^{(2)} x_i + \cdots + \beta_k^{(2)} x_k}} = e^{\beta_i^{(2)}}$$

Thus the exponentiated value of a coefficient is the relative-risk ratio for a one-unit change in the corresponding variable (risk is measured as the risk of the outcome relative to the base outcome).

▷ Example 1

Using the NHANES II dataset, [SVY] **svy: ologit** and [SVY] **svy: oprobit** model the categories of self-reported health status as ordered categories. Here we model the values of health as unordered categories using svy: mlogit.

(Continued on next page)

```
. use http://www.stata-press.com/data/r9/nhanes2f

. svyset
      pweight: finalwgt
          VCE: linearized
    Strata 1: stratid
        SU 1: psuid
       FPC 1: <zero>

. svy: mlogit health female black age age2
(running mlogit on estimation sample)

Survey: Multinomial logistic regression
```

Number of strata	=	31	Number of obs	=	10335
Number of PSUs	=	62	Population size	=	1.170e+08
			Design df	=	31
			F(16, 16)	=	36.41
			Prob > F	=	0.0000

health	Coef.	Linearized Std. Err.	t	P>|t|	[95% Conf. Interval]	
poor						
female	-.1983735	.1072747	-1.85	0.074	-.4171617	.0204147
black	.8964694	.1797728	4.99	0.000	.5298203	1.263119
age	.0990246	.032111	3.08	0.004	.0335338	.1645155
age2	-.0004749	.0003209	-1.48	0.149	-.0011294	.0001796
_cons	-5.475074	.7468576	-7.33	0.000	-6.9983	-3.951848
fair						
female	.1782371	.0726556	2.45	0.020	.030055	.3264193
black	.4429445	.122667	3.61	0.001	1927635	.0931256
age	.0024570	.0172236	0.14	0.887	-.0326702	.0375853
age2	.0002875	.0001684	1.71	0.098	-.0000559	.000631
_cons	-1.819561	.4018153	-4.53	0.000	-2.639069	-1.000053
good						
female	-.0458251	.074169	-0.62	0.541	-.1970938	.1054437
black	-.7532011	.1105444	-6.81	0.000	-.9786579	-.5277443
age	-.061369	.009794	-6.27	0.000	-.081344	-.0413939
age2	.0004166	.0001077	3.87	0.001	.000197	.0006363
_cons	1.815323	.1996917	9.09	0.000	1.408049	2.222597
excellent						
female	-.222799	.0754205	-2.95	0.006	-.3766202	-.0689778
black	-.991647	.1238806	-8.00	0.000	-1.244303	-.7389909
age	-.0293573	.0137789	-2.13	0.041	-.0574595	-.001255
age2	-.0000674	.0001505	-0.45	0.657	-.0003744	.0002396
_cons	1.499683	.286143	5.24	0.000	.9160909	2.083276

(health==average is the base outcome)

We see an interesting pattern here. It suggests that females are less likely to report the extremes of health than males; that is, it is less likely that females will report their health status as poor or excellent.

◁

Saved Results

svy: mlogit saves in e(). In addition to the items documented in [SVY] **svy**, svy: mlogit also saves the following:

Scalars

e(k_cat)	number of categories
e(ibasecat)	base category number
e(basecat)	the value of *depvar* to be treated as the base category

Macros

e(cmd)	mlogit
e(depvar)	name of dependent variable
e(eqnames)	names of equations
e(crittype)	log pseudolikelihood
e(predict)	program used to implement predict

Methods and Formulas

svy: mlogit is implemented as an ado-file.

The multinomial logit model is described in Greene (2003, chapter 21).

Suppose that there are k categorical responses, and—without loss of generality—let the base category be category 1. The probability that the response for the jth observation is equal to the ith category is

$$p_{ij} = \Pr(y_j = i) = \begin{cases} \dfrac{1}{1 + \sum\limits_{m=2}^{k} \exp(\mathbf{x}_j \boldsymbol{\beta}_m)}, & \text{if } i = 1 \\[2em] \dfrac{\exp(\mathbf{x}_j \boldsymbol{\beta}_i)}{1 + \sum\limits_{m=2}^{k} \exp(\mathbf{x}_j \boldsymbol{\beta}_m)}, & \text{if } i > 1 \end{cases}$$

where $\mathbf{x}_j$ is the row vector of observed values of the independent variables for the jth observation and $\boldsymbol{\beta}_m$ is the coefficient vector for category m. The log pseudolikelihood is

$$\ln L = \sum_j w_j \sum_{i=1}^{k} I_i(y_j) \ln p_{ik}$$

where w_j is a sampling weight and

$$I_i(y_j) = \begin{cases} 1, & \text{if } y_j = i \\ 0, & \text{otherwise} \end{cases}$$

The equation-level scores used in the linearized variance estimator are derived by taking partial derivatives of the log pseudolikelihood; see [SVY] **variance estimation**.

References

Aldrich, J. H. and F. D. Nelson. 1984. *Linear Probability, Logit, and Probit Models*. Newbury Park, CA: Sage.

Freese, J. and J. S. Long. 2000. sg155: Tests for the multinomial logit model. *Stata Technical Bulletin* 58: 19–25. Reprinted in *Stata Technical Bulletin Reprints*, vol. 10, pp. 247–255.

Greene, W. H. 2003. *Econometric Analysis*. 5th ed. Upper Saddle River, NJ: Prentice Hall.

Hamilton, L. C. 1993. sqv8: Interpreting multinomial logistic regression. *Stata Technical Bulletin* 13: 24–28. Reprinted in *Stata Technical Bulletin Reprints*, vol. 3, pp. 176–181.

——. 2004. *Statistics with Stata*. Belmont, CA: Brooks/Cole.

Hendrickx, J. 2000. sbe37: Special restrictions in multinomial logistic regression. *Stata Technical Bulletin* 56: 18–26.

Hosmer, D. W., Jr., and S. Lemeshow. 2000. *Applied Logistic Regression*. 2nd ed. New York: Wiley.

Judge, G. G., W. E. Griffiths, R. C. Hill, H. Lütkepohl, and T.-C. Lee. 1985. *The Theory and Practice of Econometrics*. 2nd ed. New York: Wiley.

Kleinbaum, D. G. and M. Klein. 2002. *Logistic Regression: A Self-Learning Text*. 2nd ed. New York: Springer.

Long, J. S. 1997. *Regression Models for Categorical and Limited Dependent Variables*. Thousand Oaks, CA: Sage.

Long, J. S. and J. Freese. 2003. *Regression Models for Categorical Dependent Variables Using Stata*. rev. ed. College Station, TX: Stata Press.

Also See

Complementary:	[SVY] **svy: mlogit postestimation**
Related:	[R] **mlogit**;
	[SVY] **svy: logistic**, [SVY] **svy: logit**, [SVY] **svy: ologit**,
	[SVY] **svy: oprobit** [SVY] **svy: probit**,
Background:	[U] **20 Estimation and postestimation commands**,
	[SVY] **estimation options**, [SVY] **poststratification**,
	[SVY] **subpopulation estimation**, [SVY] **svy**, [SVY] **variance estimation**,
	[R] **maximize**

Title

> **svy: mlogit postestimation** — Postestimation tools for svy: mlogit

Description

The following postestimation commands are available for svy: mlogit:

command	description
estat	postestimation statistics for survey data
estimates	cataloging estimation results
lincom	point estimates, standard errors, testing, and inference for linear combinations of coefficients
mfx	marginal effects or elasticities
nlcom	point estimates, standard errors, testing, and inference for nonlinear combinations of coefficients
predict	predictions, residuals, influence statistics, and other diagnostic measures
predictnl	point estimates, standard errors, testing, and inference for generalized predictions
suest	seemingly unrelated estimation
test	Wald tests for simple and composite linear hypotheses
testnl	Wald tests of nonlinear hypotheses

See [SVY] **estat**.

See the corresponding entries in the *Stata Base Reference Manual* for details.

Syntax for predict

predict $[type]$ *newvar* $[if]$ $[in]$, <u>o</u>utcome(*outcome*) $[statistic]$

predict $[type]$ { *stub** | *newvar*$_1$ ... *newvar*$_{k-1}$ } $[if]$ $[in]$, <u>sc</u>ores

where k is the number of outcomes in the model.

statistic	description
<u>p</u>r	probability of a positive outcome; the default
xb	linear prediction, $x_j\beta_i$
stdp	standard error of the linear prediction

Note that you specify one new variable with xb and stdp and specify either one or k new variables with pr.

These statistics are available both in and out of sample; type predict ... if e(sample) ... if wanted only for the estimation sample.

Options for predict

pr, the default, calculates the probability of each of the alternatives in the model or the probability of the outcome specified in outcome(). If you specify outcome(), you only need to specify one new variable; otherwise, you must specify k new variables, one for each alternative in the model.

136

xb calculates the linear prediction $\mathbf{x}_j\boldsymbol{\beta}_i$. You must also specify the outcome(*outcome*) option.

stdp calculates the standard error of the linear prediction. You must also specify the outcome(*outcome*) option.

outcome(*outcome*) specifies the outcome for which the statistic is to be calculated. equation() is a synonym for outcome(): it does not matter which you use, and the standard rules for specifying an equation() apply.

scores calculates equation-level score variables. The number of score variables created will be one less than the number of outcomes in the model. If the number of outcomes in the model were k, then

the first new variable will contain $\partial\ln L/\partial(\mathbf{x}_j\boldsymbol{\beta}_1)$;

the second new variable will contain $\partial\ln L/\partial(\mathbf{x}_j\boldsymbol{\beta}_2)$;

...

the $(k-1)$st new variable will contain $\partial\ln L/\partial(\mathbf{x}_j\boldsymbol{\beta}_{k-1})$.

Remarks

▷ Example 1

Continuing with our example from [SVY] **svy: mlogit**, we use predict to compute the probability for each the 5 alternative and save the values in the new variables pr1, ..., pr5.

```
. predict pr*
(option pr assumed; predicted probabilities)
. describe pr*
```

variable name	storage type	display format	value label	variable label
pr1	float	%9.0g		Pr(health==poor)
pr2	float	%9.0g		Pr(health==fair)
pr3	float	%9.0g		Pr(health==average)
pr4	float	%9.0g		Pr(health==good)
pr5	float	%9.0g		Pr(health==excellent)

◁

Methods and Formulas

All postestimation commands listed above are implemented as ado-files.

Also See

Complementary: [SVY] **svy: mlogit**, [SVY] **estat**;

[R] **estimates**, [R] **lincom**, [R] **mfx**, [R] **nlcom**, [R] **predict**,

[R] **predictnl**, [R] **suest**, [R] **test**, [R] **testnl**

Background: [U] **13.5 Accessing coefficients and standard errors**,

[U] **20 Estimation and postestimation commands**

Title

svy: nbreg — Negative binomial regression for survey data

Syntax

Negative binomial regression

svy [*vcetype*] [, *svy_options*] : nbreg *depvar* [*indepvars*] [*if*] [*in*] [, *nbreg_options*]

Generalized negative binomial regression

svy [*vcetype*] [, *svy_options*] : gnbreg *depvar* [*indepvars*] [*if*] [*in*] [, *gnbreg_options*]

vcetype	description
SE	
linearized	Taylor linearized variance estimation
brr	BRR variance estimation; see [SVY] **svy brr**
jackknife	jackknife variance estimation; see [SVY] **svy jackknife**

Specifying a *vcetype* overrides the default from svyset.

svy_options	description
if/in	
subpop()	identify a subpopulation
SE	
brr_options	additional options allowed with BRR variance estimation; see [SVY] *brr_options*
jackknife_options	additional options allowed with jackknife variance estimation; see [SVY] *jackknife_options*
Reporting	
level(#)	set confidence level; default is level(95)
noheader	suppress the table header
nolegend	suppress the table legend
noadjust	do not adjust model Wald statistic

svy requires that the survey-design variables be identified using svyset; see [SVY] **svyset**.

xi is allowed; see [R] **xi**.

See [U] **20 Estimation and postestimation commands** for additional capabilities of estimation commands.

Warning: Using *if* or *in* restrictions will not produce correct variance estimates for subpopulations in many cases. To compute estimates for a subpopulation, use the subpop() option. The full specification for subpop() is

subpop([*varname*] [*if*])

nbreg_options	description
Model	
<u>noco</u>nstant	suppress the constant term
dispersion(<u>m</u>ean)	parameterization of dispersion; dispersion(mean) is the default
dispersion(<u>c</u>onstant)	constant dispersion for all observations
<u>e</u>xposure(*varname_e*)	include ln(*varname_e*) in model with coefficient constrained to 1
<u>off</u>set(*varname_o*)	include *varname_o* in model with coefficient constrained to 1
<u>constr</u>aints(*constraints*)	apply specified linear constraints
Reporting	
<u>irr</u>	report incidence-rate ratios
Max options	
maximize_options	control the maximization process; seldom used

gnbreg_options	description
Model	
<u>noco</u>nstant	suppress the constant term
<u>lnal</u>pha(*varlist*)	dispersion model variables
<u>e</u>xposure(*varname_e*)	include ln(*varname_e*) in model with coefficient constrained to 1
<u>off</u>set(*varname_o*)	include *varname_o* in model with coefficient constrained to 1
<u>constr</u>aints(*constraints*)	apply specified linear constraints
Reporting	
<u>irr</u>	report incidence-rate ratios
Max options	
maximize_options	control the maximization process; seldom used

Description

svy: nbreg fits negative binomial (Poisson with overdispersion) regression models for complex survey data; see [R] **nbreg** for a description of this model involving nonsurvey data, and [SVY] **svy: poisson** for Poisson regression for survey data.

svy: gnbreg fits generalized negative binomial regression models for complex survey data; see [R] **nbreg** for this model involving nonsurvey data.

svy: gnbreg allows the shape parameter α to be estimated as a function of other variables. The parameterization of α is the same as that of the default parameterization of svy: nbreg.

Options for svy

svy_options; see [SVY] **svy**.

Options for nbreg

dispersion(mean | constant) specifies the parameterization for dispersion in the model. The default is dispersion(mean).

> dispersion(mean) specifies the model with dispersion for the jth observation equal to $1 + \alpha \exp(\mathbf{x}_j\boldsymbol{\beta} + \text{offset}_j)$; that is, the dispersion is a function of the expected mean of the count for the ith observation: $\exp(\mathbf{x}_j\boldsymbol{\beta} + \text{offset}_j)$.

> dispersion(constant) has dispersion equal to $1 + \delta$; that is, it is a constant for all observations.

> For the default model, $\alpha = 0$ corresponds to dispersion $= 1$, and, thus, it is simply a Poisson model. Likewise, for the alternative parameterization, $\delta = 0$ corresponds to dispersion $= 1$, and it is simply a Poisson model.

noconstant, exposure(*varname_e*), offset(*varname_o*), constraints(*constraints*); see [R] **estimation options**.

irr; see [SVY] *eform_option*.

maximize_options: <u>difficult</u>, <u>tech</u>nique(*algorithm_spec*), <u>iter</u>ate(*#*), [<u>no</u>]<u>log</u>, <u>trace</u>, gradient, showstep, <u>hess</u>ian, shownrtolerance, <u>tol</u>erance(*#*), <u>ltol</u>erance(*#*), gtolerance(*#*), <u>nrtol</u>erance(*#*), nonrtolerance, from(*init_specs*); see [R] **maximize**. These options are seldom used. If the maximization is taking a long time, you may wish to specify the log option to view the iteration log. The log option implies svy's noisily option; see [SVY] **svy**.

Options for gnbreg

noconstant; see [SVY] **estimation options**.

lnalpha(*varlist*) allows specifying a linear equation for $\ln(\alpha)$. Specifying lnalpha(male old) would specify $\ln(\alpha) = \alpha_0 + \alpha_1 \text{male} + \alpha_2 \text{old}$ where α_0, α_1, and α_2 are parameters to be estimated along with the other model coefficients. If this option is not specified, svy: gnbreg and svy: nbreg will produce the same results because the shape parameter will be parameterized as a constant.

exposure(*varname_e*), offset(*varname_o*), constraints(*constraints*); see [R] **estimation options**.

irr; see [SVY] *eform_option*.

> Max options

$maximize\_options$: <u>diff</u>icult, <u>tech</u>nique($algorithm\_spec$), <u>iter</u>ate($\#$), [<u>no</u>]<u>log</u>, <u>trace</u>, <u>grad</u>ient, <u>showstep</u>, <u>hessian</u>, <u>shownr</u>tolerance, <u>tol</u>erance($\#$), <u>ltol</u>erance($\#$), <u>gtol</u>erance($\#$), <u>nrtol</u>erance($\#$), <u>nonrtol</u>erance, <u>from</u>($init\_specs$); see [R] **maximize**. These options are seldom used. If the maximization is taking a long time, you may wish to specify the log option to view the iteration log. The log option implies svy's noisily option; see [SVY] **svy**.

Remarks

Negative binomial regression models the number of occurrences (counts) of an event when the event has extra-Poisson variation, that is, when it has overdispersion. The Poisson regression model is

$$y_j \sim \text{Poisson}(\mu_j)$$

where

$$\mu_j = \exp(\mathbf{x}_j \boldsymbol{\beta} + \text{offset}_j)$$

for observed counts y_j with covariates $\mathbf{x}_j$ for the jth observation. One derivation of the negative binomial mean-dispersion model is that individual units follow a Poisson regression model, but there is an omitted variable ν_j, such that e^{ν_j} follows a gamma distribution with mean 1 and variance α:

$$y_j \sim \text{Poisson}(\mu_j^*)$$

where

$$\mu_j^* = \exp(\mathbf{x}_j \boldsymbol{\beta} + \text{offset}_j + \nu_j)$$

and

$$e^{\nu_j} \sim \text{Gamma}(1/\alpha, \alpha)$$

Note that with this parameterization, a $\text{Gamma}(a, b)$ distribution will have expectation ab and variance ab^2.

We refer to α as the overdispersion parameter. The larger α is, the greater the overdispersion. The Poisson model corresponds to $\alpha = 0$. svn: nbreg parameterizes α as $\ln \alpha$. svy: gnbreg allows $\ln \alpha$ to be modeled as $\ln \alpha_j = \mathbf{z}_j \boldsymbol{\gamma}$, a linear combination of covariates $\mathbf{z}_j$.

svy: nbreg will fit two different parameterizations of the negative binomial model. The default, described above and also given by the option dispersion(mean), has dispersion for the jth observation equal to $1 + \alpha \exp(\mathbf{x}_j \boldsymbol{\beta} + \text{offset}_j)$. This is seen by noting that the above implies that

$$\mu_j^* \sim \text{Gamma}(1/\alpha, \alpha\mu_j)$$

and thus (assuming simple random sampling)

$$\text{Var}(y_j) = E\left\{\text{Var}(y_j|\mu_j^*)\right\} + \text{Var}\left\{E(y_j|\mu_j^*)\right\}$$
$$= E(\mu_j^*) + \text{Var}(\mu_j^*)$$
$$= \mu_j(1 + \alpha\mu_j)$$

The alternative parameterization, given by the option dispersion(constant), has dispersion equal to $1 + \delta$; that is, it is constant for all observations. This is so because the constant-dispersion model assumes instead that

$$\mu_j^* \sim \text{Gamma}(\mu_j/\delta, \delta)$$

and thus $\text{Var}(y_j) = \mu_j(1 + \delta)$. The Poisson model corresponds to $\delta = 0$.

Consider the population of interest to be a random sample from one of the above data generating processes. svy: nbreg estimates the parameters for this fixed population using maximum pseudo-likelihood, where the pseudolikelihood comes from one of the above parameterizations. The variance estimates from svy: nbreg measure the amount sample-to-sample variability assuming the samples come from the same survey design applied to the fixed population.

▷ Example 1

In [SVY] **svy: poisson**, we modeled the incidence of alcohol consumption using the Poisson distribution. In the following, we fit a similar model using the negative binomial distribution. Recall that drinkdays contains the number of days in the past year that a respondent had at least one alcoholic drink, ridageyr contains recoded values for age, and ridreth1 is a categorical variable for race and ethnicity. We use xi to create the dummies for the categories of ridreth1.

```
. use http://www.stata-press.com/data/r9/alq99_00

. gen  drinkdays = alq120q if alq120q <= 365
(6451 missing values generated)

. svyset
        pweight: wtmec2yr
            VCE: linearized
     Strata 1: sdmvstra
         SU 1: sdmvpsu
        FPC 1: <zero>

. xi: svy: nbreg drinkdays ridageyr i.ridreth1, irr
i.ridreth1          _Iridreth1_1-5      (naturally coded; _Iridreth1_1 omitted)
(running nbreg on estimation sample)

Survey: Negative binomial regression

Number of strata   =         13          Number of obs      =        3265
Number of PSUs     =         27          Population size    = 2.722e+08
                                         Design df          =          14
                                         F(   5,      10)   =        2.41
                                         Prob > F           =      0.1106
```

drinkdays	IRR	Linearized Std. Err.	t	P>|t|	[95% Conf. Interval]	
ridageyr	1.001339	.0032399	0.41	0.685	.9944141	1.008312
_Iridreth1_2	.6223568	.1227005	-2.41	0.031	.407752	.9499107
_Iridreth1_3	.8718195	.118232	-1.01	0.329	.6517862	1.166133
_Iridreth1_4	1.104791	.2487518	0.44	0.665	.6816366	1.790635
_Iridreth1_5	.7403963	.2329353	-0.96	0.356	.3770645	1.453827
/lnalpha	.2588911	.0843382			.0780037	.4397785
alpha	1.295493	.1092595			1.081127	1.552363

The incidence-rate ratio for ridageyr is not significantly different from 1, thus there is not enough evidence to conclude that there is any association between drinking incidence and age.

◁

Saved Results

svy: nbreg and svy: gnbreg save in e(). In addition to the items documented in [SVY] **svy**, svy: nbreg also saves the following:

Scalars
e(alpha)	the value of α if dispersion(mean)
e(delta)	the value of δ if dispersion(constant)

Macros
e(cmd)	nbreg
e(depvar)	name of dependent variable
e(offset)	offset
e(crittype)	log pseudolikelihood
e(predict)	program used to implement predict

In addition to the items documented in [SVY] **svy**, svy: gnbreg also saves the following:

Macros
e(cmd)	gnbreg
e(depvar)	name of dependent variable
e(offset1)	offset
e(crittype)	log pseudolikelihood
e(predict)	program used to implement predict

Methods and Formulas

svy: nbreg and svy: gnbreg are implemented as ado-files.

The log pseudolikelihood is

$$\ln L = \sum_j w_j \ln L_j$$

where the form of L_j (the pseudolikelihood for the jth observation) depends on how you model the dispersion parameter. The equation-level scores used in the linearized variance estimator are derived by taking partial derivatives of the log pseudolikelihood; see [SVY] **variance estimation**.

Mean-dispersion model

In this case, the negative binomial distribution can be regarded as a gamma mixture of Poisson random variables. The conditional pseudolikelihood for the jth observation is

$$f(y_j|\nu_j) = \frac{(\nu_j\mu_j)^{y_j}e^{-\nu_j\mu_j}}{\Gamma(y_j+1)}$$

where $\mu_j = \exp(\mathbf{b}_j\boldsymbol{\beta} + \text{offset}_j)$ and ν_j is unobserved but has a Gamma$(1/\alpha, \alpha)$ density.

$$g(\nu) = \frac{\nu^{(1-\alpha)/\alpha}e^{-\nu/\alpha}}{\alpha^{1/\alpha}\Gamma(1/\alpha)}$$

This gamma distribution has mean 1 and variance α, where α is the ancillary parameter. The unconditional pseudolikelihood for the jth observation is

$$L_j = f(y_j) = \int_0^\infty f(y_j \mid \nu)g(\nu)\,d\nu$$

$$= \frac{\Gamma(m + y_j)}{\Gamma(y_j + 1)\Gamma(m)}\, p_j^m (1 - p_j)^{y_j}$$

where $p_j = 1/(1 + \alpha\mu_j)$ and $m = 1/\alpha$.

In the case of svy: gnbreg, α can vary across the observations according to the parameterization $\ln\alpha_j = \mathbf{z}_j\gamma$.

Constant-dispersion model

In this case, the conditional pseudolikelihood for the jth observation is Poisson(μ_j^*), where μ_j^* has a Gamma($\mu_j/\delta, \delta$) density and δ is the dispersion parameter. The unconditional pseudolikelihood for the jth observation is

$$L_j = f(y_j) = \frac{\Gamma(m_j + y_j)}{\Gamma(y_j + 1)\Gamma(m_j)}\, p^{m_j}(1 - p)^{y_j}$$

where $p = 1/(1 + \delta)$ and $m_j = \mu_j/\delta$.

References

Cameron, A. C. and P. K. Trivedi. 1998. *Regression Analysis of Count Data*. Cambridge: Cambridge University Press.

Feller, W. 1968. *An Introduction to Probability Theory and Its Applications*, vol. 1. 3rd ed. New York: Wiley.

Hilbe, J. 1998. sg91: Robust variance estimators for MLE Poisson and negative binomial regression. *Stata Technical Bulletin* 45: 26–28. Reprinted in *Stata Technical Bulletin Reprints*, vol. 8, pp. 177–180.

Long, J. S. 1997. *Regression Models for Categorical and Limited Dependent Variables*. Thousand Oaks, CA: Sage.

Long, J. S. and J. Freese. 2001. Predicted probabilities for count models. *Stata Journal* 1: 51–57.

———. 2003. *Regression Models for Categorical Dependent Variables Using Stata*. rev. ed. College Station, TX: Stata Press.

Also See

Complementary:	[SVY] **svy: nbreg postestimation**
Related:	[R] **nbreg**;
	[SVY] **svy: poisson**, [SVY] **svy: regress**
Background:	[U] **20 Estimation and postestimation commands**,
	[SVY] **estimation options**, [SVY] **poststratification**,
	[SVY] **subpopulation estimation**, [SVY] **svy**, [SVY] **variance estimation**,
	[R] **maximize**

Title

svy: nbreg postestimation — Postestimation tools for svy: nbreg

Description

The following postestimation commands are available for svy: nbreg and svy: gnbreg:

command	description
estat	postestimation statistics for survey data
estimates	cataloging estimation results
lincom	point estimates, standard errors, testing, and inference for linear combinations of coefficients
mfx	marginal effects or elasticities
nlcom	point estimates, standard errors, testing, and inference for nonlinear combinations of coefficients
predict	predictions, residuals, influence statistics, and other diagnostic measures
predictnl	point estimates, standard errors, testing, and inference for generalized predictions
suest	seemingly unrelated estimation
test	Wald tests for simple and composite linear hypotheses
testnl	Wald tests of nonlinear hypotheses

See [SVY] **estat**.

See the corresponding entries in the *Stata Base Reference Manual* for details.

Syntax for predict

> predict [*type*] *newvarname* [*if*] [*in*] [, *statistic* <u>nooff</u>set]

> predict [*type*] { *stub** | *newvar*$_{\text{reg}}$ *newvar*$_{\text{disp}}$ } [*if*] [*in*] , <u>sc</u>ores

statistic	description
n	predicted number of events; the default
ir	incidence rate
xb	linear prediction, $\mathbf{x}_j\beta$
stdp	standard error of the linear prediction

In addition, relevant only after svy: gnbreg are

statistic	description
<u>alpha</u>	predicted values of α
<u>lnalpha</u>	predicted values of $\ln(\alpha)$
<u>stdplna</u>	standard error of the predicted $\ln(\alpha)$

These statistics are available both in and out of sample; type predict ... if e(sample) ... if wanted only for the estimation sample.

145

Options for predict

n, the default, calculates the predicted number of events, which is $\exp(\mathbf{x}_j\boldsymbol{\beta})$ if neither offset() nor exposure() was specified when the model was fitted; $\exp(\mathbf{x}_j\boldsymbol{\beta} + \text{offset}_j)$ if offset() was specified; or $\exp(\mathbf{x}_j\boldsymbol{\beta}) \times \text{exposure}_j$ if exposure() was specified.

ir calculates the incidence rate $\exp(\mathbf{x}_j\boldsymbol{\beta})$, which is the predicted number of events when exposure is 1. This is equivalent to specifying both n and nooffset options.

xb calculates the linear prediction, which is $\mathbf{x}_j\boldsymbol{\beta}$ if neither offset() nor exposure() was specified; $\mathbf{x}_j\boldsymbol{\beta} + \text{offset}_j$ if offset() was specified; or $\mathbf{x}_j\boldsymbol{\beta} + \ln(\text{exposure}_j)$ if exposure() was specified; see nooffset below.

stdp calculates the standard error of the linear prediction.

alpha, lnalpha, and stdplna are relevant after svy: gnbreg estimation only; they produce the predicted values of α, $\ln(\alpha)$, and the standard error of the predicted $\ln(\alpha)$, respectively.

nooffset is relevant if you specified offset() or exposure() when you fitted the model. It modifies the calculations made by predict so that they ignore the offset or exposure variable; the linear prediction is treated as $\mathbf{x}_j\boldsymbol{\beta}$ rather than as $\mathbf{x}_j\boldsymbol{\beta} + \text{offset}_j$ or $\mathbf{x}_j\boldsymbol{\beta} + \ln(\text{exposure}_j)$. Specifying predict ... , nooffset is equivalent to specifying predict ... , ir.

scores calculates equation-level score variables.

The first new variable will contain $\partial \ln L / \partial(\mathbf{x}_j\boldsymbol{\beta})$.

The second new variable will contain $\partial \ln L / \partial(\ln \alpha_j)$ for dispersion(mean) and gnbreg.

The second new variable will contain $\partial \ln L / \partial(\ln \delta)$ for dispersion(constant).

Remarks

▷ Example 1

Continuing with our example from [SVY] **svy: nbreg**, we use predict to compute the incidence rate for alcohol consumption for each observation in the estimation sample and save the values in the new variable ir_drink. We then use summarize to make a quick comparison of the average and range of the values in drinkdays and ir_drink.

```
. predict ir_drink if e(sample), ir
(6700 missing values generated)
. sum ir_drink drinkdays if e(sample)
```

Variable	Obs	Mean	Std. Dev.	Min	Max
ir_drink	3265	3.152501	.4297346	1.986608	3.951371
drinkdays	3265	3.227871	12.67914	0	365

◁

Methods and Formulas

All postestimation commands listed above are implemented as ado-files.

The following formulas use the same notation as in [SVY] **svy: nbreg**.

Mean-dispersion model

The equation-level scores are given by

$$\text{score}(\mathbf{x}\boldsymbol{\beta})_j = p_j(y_j - \mu_j)$$

$$\text{score}(\tau)_j = -m\left\{\frac{\alpha(\mu_j - y_j)}{1 + \alpha\mu_j} - \ln(1 + \alpha\mu_j) + \psi(y_j + m) - \psi(m)\right\}$$

where $\tau_j = \ln\alpha_j$.

Constant-dispersion model

The equation-level scores are given by

$$\text{score}(\mathbf{x}\boldsymbol{\beta})_j = m_j\left\{\psi(y_j + m_j) - \psi(m_j) + \ln(p)\right\}$$

$$\text{score}(\tau)_j = y_j - (y_j + m_j)(1 - p) - \text{score}(\mathbf{x}\boldsymbol{\beta})_j$$

where $\tau_j = \ln\delta$.

Also See

Complementary:	[SVY] **svy: nbreg**, [SVY] **estat**; [R] **estimates**, [R] **lincom**, [R] **mfx**, [R] **nlcom**, [R] **predict**, [R] **predictnl**, [R] **suest**, [R] **test**, [R] **testnl**
Background:	[U] **13.5 Accessing coefficients and standard errors**, [U] **20 Estimation and postestimation commands**

Title

> **svy: ologit** — Ordered logistic regression for survey data

Syntax

svy [*vcetype*] [, *svy_options*] : ologit *depvar* [*indepvars*] [*if*] [*in*] [, *options*]

vcetype	description
SE	
linearized	Taylor linearized variance estimation
brr	BRR variance estimation; see [SVY] **svy brr**
jackknife	jackknife variance estimation; see [SVY] **svy jackknife**

Specifying a *vcetype* overrides the default from svyset.

svy_options	description
if/in	
subpop()	identify a subpopulation
SE	
brr_options	additional options allowed with BRR variance estimation; see [SVY] ***brr_options***
jackknife_options	additional options allowed with jackknife variance estimation; see [SVY] ***jackknife_options***
Reporting	
level(#)	set confidence level; default is level(95)
noheader	suppress the table header
nolegend	suppress the table legend
noadjust	do not adjust model Wald statistic

svy requires that the survey-design variables be identified using svyset; see [SVY] **svyset**.

xi is allowed; see [R] **xi**.

See [U] **20 Estimation and postestimation commands** for additional capabilities of estimation commands.

Warning: Using *if* or *in* restrictions will not produce correct variance estimates for subpopulations in many cases. To compute estimates for a subpopulation, use the subpop() option. The full specification for subpop() is

subpop([*varname*] [*if*])

options	description
Model	
offset(*varname*)	include *varname* in model with coefficient constrained to 1
Reporting	
or	report odds ratios
Max options	
maximize_options	control the maximization process; seldom used

Description

svy: ologit fits ordered logistic regression models for complex survey data. In the ordered logistic regression model, *depvar* is an ordinal variable that takes on two or more outcomes that also has a natural ordering.

See [R] **ologit** for a description of this model involving nonsurvey data, [SVY] **svy: logistic** for logistic regression reporting odds ratios, [SVY] **svy: logit** for logistic regression, [SVY] **svy: probit** for probit regression, [SVY] **svy: mlogit** for multinomial logistic regression, and [SVY] **svy: oprobit** for ordered probit regression for survey data.

Options

svy_options; see [SVY] **svy**.

⌐ Model ⌐

offset(*varname*); see [SVY] **estimation options**.

⌐ Reporting ⌐

or; see [SVY] *eform_option*.

⌐ Max options ⌐

maximize_options: iterate(#), [no]log, trace, tolerance(#), ltolerance(#); see [R] **maximize**. These options are seldom used. If the maximization is taking a long time, you may wish to specify the log option to view the iteration log. The log option implies svy's noisily option; see [SVY] **svy**.

Remarks

Ordered logistic models are used to estimate relationships between an ordinal dependent variable and a set of independent variables. An *ordinal* variable is a variable that is categorical and ordered, for instance, "poor", "good", and "excellent", which might indicate a person's current health status or the repair record of a car. If there are only two outcomes, see [SVY] **svy: logistic**, [SVY] **svy: logit**, and [SVY] **svy: probit**. This entry is concerned only with more than two outcomes. If the outcomes cannot be ordered (e.g., residency in the north, east, south, or west), see [SVY] **svy: mlogit**. This entry is concerned only with models in which the outcomes can be ordered.

In ordered logistic, an underlying outcome measurement is modeled as a linear function of the independent variables and a set of cutpoints. The probability of observing outcome i corresponds to the probability that the estimated linear function, plus random error, is within the range of the cutpoints estimated for the outcome:

$$\Pr(\text{outcome}_j = i) = \Pr(\kappa_{i-1} < \beta_1 x_{1j} + \beta_2 x_{2j} + \cdots + \beta_k x_{kj} + u_j \leq \kappa_i)$$

u_j is assumed to be logistically distributed. In either case, we estimate the coefficients β_1, β_2, ..., β_k together with the cutpoints κ_1, κ_2, ..., κ_{k-1}, where k is the number of possible outcomes. κ_0 is taken as $-\infty$, and κ_k is taken as $+\infty$. All of this is a direct generalization of the ordinary two-outcome logistic regression model.

▷ Example 1

In the NHANES II dataset, we have a variable `health` containing self-reported health status, which takes on the values 1–5, with 1 being "poor" and 5 being "excellent". Since this is an ordered categorical variable, it makes sense to model it using `svy: ologit`. As predictors, we use some basic demographic variables: `female` is an indicator of female individual, `black` is an indicator for black individuals, `age` in years, and `age2` (age squared).

```
. use http://www.stata-press.com/data/r9/nhanes2f
. svyset
      pweight: finalwgt
          VCE: linearized
    Strata 1: stratid
        SU 1: psuid
       FPC 1: <zero>
. svy: ologit health female black age age2
(running ologit on estimation sample)
Survey: Ordered logistic regression
```

Number of strata	=	31	Number of obs	=	10335
Number of PSUs	=	62	Population size	=	1.170e+08
			Design df	=	31
			F(4, 28)	=	223.27
			Prob > F	=	0.0000

health	Coef.	Linearized Std. Err.	t	P>|t|	[95% Conf. Interval]
female	-.1615219	.0523678	-3.08	0.004	-.2683266 -.0547171
black	-.986568	.0790276	-12.48	0.000	-1.147746 -.8253901
age	-.0119491	.0082974	-1.44	0.160	-.0288717 .0049736
age2	-.0003234	.000091	-3.55	0.001	-.000509 -.0001377
/cut1	-4.566229	.1632559	-27.97	0.000	-4.899192 -4.233266
/cut2	-3.057415	.1699943	-17.99	0.000	-3.404121 -2.710709
/cut3	-1.520596	.1714341	-8.87	0.000	-1.870238 -1.170954
/cut4	-.242785	.1703964	-1.42	0.164	-.5903107 .1047407

According to our model, after controlling for the other factors, females give self-reports of poorer health status than males, blacks report much poorer health status than nonblacks, and older people report worse health than younger people.

◁

Saved Results

`svy: ologit` saves in `e()`. In addition to the items documented in [SVY] **svy**, `svy: ologit` also saves the following:

Scalars
    e(k_cat)   number of categories

Macros
    e(cmd)   ologit
    e(depvar)   name of dependent variable
    e(offset)   offset
    e(crittype)   log pseudolikelihood
    e(predict)   program used to implement predict

Methods and Formulas

`svy: ologit` is implemented as an ado-file.

The ordered logit model is described in Greene (2003, chapter 21).

Suppose that there are k categorical responses. The probability that the response for the jth observation is equal to the ith category is

$$p_{ij} = \Pr(y_j = i) = \frac{1}{1 + \exp(-\kappa_i + \mathbf{x}_j\boldsymbol{\beta})} - \frac{1}{1 + \exp(-\kappa_{i-1} + \mathbf{x}_j\boldsymbol{\beta})}$$

where κ_i is the ith cutpoint, $\mathbf{x}_j$ is the row vector of observed values of the independent variables for the jth observation, and $\boldsymbol{\beta}$ is the vector of regression coefficients. Note that κ_0 is defined as $-\infty$ and κ_k as $+\infty$. The log pseudolikelihood is

$$\ln L = \sum_{j=1}^{N} w_j \sum_{i=1}^{k} I_i(y_j) \ln p_{ij}$$

where w_j is a sampling weight and

$$I_i(y_j) = \begin{cases} 1, \text{ if } y_j = i \\ 0, \text{ otherwise} \end{cases}$$

The equation-level scores used in the linearized variance estimator are derived by taking partial derivatives of the log pseudolikelihood; see [SVY] **variance estimation**.

References

Aitchison, J. and S. D. Silvey. 1957. The generalization of probit analysis to the case of multiple responses. *Biometrika* 44: 131–140.

Anderson, J. A. 1984. Regression and ordered categorical variables (with discussion). *Journal of the Royal Statistical Society, Series B* 46: 1–30.

Brant, R. 1990. Assessing proportionality in the proportional odds model for ordinal logistic regression. *Biometrics* 46: 1171–1178.

Greene, W. H. 2003. *Econometric Analysis.* 5th ed. Upper Saddle River, NJ: Prentice Hall.

Greenland, S. 1985. An application of logistic models to the analysis of ordinal response. *Biometrical Journal* 27: 189–197.

Kleinbaum, D. G. and M. Klein. 2002. *Logistic Regression: A Self-Learning Text.* 2nd ed. New York: Springer.

Long, J. S. 1997. *Regression Models for Categorical and Limited Dependent Variables.* Thousand Oaks, CA: Sage.

Long, J. S. and J. Freese. 2003. *Regression Models for Categorical Dependent Variables Using Stata.* rev. ed. College Station, TX: Stata Press.

McCullagh, P. 1977. A logistic model for paired comparisons with ordered categorical data. *Biometrika* 64: 449–453.

———. 1980. Regression models for ordinal data (with discussion). *Journal of the Royal Statistical Society, Series B* 42: 109–142.

McCullagh, P. and J. A. Nelder. 1989. *Generalized Linear Models.* 2nd ed. London: Chapman & Hall.

Zavoina, W. and R. D. McKelvey. 1975. A statistical model for the analysis of ordinal level dependent variables. *Journal of Mathematical Sociology* 4: 103–120.

Also See

Complementary:	[SVY] **svy: ologit postestimation**
Related:	[R] **ologit**;
	[SVY] **svy: logistic**, [SVY] **svy: logit**, [SVY] **svy: mlogit**,
	[SVY] **svy: oprobit**, [SVY] **svy: probit**
Background:	[U] **20 Estimation and postestimation commands**,
	[SVY] **estimation options**, [SVY] **poststratification**,
	[SVY] **subpopulation estimation**, [SVY] **svy**, [SVY] **variance estimation**,
	[R] **maximize**

Title

svy: ologit postestimation — Postestimation tools for svy: ologit

Description

The following postestimation commands are available for svy: ologit:

command	description
estat	postestimation statistics for survey data
estimates	cataloging estimation results
lincom	point estimates, standard errors, testing, and inference for linear combinations of coefficients
mfx	marginal effects or elasticities
nlcom	point estimates, standard errors, testing, and inference for nonlinear combinations of coefficients
predict	predictions, residuals, influence statistics, and other diagnostic measures
predictnl	point estimates, standard errors, testing, and inference for generalized predictions
suest	seemingly unrelated estimation
test	Wald tests for simple and composite linear hypotheses
testnl	Wald tests of nonlinear hypotheses

See [SVY] **estat**.

See the corresponding entries in the *Stata Base Reference Manual* for details.

Syntax for predict

predict [*type*] *newvars* [*if*] [*in*] [, *statistic* <u>ou</u>tcome(*outcome*) <u>nooff</u>set]

predict [*type*] { *stub** | *newvar*$_{\mathrm{reg}}$ *newvar*$_{\kappa_1}$ ... *newvar*$_{\kappa_{k-1}}$ } [*if*] [*in*] , <u>sc</u>ores

statistic	description
<u>pr</u>	probability of a positive outcome; the default
xb	linear prediction, $\mathbf{x}_j \beta$
stdp	standard error of the linear prediction

Note that you specify one new variable with xb and stdp and specify either one or k new variables with pr.

These statistics are available both in and out of sample; type predict ... if e(sample) ... if wanted only for the estimation sample.

(*Continued on next page*)

Options for predict

pr, the default, calculates the probability of each of the alternatives in the model or the probability of the outcome specified in outcome(). If you specify outcome(), you only need to specify one new variable; otherwise, you must specify k new variables, one for each alternative in the model.

xb calculates the linear prediction. You specify one new variable; for example, predict *myxb*, xb. The linear prediction is defined, ignoring the contribution of the estimated cutpoints.

stdp calculates the standard error of the linear prediction. You specify one new variable; for example, predict *se_of_myxb*, stdp.

outcome(*outcome*) specifies the outcome for which the predicted probabilities are to be calculated. equation() is a synonym for outcome(): it does not matter which you use, and the standard rules for specifying an equation() apply.

nooffset is relevant if you specified offset() when you fitted the model. It modifies the calculations made by predict so that they ignore the offset variable; the linear prediction is treated as $\mathbf{x}_j\beta$ rather than as $\mathbf{x}_j\beta + \text{offset}_j$.

scores calculates equation-level score variables. The number of score variables created will equal the number of outcomes in the model. If the number of outcomes in the model were k, then

the first new variable will contain $\partial\ln L/\partial(\mathbf{x}_j\beta)$.

the second new variable will contain $\partial\ln L/\partial\kappa_1$;

the third new variable will contain $\partial\ln L/\partial\kappa_2$;

. . .

the kth new variable will contain $\partial\ln L/\partial\kappa_{k-1}$, where κ_i refers to the ith cutpoint.

Remarks

▷ Example 1

Continuing with our example from [SVY] **svy: ologit**, we use predict to compute the probability for reporting a poor health status for each observation in the dataset and save the values in the new variable pr_poor.

```
. predict pr_poor, outcome(1)
(option pr assumed; predicted probability)
. describe pr_poor

              storage  display   value
variable name   type   format    label       variable label

pr_poor        float   %9.0g                 Pr(health==1)
```

◁

Methods and Formulas

All postestimation commands listed above are implemented as ado-files.

Also See

Complementary:	[SVY] **svy: ologit**, [SVY] **estat**;
	[R] **estimates**, [R] **lincom**, [R] **mfx**, [R] **nlcom**, [R] **predict**,
	[R] **predictnl**, [R] **suest**, [R] **test**, [R] **testnl**
Background:	[U] **13.5 Accessing coefficients and standard errors**,
	[U] **20 Estimation and postestimation commands**

Title

svy: oprobit — Ordered probit regression for survey data

Syntax

svy [*vcetype*] [, *svy_options*] : <u>oprob</u>it *depvar* [*indepvars*] [*if*] [*in*] [, *options*]

vcetype	description
SE	
<u>linear</u>ized	Taylor linearized variance estimation
brr	BRR variance estimation; see [SVY] **svy brr**
<u>jack</u>knife	jackknife variance estimation; see [SVY] **svy jackknife**

Specifying a *vcetype* overrides the default from svyset.

svy_options	description
if/in	
<u>subpop</u>()	identify a subpopulation
SE	
brr_options	additional options allowed with BRR variance estimation; see [SVY] ***brr_options***
jackknife_options	additional options allowed with jackknife variance estimation; see [SVY] ***jackknife_options***
Reporting	
<u>level</u>(#)	set confidence level; default is level(95)
<u>nohead</u>er	suppress the table header
<u>noleg</u>end	suppress the table legend
<u>noadj</u>ust	do not adjust model Wald statistic

svy requires that the survey-design variables be identified using svyset; see [SVY] **svyset**.

xi is allowed; see [R] **xi**.

See [U] **20 Estimation and postestimation commands** for additional capabilities of estimation commands.

Warning: Using *if* or *in* restrictions will not produce correct variance estimates for subpopulations in many cases. To compute estimates for a subpopulation, use the subpop() option. The full specification for subpop() is
<u>subpop</u>([*varname*] [*if*])

options	description
Model	
<u>off</u>set(*varname*)	include *varname* in model with coefficient constrained to 1
Max options	
maximize_options	control the maximization process; seldom used

156

Description

svy: oprobit fits ordered probit regression models for complex survey data. In the ordered probit regression model, *depvar* is an ordinal variable that takes on two or more outcomes that also has a natural ordering.

See [R] **oprobit** for a description of this model involving nonsurvey data, [SVY] **svy: logistic** for logistic regression reporting odds ratios, [SVY] **svy: logit** for logistic regression, [SVY] **svy: probit** for probit regression, [SVY] **svy: mlogit** for multinomial logistic regression, and [SVY] **svy: ologit** for ordered logistic regression for survey data.

Options

svy_options; see [SVY] **svy**.

┌─── Model ───

offset(*varname*); see [SVY] **estimation options**.

┌─── Max options ───

maximize_options: iterate(#), [no]log, trace, tolerance(#), ltolerance(#); see [R] **maximize**. These options are seldom used. If the maximization is taking a long time, you may wish to specify the log option to view the iteration log. The log option implies svy's noisily option; see [SVY] **svy**.

Remarks

Ordered probit models are used to estimate relationships between an ordinal dependent variable and a set of independent variables. An *ordinal* variable is a variable that is categorical and ordered, for instance, "poor", "good", and "excellent", which might indicate a person's current health status or the repair record of a car. If there are only two outcomes, see [SVY] **svy: logistic**, [SVY] **svy: logit**, and [SVY] **svy: probit**. This entry is concerned only with more than two outcomes. If the outcomes cannot be ordered (e.g., residency in the north, east, south, or west), see [SVY] **svy: mlogit**. This entry is concerned only with models in which the outcomes can be ordered.

In ordered probit, an underlying outcome measurement is modeled as a linear function of the independent variables and a set of cutpoints. The probability of observing outcome i corresponds to the probability that the estimated linear function, plus random error, is within the range of the cutpoints estimated for the outcome:

$$\Pr(\text{outcome}_j = i) = \Pr(\kappa_{i-1} < \beta_1 x_{1j} + \beta_2 x_{2j} + \cdots + \beta_k x_{kj} + u_j \le \kappa_i)$$

u_j is assumed to be normally distributed. In either case, we estimate the coefficients β_1, β_2, ..., β_k together with the cutpoints κ_1, κ_2, ..., κ_{k-1}, where k is the number of possible outcomes. κ_0 is taken as $-\infty$, and κ_k is taken as $+\infty$. All of this is a direct generalization of the ordinary two-outcome probit regression model.

▷ Example 1

Using the setup from Example 1 in [SVY] **svy: ologit**, we model the categories of the health variable (1 being "poor" to 5 being "excellent") in the NHANES II dataset using svy: oprobit.

```
. use http://www.stata-press.com/data/r9/nhanes2f

. svyset
      pweight: finalwgt
          VCE: linearized
     Strata 1: stratid
         SU 1: psuid
        FPC 1: <zero>

. svy: oprobit health female black age age2
(running oprobit on estimation sample)

Survey: Ordered probit regression
```

Number of strata	=	31		Number of obs	=	10335
Number of PSUs	=	62		Population size	=	1.170e+08
				Design df	=	31
				F(4, 28)	=	225.80
				Prob > F	=	0.0000

health	Coef.	Linearized Std. Err.	t	P>|t|	[95% Conf. Interval]	
female	-.0907319	.0308588	-2.94	0.006	-.1536688	-.0277949
black	-.5701119	.0466797	-12.21	0.000	-.6653158	-.474908
age	-.0115112	.0049363	-2.33	0.026	-.0215788	-.0014435
age2	-.0001405	.0000537	-2.62	0.014	-.0002499	-.000031
/cut1	-2.697512	.09917	-27.20	0.000	-2.89977	-2.495253
/cut2	-1.905636	.102841	-18.53	0.000	-2.115382	-1.695891
/cut3	-.9960377	.1030969	-9.66	0.000	-1.206305	-.7857703
/cut4	-.2198152	.1027691	-2.14	0.040	-.4294141	-.0102164

Not surprisingly, we come to similar conclusions. After controlling for the other factors, females give self-reports of poorer health status than males, blacks report much poorer health status than nonblacks, and older people report worse health than younger people.

◁

Saved Results

svy: oprobit saves in e(). In addition to the items documented in [SVY] **svy**, svy: oprobit also saves the following:

Scalars
    e(k_cat)   number of categories

Macros
    e(cmd)   oprobit
    e(depvar)   name of dependent variable
    e(offset)   offset
    e(crittype)   log pseudolikelihood
    e(predict)   program used to implement predict

Methods and Formulas

`svy: oprobit` is implemented as an ado-file.

The ordered probit model is described in Greene (2003, chapter 21).

Suppose that there are k categorical responses. The probability that the response for the jth observation is equal to the ith category is

$$p_{ik} = \Pr(y_j = i) = \Phi(\kappa_i - \mathbf{x}_j\boldsymbol{\beta}) - \Phi(\kappa_{i-1} - \mathbf{x}_j\boldsymbol{\beta})$$

where $\Phi()$ is the standard normal cumulative distribution function, κ_i is the ith cutpoint, $\mathbf{x}_j$ is the row vector of observed values of the independent variables for the jth observation, and $\boldsymbol{\beta}$ is the vector of regression coefficients. Note that κ_0 is defined as $-\infty$ and κ_k as $+\infty$. The log pseudolikelihood is

$$\ln L = \sum_{j=1}^{N} w_j \sum_{i=1}^{k} I_i(y_j) \ln p_{ik}$$

where w_j is a sampling weight and

$$I_i(y_j) = \begin{cases} 1, \text{ if } y_j = i \\ 0, \text{ otherwise} \end{cases}$$

The equation-level scores used in the linearized variance estimator are derived by taking partial derivatives of the log pseudolikelihood; see [SVY] **variance estimation**.

References

Aitchison, J. and S. D. Silvey. 1957. The generalization of probit analysis to the case of multiple responses. *Biometrika* 44: 131–140.

Greene, W. H. 2003. *Econometric Analysis*. 5th ed. Upper Saddle River, NJ: Prentice Hall.

Long, J. S. 1997. *Regression Models for Categorical and Limited Dependent Variables*. Thousand Oaks, CA: Sage.

Long, J. S. and J. Freese. 2003. *Regression Models for Categorical Dependent Variables Using Stata*. rev. ed. College Station, TX: Stata Press.

Also See

Complementary:	[SVY] **svy: oprobit postestimation**
Related:	[R] **oprobit**;
	[SVY] **svy: logistic**, [SVY] **svy: logit**, [SVY] **svy: mlogit**,
	[SVY] **svy: ologit**, [SVY] **svy: probit**
Background:	[U] **20 Estimation and postestimation commands**,
	[SVY] **estimation options**, [SVY] **poststratification**,
	[SVY] **subpopulation estimation**, [SVY] **svy**, [SVY] **variance estimation**,
	[R] **maximize**

Title

svy: oprobit postestimation — Postestimation tools for svy: oprobit

Description

The following postestimation commands are available for svy: oprobit:

command	description
estat	postestimation statistics for survey data
estimates	cataloging estimation results
lincom	point estimates, standard errors, testing, and inference for linear combinations of coefficients
mfx	marginal effects or elasticities
nlcom	point estimates, standard errors, testing, and inference for nonlinear combinations of coefficients
predict	predictions, residuals, influence statistics, and other diagnostic measures
predictnl	point estimates, standard errors, testing, and inference for generalized predictions
suest	seemingly unrelated estimation
test	Wald tests for simple and composite linear hypotheses
testnl	Wald tests of nonlinear hypotheses

See [SVY] **estat**.

See the corresponding entries in the *Stata Base Reference Manual* for details.

Syntax for predict

predict [*type*] *newvars* [*if*] [*in*] [, *statistic* $\underline{o}utcome(outcome)$ $\underline{nooff}set$]

predict [*type*] { *stub** | *newvar*$_{reg}$ *newvar*$_{\kappa_1}$ ... *newvar*$_{\kappa_{k-1}}$ } [*if*] [*in*] , $\underline{sc}ores$

statistic	description
$\underline{p}r$	probability of a positive outcome; the default
$\underline{x}b$	linear prediction, $x_j\beta$
stdp	standard error of the linear prediction

Note that you specify one new variable with xb and stdp and specify either one or k new variables with pr.

These statistics are available both in and out of sample; type predict ... if e(sample) ... if wanted only for the estimation sample.

Options for predict

pr, the default, calculates the probability of each of the alternatives in the model or the probability of the outcome specified in outcome(). If you specify outcome(), you only need to specify one new variable; otherwise, you must specify k new variables, one for each alternative in the model.

xb calculates the linear prediction. You specify one new variable; for example, predict *myxb*, xb. The linear prediction is defined ignoring the contribution of the estimated cutpoints.

stdp calculates the standard error of the linear prediction. You specify one new variable; for example, predict *se_of_myxb*, stdp.

outcome(*outcome*) specifies the outcome for which the predicted probabilities are to be calculated. equation() is a synonym for outcome(): it does not matter which you use, and the standard rules for specifying an equation() apply.

nooffset is relevant if you specified offset() when you fitted the model. It modifies the calculations made by predict so that they ignore the offset variable; the linear prediction is treated as $\mathbf{x}_j\beta$ rather than as $\mathbf{x}_j\beta + \text{offset}_j$.

scores calculates equation-level score variables. The number of score variables created will equal the number of outcomes in the model. If the number of outcomes in the model were k, then

the first new variable will contain $\partial \ln L / \partial(\mathbf{x}_j\mathbf{b})$;

the second new variable will contain $\partial \ln L / \partial \kappa_1$;

the third new variable will contain $\partial \ln L / \partial \kappa_2$;

. . .

the kth new variable will contain $\partial \ln L / \partial \kappa_{k-1}$, where κ_i refers to the ith cutpoint.

Remarks

▷ Example 1

Continuing with our example from [SVY] **svy: oprobit**, we use predict to compute the probability for reporting an average health status for each observation in the dataset and save the values in the new variable pr_avg.

```
. predict pr_avg, outcome(3)
(option pr assumed; predicted probability)
. describe pr_avg
             storage  display    value
variable name  type   format     label      variable label

pr_avg        float   %9.0g                 Pr(health==3)
```

◁

Methods and Formulas

All postestimation commands listed above are implemented as ado-files.

Also See

Complementary: [SVY] **svy: oprobit**, [SVY] **estat**;

                    [R] **estimates**, [R] **lincom**, [R] **mfx**, [R] **nlcom**, [R] **predict**,

                    [R] **predictnl**, [R] **suest**, [R] **test**, [R] **testnl**

Background: [U] **13.5 Accessing coefficients and standard errors**,

                    [U] **20 Estimation and postestimation commands**

Title

svy: poisson — Poisson regression for survey data

Syntax

svy [*vcetype*] [, *svy_options*] : poisson *depvar* [*indepvars*] [*if*] [*in*] [, *options*]

vcetype	description
SE	
linearized	Taylor linearized variance estimation
brr	BRR variance estimation; see [SVY] **svy brr**
jackknife	jackknife variance estimation; see [SVY] **svy jackknife**

Specifying a *vcetype* overrides the default from svyset.

svy_options	description
if/in	
subpop()	identify a subpopulation
SE	
brr_options	additional options allowed with BRR variance estimation; see [SVY] *brr_options*
jackknife_options	additional options allowed with jackknife variance estimation; see [SVY] *jackknife_options*
Reporting	
level(#)	set confidence level; default is level(95)
noheader	suppress the table header
nolegend	suppress the table legend
noadjust	do not adjust model Wald statistic

svy requires that the survey-design variables be identified using svyset; see [SVY] **svyset**.

xi is allowed; see [R] **xi**.

See [U] **20 Estimation and postestimation commands** for additional capabilities of estimation commands.

Warning: Using *if* or *in* restrictions will not produce correct variance estimates for subpopulations in many cases. To compute estimates for a subpopulation, use the subpop() option. The full specification for subpop() is

subpop([*varname*] [*if*])

(Continued on next page)

163

options	description
Model	
<u>nocon</u>stant	suppress the constant term
<u>exposure</u>($varname_e$)	include ln($varname_e$) in model with coefficient constrained to 1
<u>off</u>set($varname_o$)	include $varname_o$ in model with coefficient constrained to 1
<u>constr</u>aints(*constraints*)	apply specified linear constraints
Reporting	
<u>irr</u>	report incidence-rate ratios
Max options	
maximize_options	control the maximization process; seldom used

Description

svy: poisson fits Poisson regression models for complex survey data; see [R] **poisson** for a description of this model involving nonsurvey data, [SVY] **svy: nbreg** for negative binomial regression for survey data.

Options

svy_options; see [SVY] **svy**.

⌐▔▔▔▔▔⌐ Model ⌐▔▔▔

noconstant, exposure($varname_e$), offset($varname_o$), constraints(*constraints*); see [R] **estimation options**.

⌐▔▔▔▔▔⌐ Reporting ⌐▔▔▔

irr. see [SVY] *eform_option*.

⌐▔▔▔▔▔⌐ Max options ⌐▔▔▔▔▔▔▔▔▔▔▔▔▔▔▔▔▔▔▔▔▔▔▔▔▔▔▔▔▔▔▔▔▔▔▔▔▔▔▔

maximize_options: <u>dif</u>ficult, <u>tech</u>nique(*algorithm_spec*), <u>iter</u>ate(*#*), [<u>no</u>]<u>log</u>, <u>trace</u>, <u>grad</u>ient, <u>showstep</u>, <u>hess</u>ian, <u>shownr</u>tolerance, <u>tol</u>erance(*#*), <u>ltol</u>erance(*#*), <u>gtol</u>erance(*#*), <u>nrtol</u>erance(*#*), <u>nonrtol</u>erance, from(*init_specs*); see [R] **maximize**. These options are seldom used. If the maximization is taking a long time, you may wish to specify the log option to view the iteration log. The log option implies svy's noisily option; see [SVY] **svy**.

Remarks

The basic idea of Poisson regression was outlined by Coleman (1964, 378–379). See Cameron and Trivedi (1998) and Feller (1968, 156–164) for information about the Poisson distribution. See Cameron and Trivedi (1998), Long (1997, chapter 8), Long and Freese (2003, chapter 7), McNeil (1996, chapter 6), and Selvin (2004, chapter 9) for an introduction to Poisson regression. Also see Selvin (2004, chapter 5) for a discussion of the analysis of spatial distributions, which includes a discussion of the Poisson distribution. An early example of Poisson regression was Cochran (1940).

Poisson regression fits models of the number of occurrences (counts) of an event. The Poisson distribution has been applied to diverse events, such as the number of soldiers kicked to death by horses in the Prussian army (Bortkewitsch 1898); the pattern of hits by buzz bombs launched against London during World War II (Clarke 1946); telephone connections to a wrong number (Thorndike 1926); and disease incidence, typically with respect to time, but occasionally with respect to space. The basic assumptions are as follows:

1. There is a quantity called the *incidence rate* that is the rate at which events occur. Examples are 5 per second, 20 per 1,000 person-years, 17 per square meter, and 38 per cubic centimeter.

2. The incidence rate can be multiplied by *exposure* to obtain the expected number of observed events. For example, a rate of 5 per second multiplied by 30 seconds means that 150 events are expected; a rate of 20 per 1,000 person-years multiplied by 2,000 person-years means that 40 events are expected; and so on.

3. Over very small exposures ϵ, the probability of finding more than one event is small compared with ϵ.

4. Nonoverlapping exposures are mutually independent.

With these assumptions, to find the probability of k events in an exposure of size E, you divide E into n subintervals $E_1, E_2, \ldots, E_n$, and approximate the answer as the binomial probability of observing k successes in n trials. If you let $n \to \infty$, you obtain the Poisson distribution.

In the Poisson regression model, the incidence rate for the jth observation is assumed to be given by

$$r_j = e^{\beta_0 + \beta_1 x_{1,j} + \cdots + \beta_k x_{k,j}}$$

If E_j is the exposure, the expected number of events, C_j, will be

$$C_j = E_j e^{\beta_0 + \beta_1 x_{1,j} + \cdots + \beta_k x_{k,j}}$$
$$= e^{\ln(E_j) + \beta_0 + \beta_1 x_{1,j} + \cdots + \beta_k x_{k,j}}$$

This model is fitted by `svy: poisson`. Without the `exposure()` or `offset()` options, E_j is assumed to be 1 (equivalent to assuming that exposure is unknown), and controlling for exposure, if necessary, is your responsibility.

Comparing rates is most easily done by calculating *incidence-rate ratios* (IRR). For instance, what is the relative incidence rate of chromosome interchanges in cells as the intensity of radiation increases; the relative incidence rate of telephone connections to a wrong number as load increases; or the relative incidence rate of deaths due to cancer for females relative to males? That is, you want to hold all the xs in the model constant except one, say, the ith. The incidence-rate ratio for a one-unit change in x_i is

$$\frac{e^{\ln(E) + \beta_1 x_1 + \cdots + \beta_i (x_i + 1) + \cdots + \beta_k x_k}}{e^{\ln(E) + \beta_1 x_1 + \cdots + \beta_i x_i + \cdots + \beta_k x_k}} = e^{\beta_i}$$

More generally, the incidence-rate ratio for a Δx_i change in x_i is $e^{\beta_i \Delta x_i}$.

Consider the population of interest to be a random sample from the above data generating process. `svy: poisson` estimates the parameters for this fixed population using maximum pseudolikelihood, where the pseudolikelihood comes from the Poisson distribution. The variance estimates from `svy: poisson` measure the amount sample-to-sample variability assuming the samples come from the same survey design applied to the fixed population.

▷ Example 1

Suppose that we were interesting in modeling the incidence of alcohol consumption. The `alq.xpt` dataset from the NHANES 1999–2000 survey contains information about alcohol consumption for adults over the age of 20 years. We merged this dataset with the demographic dataset (`demo.xpt`) to create `alq99_00.dta`. The variable `alq120q` contains the response to the question, "In the past 12 months, how often did you drink any type of alcoholic beverage?" We'll assume the recorded value is the number of days that the respondent had at least one alcoholic drink, so the range of valid values is 0 to 365. The codebook for this variable states that 777 indicates a refusal to answer the question and 999 indicates a "don't know" answer.

In the following example, we read in the survey data, check that the survey design characteristics are already `svyset`, generate a new variable called `drinkdays` that contains the valid values of `alq120q`, and check for singleton sampling units that might result due to missing values in `drinkdays`.

```
. use http://www.stata-press.com/data/r9/alq99_00

. svyset
      pweight: wtmec2yr
          VCE: linearized
     Strata 1: sdmvstra
        SU 1: sdmvpsu
       FPC 1: <zero>

. gen  drinkdays = alq120q if alq120q <= 365
(6451 missing values generated)

. svydes drinkdays

Survey: Describing stage 1 sampling units

      pweight: wtmec2yr
          VCE: linearized
     Strata 1: sdmvstra
        SU 1: sdmvpsu
       FPC 1: <zero>
```

Stratum	#Units included	#Units omitted	#Obs with complete data	#Obs with missing data	#Obs per included Unit min	mean	max
1	3	0	392	673	114	130.7	142
2	2	0	213	481	87	106.5	126
3	2	0	283	504	134	141.5	149
4	2	0	296	562	138	148.0	158
5	2	0	270	479	128	135.0	142
6	2	0	277	453	133	138.5	144
7	2	0	324	535	149	162.0	175
8	2	0	258	491	120	129.0	138
9	2	0	229	461	104	114.5	125
10	2	0	237	409	117	118.5	120
11	2	0	273	464	134	136.5	139
12	2	0	273	542	129	136.5	144
13	2	0	189	397	86	94.5	103
13	27	0	3514	6451	86	130.1	175

9965

We see that none of the PSUs have been dropped due to missing values in `drinkdays`. Now we can use `svy: poisson` to model the `drinkdays` as a function of `ridageyr` (recoded values of age) and `ridreth1` (recoded categories of race/ethnicity). Note that we use the `irr` option so that `svy: poisson` will report the incidence-rate ratio estimates instead of the coefficient estimates.

```
. xi: svy: poisson drinkdays ridageyr i.ridreth1, irr
i.ridreth1        _Iridreth1_1-5      (naturally coded; _Iridreth1_1 omitted)
(running poisson on estimation sample)
```

Survey: Poisson regression

Number of strata	=	13	Number of obs	=	3265
Number of PSUs	=	27	Population size	=	2.722e+08
			Design df	=	14
			F(5, 10)	=	2.40
			Prob > F	=	0.1122

drinkdays	IRR	Linearized Std. Err.	t	P>|t|	[95% Conf. Interval]	
ridageyr	1.001252	.0033521	0.37	0.714	.9940877	1.008467
_Iridreth1_2	.6216791	.125314	-2.36	0.033	.4034659	.9579121
_Iridreth1_3	.8715129	.1213347	-0.99	0.340	.6465348	1.174778
_Iridreth1_4	1.102014	.252548	0.42	0.678	.6740978	1.801571
_Iridreth1_5	.7435355	.2324936	-0.95	0.359	.3802277	1.453984

The incidence-rate ratio for `ridageyr` is not significantly different from 1, thus there is not enough evidence to conclude that there is any association between drinking incidence and age.

◁

Saved Results

svy: poisson saves in e(). In addition to the items documented in [SVY] **svy**, svy: poisson also saves the following:

Macros
e(cmd)	poisson
e(depvar)	name of dependent variable
e(offset)	offset
e(crittype)	log pseudolikelihood
e(predict)	program used to implement predict

Methods and Formulas

svy: poisson is implemented as an ado-file.

The Poisson probability mass function is

$$\Pr(Y = y) = \frac{e^{-\lambda}\lambda^y}{\Gamma(y + 1)}$$

In Poisson regression, $\ln \lambda$ is modeled as a linear function of independent variables, plus an optional offset.

$$\ln \lambda_j = \xi_j = \mathbf{x}_j \boldsymbol{\beta} + \text{offset}_j$$

The log pseudolikelihood is

$$\ln L = \sum_{j=1}^{N} w_j \left[-e^{\xi_j} y_j + \xi_j y_j - \ln\{\Gamma(y_j + 1)\} \right]$$

where w_j is a sampling weight. The equation-level scores used in the linearized variance estimator are derived by taking partial derivatives of the log pseudolikelihood; see [SVY] **variance estimation**.

References

Bortkewitsch, L. von. 1898. *Das Gesetz der Kleinen Zahlen*. Leipzig: Teubner.

Bru, B. 2001. Siméon-Denis Poisson. In *Statisticians of the Centuries*, ed. C. C. Heyde and E. Seneta, 123–126. New York: Springer.

Cameron, A. C. and P. K. Trivedi. 1998. *Regression Analysis of Count Data*. Cambridge: Cambridge University Press.

Chatterjee, S., A. S. Hadi, and B. Price. 2000. *Regression Analysis by Example*. 3rd ed. New York: Wiley.

Clarke, R. D. 1946. An application of the Poisson distribution. *Journal of the Institute of Actuaries* 22: 48.

Cochran, W. G. 1940. The analysis of variance when experimental errors follow the Poisson or binomial laws. *Annals of Mathematical Statistics* 11: 335–347. Reprinted as paper 22 in Cochran (1982).

——. 1977. *Sampling Techniques*. 3rd ed. New York: Wiley.

——. 1982. *Contributions to Statistics*. New York: Wiley.

Coleman, J. S. 1964. *Introduction to Mathematical Sociology*. New York: Free Press.

Doll, R. and A. B. Hill. 1966. Mortality of British doctors in relation to smoking; observations on coronary thrombosis. In *Epidemiological Approaches to the Study of Cancer and Other Chronic Diseases*, ed. W. Haenszel. *National Cancer Institute Monograph* 19: 204–268.

Feller, W. 1968. *An Introduction to Probability Theory and Its Applications*, vol. 1. 3rd ed. New York: Wiley.

Hilbe, J. 1998. sg91: Robust variance estimators for MLE Poisson and negative binomial regression. *Stata Technical Bulletin* 45: 26–28. Reprinted in *Stata Technical Bulletin Reprints*, vol. 8, pp. 177–180.

——. 1999. sg102: Zero-truncated Poisson and negative binomial regression. *Stata Technical Bulletin* 47: 37–40. Reprinted in *Stata Technical Bulletin Reprints*, vol. 8, pp. 233–236.

Long, J. S. 1997. *Regression Models for Categorical and Limited Dependent Variables*. Thousand Oaks, CA: Sage.

Long, J. S. and J. Freese. 2001. Predicted probabilities for count models. *Stata Journal* 1: 51–57.

——. 2003. *Regression Models for Categorical Dependent Variables Using Stata*. rev. ed. College Station, TX: Stata Press.

McNeil, D. 1996. *Epidemiological Research Methods*. Chichester, UK: Wiley.

Poisson, S. D. 1837. *Recherches sur la probabilité des jugements en matière criminelle et en matière civile, précédés des règles générales du calcul des probabilités*. Paris: Bachelier.

Selvin, S. 2004. *Statistical Analysis of Epidemiologic Data*. 3rd ed. New York: Oxford University Press.

Thorndike, F. 1926. Applications of Poisson's probability summation. *Bell System Technical Journal* 5: 604–624.

Also See

Complementary:	[SVY] **svy: poisson postestimation**
Related:	[R] **poisson**;
	[SVY] **svy: nbreg**, [SVY] **svy: regress**
Background:	[U] **20 Estimation and postestimation commands**,
	[SVY] **estimation options**, [SVY] **poststratification**,
	[SVY] **subpopulation estimation**, [SVY] **svy**, [SVY] **variance estimation**,
	[R] **maximize**

Title

svy: poisson postestimation — Postestimation tools for svy: poisson

Description

The following postestimation commands are available for svy: poisson:

command	description
estat	postestimation statistics for survey data
estimates	cataloging estimation results
lincom	point estimates, standard errors, testing, and inference for linear combinations of coefficients
mfx	marginal effects or elasticities
nlcom	point estimates, standard errors, testing, and inference for nonlinear combinations of coefficients
predict	predictions, residuals, influence statistics, and other diagnostic measures
predictnl	point estimates, standard errors, testing, and inference for generalized predictions
suest	seemingly unrelated estimation
test	Wald tests for simple and composite linear hypotheses
testnl	Wald tests of nonlinear hypotheses

See [SVY] **estat**.

See the corresponding entries in the *Stata Base Reference Manual* for details.

Syntax for predict

predict [*type*] *newvarname* [*if*] [*in*] [, *statistic* <u>nooff</u>set]

statistic	description
n	predicted number of events; the default
ir	incidence rate (equivalent to predict ... , n nooffset)
xb	linear prediction, $x_j\beta$
stdp	standard error of the linear prediction
<u>sc</u>ore	first derivative of the log pseudolikelihood with respect to $x_j\beta$

These statistics are available both in and out of sample; type predict ... if e(sample) ... if wanted only for the estimation sample.

Options for predict

n, the default, calculates the predicted number of events, which is $\exp(x_j\beta)$ if neither offset() nor exposure() was specified when the model was fitted; $\exp(x_j\beta + \text{offset}_j)$ if offset() was specified; or $\exp(x_j\beta) \times \text{exposure}_j$ if exposure() was specified.

ir calculates the incidence rate $\exp(\mathbf{x}_j\boldsymbol{\beta})$, which is the predicted number of events when exposure is 1. This is equivalent to specifying both n and nooffset options.

xb calculates the linear prediction, which is $\mathbf{x}_j\boldsymbol{\beta}$ if neither offset() nor exposure() was specified; $\mathbf{x}_j\boldsymbol{\beta} + \text{offset}_j$ if offset() was specified; or $\mathbf{x}_j\boldsymbol{\beta} + \ln(\text{exposure}_j)$ if exposure() was specified; see nooffset below.

stdp calculates the standard error of the linear prediction.

nooffset is relevant if you specified offset() or exposure() when you fitted the model. It modifies the calculations made by predict so that they ignore the offset or exposure variable; the linear prediction is treated as $\mathbf{x}_j\boldsymbol{\beta}$ rather than as $\mathbf{x}_j\boldsymbol{\beta} + \text{offset}_j$ or $\mathbf{x}_j\boldsymbol{\beta} + \ln(\text{exposure}_j)$. Specifying predict ..., nooffset is equivalent to specifying predict ..., ir.

score calculates the equation-level score, $\partial \ln L/\partial(\mathbf{x}_j\boldsymbol{\beta})$.

Remarks

▷ Example 1

Continuing with our example from [SVY] **svy: poisson**, we use predict to compute the incidence rate for alcohol consumption for each observation in the estimation sample and save the values in the new variable ir_drink. We then use summarize to make a quick comparison of the average and range of the values in drinkdays and ir_drink.

```
. predict ir_drink if e(sample), ir
(6700 missing values generated)

. sum ir_drink drinkdays if e(sample)
```

Variable	Obs	Mean	Std. Dev.	Min	Max
ir_drink	3265	3.153157	.4264748	1.991329	3.925883
drinkdays	3265	3.227871	12.67914	0	365

◁

Methods and Formulas

All postestimation commands listed above are implemented as ado-files.

The equation-level scores are given by

$$\text{score}_j = y_j - e^{\xi_j}$$

Also See

Complementary: [SVY] **svy: poisson**, [SVY] **estat**;
[R] **estimates**, [R] **lincom**, [R] **mfx**, [R] **nlcom**, [R] **predict**,
[R] **predictnl**, [R] **suest**, [R] **test**, [R] **testnl**

Background: [U] **13.5 Accessing coefficients and standard errors**,
[U] **20 Estimation and postestimation commands**

Title

svy: probit — Probit regression for survey data

Syntax

svy [*vcetype*] [, *svy_options*] : <u>prob</u>it *depvar* [*indepvars*] [*if*] [*in*] [, *options*]

vcetype	description
SE	
<u>linear</u>ized	Taylor linearized variance estimation
brr	BRR variance estimation; see [SVY] **svy brr**
jackknife	jackknife variance estimation; see [SVY] **svy jackknife**

Specifying a *vcetype* overrides the default from svyset.

svy_options	description
if/in	
<u>subp</u>op()	identify a subpopulation
SE	
brr_options	additional options allowed with BRR variance estimation; see [SVY] *brr_options*
jackknife_options	additional options allowed with jackknife variance estimation; see [SVY] *jackknife_options*
Reporting	
<u>level</u>(#)	set confidence level; default is level(95)
<u>nohe</u>ader	suppress the table header
<u>nol</u>egend	suppress the table legend
<u>noadj</u>ust	do not adjust model Wald statistic

svy requires that the survey-design variables be identified using svyset; see [SVY] **svyset**.

xi is allowed; see [R] **xi**.

See [U] **20 Estimation and postestimation commands** for additional capabilities of estimation commands.

Warning: Using *if* or *in* restrictions will not produce correct variance estimates for subpopulations in many cases. To compute estimates for a subpopulation, use the subpop() option. The full specification for subpop() is
<u>subp</u>op([*varname*] [*if*])

options	description
Model	
<u>nocon</u>stant	suppress the constant term
<u>off</u>set(*varname*)	include *varname* in model with coefficient constrained to 1
asis	retain perfect predictor variables
Max options	
maximize_options	control the maximization process; seldom used

Description

svy: probit fits probit regression models for complex survey data In the probit regression model, *depvar* is a 0/1 variable (or, more precisely, a 0/non-0 variable).

See [R] **probit** for a description of this model involving nonsurvey data, [SVY] **svy: logistic** for logistic regression reporting odds ratios, [SVY] **svy: logit** for logistic regression, [SVY] **svy: mlogit** for multinomial logistic regression, [SVY] **svy: ologit** for ordered logistic regression, and [SVY] **svy: oprobit** for ordered probit regression for survey data.

Options

svy_options; see [SVY] **svy**.

⌐‾‾⌐ Model ⌐

noconstant, offset(*varname*); see [SVY] **estimation options**.

asis forces retention of perfect predictor variables and their associated perfectly predicted observations and may produce instabilities in maximization; see [R] **probit**.

⌐‾‾⌐ Max options ⌐

maximize_options: iterate(*#*), [no]log, trace, tolerance(*#*), ltolerance(*#*); see [R] **maximize**. These options are seldom used. If the maximization is taking a long time, you may wish to specify the log option to view the iteration log. The log option implies svy's noisily option; see [SVY] **svy**.

Remarks

If y is the binary reponse variable and the vector of predictors is $\mathbf{x}$, then probit regression models the probability of a positive outcome by

$$\Pr(y = 1; \mathbf{x}) = \Phi(\mathbf{x}\boldsymbol{\beta})$$

where $\Phi()$ is the standard cumulative normal distribution function, and $\boldsymbol{\beta}$ is the vector of coefficients for the predictors $\mathbf{x}$. svy: probit estimates $\boldsymbol{\beta}$ for the population using the survey data sampled from it.

▷ Example 1

In the following example, we fit a probit regression of the incidence of high blood pressure on some demographic variables for the subpopulation indicated by the female variable using the NHANES II dataset.

```
. use http://www.stata-press.com/data/r9/nhanes2d
. svyset
      pweight: finalwgt
          VCE: linearized
    Strata 1: strata
       SU 1: psu
      FPC 1: <zero>
```

```
. svy, subpop(female): probit highbp height weight age age2 black
(running probit on estimation sample)

Survey: Probit regression

Number of strata   =        31              Number of obs       =       10351
Number of PSUs     =        62              Population size      = 1.172e+08
                                            Subpop. no. of obs  =        5436
                                            Subpop. size        =    60998033
                                            Design df           =          31
                                            F(   5,     27)     =       58.64
                                            Prob > F            =      0.0000
```

highbp	Coef.	Linearized Std. Err.	t	P>|t|	[95% Conf. Interval]	
height	-.0145621	.004785	-3.04	0.005	-.0243213	-.004803
weight	.023917	.0023869	10.02	0.000	.0190489	.0287852
age	.0799438	.0196039	4.08	0.000	.0399615	.1199262
age2	-.0005141	.0001867	-2.75	0.010	-.0008949	-.0001333
black	.2543391	.1114459	2.28	0.029	.0270436	.4816345
_cons	-3.234614	.9560131	-3.38	0.002	-5.184415	-1.284812

Our results show that older women are more likely to have high blood than younger women.

◁

Saved Results

svy: probit saves in e(). In addition to the items documented in [SVY] **svy**, svy: probit also saves the following:

Macros
    e(cmd)   probit
    e(depvar)   name of dependent variable
    e(offset)   offset
    e(crittype)   log pseudolikelihood
    e(predict)   program used to implement predict

Methods and Formulas

svy: probit is implemented as an ado-file.

The log pseudolikelihood is

$$\ln L = \sum_{j \in S} w_j \ln \Phi(\mathbf{x}_j \boldsymbol{\beta}) + \sum_{j \notin S} w_j \ln\{1 - \Phi(\mathbf{x}_j \boldsymbol{\beta})\}$$

where S is the set of all observations such that $y_j \neq 0$, $\Phi()$ is the standard cumulative normal and w_j is a sampling weight. The equation-level scores used in the linearized variance estimator are derived by taking partial derivatives of the log pseudolikelihood; see [SVY] **variance estimation**.

References

Aldrich, J. H. and F. D. Nelson. 1984. *Linear Probability, Logit, and Probit Models.* Newbury Park, CA: Sage.

Bliss, C. I. 1934. The method of probits. *Science* 79: 38–39, 409–410.

Eltinge, J. L. and W. M. Sribney. 1996. svy4: Linear, logistic, and probit regressions for survey data. *Stata Technical Bulletin* 31: 26–31. Reprinted in *Stata Technical Bulletin Reprints*, vol. 6, pp. 239–245.

Johnston, J. and J. DiNardo. 1997. *Econometric Methods.* 4th ed. New York: McGraw–Hill.

Long, J. S. 1997. *Regression Models for Categorical and Limited Dependent Variables.* Thousand Oaks, CA: Sage.

Long, J. S. and J. Freese. 2003. *Regression Models for Categorical Dependent Variables Using Stata.* rev. ed. College Station, TX: Stata Press.

Powers, D. A. and Y. Xie. 2000. *Statistical Methods for Categorical Data Analysis.* San Diego, CA: Academic Press.

Also See

Complementary:	[SVY] **svy: probit postestimation**
Related:	[R] **probit**;
	[SVY] **svy: logistic**, [SVY] **svy: logit**, [SVY] **svy: mlogit**,
	[SVY] **svy: ologit**, [SVY] **svy: oprobit**
Background:	[U] **20 Estimation and postestimation commands**,
	[SVY] **estimation options**, [SVY] **poststratification**,
	[SVY] **subpopulation estimation**, [SVY] **svy**, [SVY] **variance estimation**,
	[R] **maximize**

Title

svy: probit postestimation — Postestimation tools for svy: probit

Description

The following postestimation commands are available for svy: probit:

command	description
estat	postestimation statistics for survey data
estimates	cataloging estimation results
lincom	point estimates, standard errors, testing, and inference for linear combinations of coefficients
mfx	marginal effects or elasticities
nlcom	point estimates, standard errors, testing, and inference for nonlinear combinations of coefficients
predict	predictions, residuals, influence statistics, and other diagnostic measures
predictnl	point estimates, standard errors, testing, and inference for generalized predictions
suest	seemingly unrelated estimation
test	Wald tests for simple and composite linear hypotheses
testnl	Wald tests of nonlinear hypotheses

See [SVY] **estat**.

See the corresponding entries in the *Stata Base Reference Manual* for details.

Syntax for predict

predict [*type*] *newvarname* [*if*] [*in*] [, *statistic* <u>nooff</u>set]

statistic	description
<u>pr</u>	probability of a positive outcome; the default
xb	linear prediction, $x_j\beta$
stdp	standard error of the prediction
<u>sco</u>re	first derivative of the log pseudolikelihood with respect to $x_j\beta$

These statistics are available both in and out of sample; type predict ... if e(sample) ... if wanted only for the estimation sample.

Options for predict

pr, the default, calculates the probability of a positive outcome.

xb calculates the linear prediction $x_j\beta$.

stdp calculates the standard error of the linear prediction.

score calculates the equation-level score, $\partial \ln L / \partial(x_j\beta)$.

nooffset is relevant if you specified offset() when you fitted the model. It modifies the calculations made by predict so that they ignore the offset variable; the linear prediction is treated as $\mathbf{x}_j\beta$ rather than as $\mathbf{x}_j\beta + \text{offset}_j$.

Remarks

▷ Example 1

Continuing with our example from [SVY] **svy: probit**, we use predict to compute the probability of high blood pressure for each covariate pattern in the dataset and save the values in the new variable p_highbp.

```
. predict p_highbp, pr
```

◁

Methods and Formulas

All postestimation commands listed above are implemented as ado-files.

Also See

Complementary:	[SVY] **svy: probit**, [SVY] **estat**;
	[R] **estimates**, [R] **lincom**, [R] **mfx**, [R] **nlcom**, [R] **predict**,
	[R] **predictnl**, [R] **suest**, [R] **test**, [R] **testnl**
Background:	[U] **13.5 Accessing coefficients and standard errors**,
	[U] **20 Estimation and postestimation commands**

Title

svy: proportion — Estimate proportions for survey data

Syntax

svy [*vcetype*] [, *svy_options*] : proportion *varlist* [*if*] [*in*] [, *options*]

vcetype	description
SE	
linearized	Taylor linearized variance estimation
brr	BRR variance estimation; see [SVY] **svy brr**
jackknife	jackknife variance estimation; see [SVY] **svy jackknife**

Specifying a *vcetype* overrides the default from svyset.

svy_options	description
if/in/over	
subpop()	identify a subpopulation
SE	
brr_options	additional options allowed with BRR variance estimation; see [SVY] ***brr_options***
jackknife_options	additional options allowed with jackknife variance estimation; see [SVY] ***jackknife_options***
Reporting	
level(#)	set confidence level; default is level(95)
noheader	suppress the table header
nolegend	suppress the table legend

svy requires that the survey-design variables be identified using svyset; see [SVY] **svyset**.

See [U] **20 Estimation and postestimation commands** for additional capabilities of estimation commands.

Warning: Using *if* or *in* restrictions will not produce correct variance estimates for subpopulations in many cases. To compute estimates for a subpopulation, use the subpop() option. The full specification for subpop() is

subpop([*varname*] [*if*])

178

options	description
Model	
<u>stdize</u>(*varname*)	variable identifying strata for standardization
<u>stdweight</u>(*varname*)	weight variable for standardization
<u>nostdr</u>escale	do not rescale the standard weight variable
<u>nolabel</u>	suppress value labels from *varlist*
<u>miss</u>ing	treat missing values like other values
if/in/over	
over(*varlist* [, <u>nolabel</u>])	identify multiple subpopulations

Description

svy: proportion produces estimates of finite-population proportions for the categories identified by the values in each variable of *varlist* from survey data; see [R] **proportion** for a description of sample proportions from nonsurvey data.

Options

svy_options; see [SVY] **svy**.

⌐ Model ⌐

stdize(*varname*) specifies that the point estimates be adjusted by direct standardization across the strata identified by *varname*. This option requires the stdweight() option.

stdweight(*varname*) specifies the weight variable associated with the standard strata identified in the stdize() option. The standardization weights must be constant within the standard strata.

nostdrescale prevents the standardization weights from being rescaled within the over() groups. This option requires stdize() but is ignored if the over() option is not specified.

nolabel requests that value labels attached to the variables in *varlist* be ignored.

missing specifies that missing values in *varlist* be treated as valid categories, rather than be omitted from the analysis (the default).

⌐ if/in/over ⌐

over(*varlist* [, <u>nolabel</u>]) specifies that estimates be computed for multiple subpopulations.

The subpopulations are identified by the different values of the variables in *varlist*.

When over() is supplied with a single variable name, such as over(*varname*), the value labels of *varname* are used to identify the subpopulations. If *varname* does not have labeled values (or there are unlabeled values), the values themselves are used, provided that they are non-negative integers. Non-integer values, negative values, and labels that are not valid Stata names will be substituted with a default identifier.

When supplied with multiple variable names, a subpopulation index (starting at 1) is used to identify subpopulations. In this case, the index is listed with the values that identify the subpopulations.

nolabel requests that value labels attached to the variables identifying the subpopulations be ignored.

Remarks

Estimating proportions can be done by using svy: mean or svy: proportion; however, you will find that svy: proportion is generally easier to use with variables that have multiple categories. svy: proportion also produces a full covariance matrix, enabling the use of postestimation commands to draw inferences and make comparisons of proportions (and functions of proportions) within categories of a variable, between variables, and between subpopulations.

▷ Example 1

In the NHANES II (McDowell et al. 1981) dataset, the survey characteristics are already set. The variable heartatk equals 1 if a person has ever had a heart attack and equals 0 otherwise.

```
. use http://www.stata-press.com/data/r9/nhanes2
. svyset
       pweight: finalwgt
           VCE: linearized
     Strata 1: strata
        SU 1: psu
       FPC 1: <zero>
. describe heartatk
                storage   display    value
variable name    type    format     label        variable label

heartatk         byte    %9.0g                    heart attack, 1=yes, 0=no
```

The mean of heartatk is an estimate of the proportion of persons who have had heart attacks.

```
. svy: mean heartatk
(running mean on estimation sample)
Survey: Mean estimation
Number of strata =      31          Number of obs    =     10349
Number of PSUs   =      62          Population size  = 1.2e+08
                                    Design df        =        31
```

		Linearized	
	Mean	Std. Err.	[95% Conf. Interval]
heartatk	.0297383	.0018484	.0259684 .0335081

We also could have obtained this estimate by using svy: proportion.

```
. svy: proportion heartatk
(running proportion on estimation sample)
Survey: Proportion estimation
Number of strata =      31          Number of obs    =     10349
Number of PSUs   =      62          Population size  = 1.2e+08
                                    Design df        =        31
```

		Linearized	Binomial Wald
	Proportion	Std. Err.	[95% Conf. Interval]
heartatk			
0	.9702617	.0018484	.9664919 .9740316
1	.0297383	.0018484	.0259684 .0335081

◁

▷ Example 2: Proportions from multiple variables

The svy: mean command produces less output than svy: proportion — it calculates the proportion for the category identified by the indicator variable heartatk. svy: mean requires that we specify a separate indicator variable for each proportion that we wish to estimate. With svy: proportion, we do not have to create indicator variables.

Here we estimate the proportions for each race and age group in the NHANES II data.

```
. svy: proportion race agegrp
(running proportion on estimation sample)

Survey: Proportion estimation

Number of strata =        31          Number of obs     =    10351
Number of PSUs   =        62          Population size   = 1.2e+08
                                      Design df         =       31

            _prop_4: agegrp = age20-29
            _prop_5: agegrp = age30-39
            _prop_6: agegrp = age40-49
            _prop_7: agegrp = age50-59
            _prop_8: agegrp = age60-69
            _prop_9: agegrp = age 70+
```

	Proportion	Linearized Std. Err.	Binomial Wald [95% Conf. Interval]	
race				
White	.8791545	.016689	.845117	.9131919
Black	.0955059	.0127491	.069504	.1215079
Other	.0253396	.0105423	.0038385	.0468408
agegrp				
_prop_4	.2804574	.0071815	.2658107	.2951042
_prop_5	.2043014	.005756	.192562	.2160407
_prop_6	.1683637	.0041574	.1598846	.1768427
_prop_7	.1671604	.0050705	.1568191	.1775017
_prop_8	.1334892	.0038819	.1255721	.1414063
_prop_9	.0462279	.0029737	.040163	.0522928

◁

(*Continued on next page*)

▷ Example 3: Proportions for subpopulations

svy: proportion also allows the over() and subpop() options for subpopulation estimates.

```
. svy: proportion agegrp, over(race)
(running proportion on estimation sample)

Survey: Proportion estimation

Number of strata =        31        Number of obs     =      10351
Number of PSUs   =        62        Population size    =   1.2e+08
                                    Design df          =         31

          _prop_1: agegrp = age20-29
          _prop_2: agegrp = age30-39
          _prop_3: agegrp = age40-49
          _prop_4: agegrp = age50-59
          _prop_5: agegrp = age60-69
          _prop_6: agegrp = age 70+

            White: race = White
            Black: race = Black
            Other: race = Other
```

Over	Proportion	Linearized Std. Err.	Binomial Wald [95% Conf. Interval]	
_prop_1				
White	.2742205	.0072859	.2593609	.2890801
Black	.3293883	.0196062	.2894011	.3693754
Other	.3124264	.0477634	.2150123	.4098405
_prop_2				
White	.2031529	.0066023	.1896874	.2166184
Black	.2144945	.0129634	.1880555	.2409336
Other	.2057292	.027031	.1505991	.2608593
_prop_3				
White	.1690956	.0046802	.1595502	.178641
Black	.1582656	.0138216	.1300762	.186455
Other	.1810277	.0199529	.1403334	.221722
_prop_4				
White	.1682846	.0059082	.1562347	.1803344
Black	.1587381	.0120459	.1341704	.1833058
Other	.1599011	.0249102	.1090965	.2107058
_prop_5				
White	.1374726	.0041022	.1291062	.1458391
Black	.1016009	.0077398	.0858154	.1173864
Other	.1154734	.0381939	.0375763	.1933704
_prop_6				
White	.0477738	.0032648	.0411152	.0544323
Black	.0375127	.0052931	.0267173	.048308
Other	.0254422	.0110666	.0028717	.0480127

◁

Saved Results

svy: proportion saves in e(). In addition to the items documented in [SVY] **svy**, svy: proportion also saves the following:

Scalars
    e(N_over)   number of subpopulations

Macros

e(cmd)	proportion	e(varlist)	*varlist*
e(over)	*varlist* from over()	e(stdize)	*varname* from stdize()
e(over_labels)	labels from over() variables	e(stdweight)	*varname* from stdweight()
e(over_namelist)	names from e(over_labels)	e(namelist)	proportion identifiers
		e(label#)	labels from #th variable in *varlist*

Matrices
    e(_N)   vector of sample sizes
    e(_N_subp)   vector of subpopulation size estimates

Methods and Formulas

svy: proportion is implemented as an ado-file.

A proportion is simply the mean of an indicator variable (y_j only takes on the values 0 and 1, if it is not missing); see the *Methods and Formulas* section in [SVY] **svy: mean**.

References

Cochran, W. G. 1977. *Sampling Techniques*. 3rd ed. New York: Wiley.

Eltinge, J. L. and W. M. Sribney. 1996. svy2: Estimation of means, totals, ratios, and proportions for survey data. *Stata Technical Bulletin* 31: 6–23. Reprinted in *Stata Technical Bulletin Reprints*, vol. 6, pp. 213–235.

Kish, L. 1965. *Survey Sampling*. New York: Wiley.

McDowell, A., A. Engel, J. T. Massey, and K. Maurer. 1981. Plan and operation of the Second National Health and Nutrition Examination Survey, 1976–1980. *Vital and Health Statistics* 15(1). Hyattsville, MD: National Center for Health Statistics.

Wolter, K. M. 1985. *Introduction to Variance Estimation*. New York: Springer.

Also See

Complementary: [SVY] **svy: proportion postestimation**

Related: [R] **proportion**;
                [SVY] **svy: mean**, [SVY] **svy: ratio**, [SVY] **svy: total**

Background: [U] **20 Estimation and postestimation commands**,
                [SVY] **estimation options**, [SVY] **direct standardization**,
                [SVY] **poststratification**, [SVY] **subpopulation estimation**,
                [SVY] **svy**, [SVY] **variance estimation**

Title

svy: proportion postestimation — Postestimation tools for svy: proportion

Description

The following postestimation commands are available for `svy: proportion`:

command	description
estat	postestimation statistics for survey data
estimates	cataloging estimation results
lincom	point estimates, standard errors, testing, and inference for linear combinations of descriptive statistics
nlcom	point estimates, standard errors, testing, and inference for nonlinear combinations of descriptive statistics
test	Wald tests for simple and composite linear hypotheses
testnl	Wald tests of nonlinear hypotheses

See [SVY] **estat**.

See the corresponding entries in the *Stata Base Reference Manual* for details on the other postestimation commands.

`predict` is not allowed after `svy: proportion`.

Remarks

▷ Example 1

In the NHANES II (McDowell et al. 1981) dataset, `heartatk` indicates if a person has ever had a heart attack, and `agegrp` identifies age groups.

```
. use http://www.stata-press.com/data/r9/nhanes2
. svyset
      pweight: finalwgt
          VCE: linearized
    Strata 1: strata
       SU 1: psu
      FPC 1: <zero>
. describe heartatk agegrp

              storage   display    value
variable name   type    format     label      variable label

heartatk        byte    %9.0g                 heart attack, 1=yes, 0=no
agegrp          byte    %8.0g      agegrp      Age groups 1-6
. label list agegrp
agegrp:
           1 age20-29
           2 age30-39
           3 age40-49
           4 age50-59
           5 age60-69
           6 age 70+
```

We can estimate the proportion of people who have ever had a heart attack for each subpopulation defined by the age group variable.

```
. svy: proportion heartatk, over(agegrp)
(running proportion on estimation sample)

Survey: Proportion estimation

Number of strata =        31          Number of obs    =     10349
Number of PSUs   =        62          Population size  = 1.2e+08
                                      Design df        =        31

         _prop_1: heartatk = 0
         _prop_2: heartatk = 1

      _subpop_1: agegrp = age20-29
      _subpop_2: agegrp = age30-39
      _subpop_3: agegrp = age40-49
      _subpop_4: agegrp = age50-59
      _subpop_5: agegrp = age60-69
      _subpop_6: agegrp = age 70+
```

Over	Proportion	Linearized Std. Err.	Binomial Wald [95% Conf. Interval]	
_prop_1				
_subpop_1	.999621	.0003798	.9988464	1.000396
_subpop_2	.9978977	.0010767	.9957018	1.000094
_subpop_3	.9850219	.0042378	.9763788	.9936649
_subpop_4	.9451288	.0069638	.9309261	.9593316
_subpop_5	.9095761	.0064351	.8964515	.9227006
_subpop_6	.8824748	.0110165	.8600065	.9049431
_prop_2				
_subpop_1	.000379	.0003798	-.0003957	.0011536
_subpop_2	.0021023	.0010767	-.0000935	.0042982
_subpop_3	.0149781	.0042378	.0063351	.0236212
_subpop_4	.0548712	.0069638	.0406684	.0690739
_subpop_5	.0904239	.0064351	.0772994	.1035485
_subpop_6	.1175252	.0110165	.0950569	.1399935

Here we use the test command to jointly test that the proportion of people who have had a heart attack is the same between adults in their 20s, 30s, and 40s.

```
. test [_prop_2]_subpop_1 = [_prop_2]_subpop_2 = [_prop_2]_subpop_3

Adjusted Wald test

 ( 1)  [_prop_2]_subpop_1 - [_prop_2]_subpop_2 = 0
 ( 2)  [_prop_2]_subpop_1 - [_prop_2]_subpop_3 = 0

       F( 2,    30) =    7.51
            Prob > F =   0.0023
```

◁

Methods and Formulas

All postestimation commands listed above are implemented as ado-files.

Also See

Complementary:	[SVY] **svy: proportion**, [SVY] **estat**;
	[R] **estimates**, [R] **lincom**, [R] **nlcom**, [R] **test**, [R] **testnl**
Background:	[U] **13.5 Accessing coefficients and standard errors**,
	[U] **20 Estimation and postestimation commands**

Title

svy: ratio — Estimate ratios for survey data

Syntax

Basic syntax

svy: ratio [*name:*] *varname* [*/*] *varname*

Full syntax

svy [*vcetype*] [, *svy_options*] :

    ratio ([*name:*] *varname* [*/*] *varname*)

        [([*name:*] *varname* [*/*] *varname*) ...] [*if*] [*in*] [, *options*]

vcetype	description
SE	
linearized	Taylor linearized variance estimation
brr	BRR variance estimation; see [SVY] **svy brr**
jackknife	jackknife variance estimation; see [SVY] **svy jackknife**

Specifying a *vcetype* overrides the default from svyset.

svy_options	description
if/in/over	
subpop()	identify a subpopulation
SE	
brr_options	additional options allowed with BRR variance estimation; see [SVY] ***brr_options***
jackknife_options	additional options allowed with jackknife variance estimation; see [SVY] ***jackknife_options***
Reporting	
level(#)	set confidence level; default is level(95)
noheader	suppress the table header
nolegend	suppress the table legend

svy requires that the survey-design variables be identified using svyset; see [SVY] **svyset**.

See [U] **20 Estimation and postestimation commands** for additional capabilities of estimation commands.

Warning: Using *if* or *in* restrictions will not produce correct variance estimates for subpopulations in many cases. To compute estimates for a subpopulation, use the subpop() option. The full specification for subpop() is

    subpop([*varname*] [*if*])

options	description
Model	
<u>stdize</u>(*varname*)	variable identifying strata for standardization
<u>stdw</u>eight(*varname*)	weight variable for standardization
<u>nostdr</u>escale	do not rescale the standard weight variable
if/in/over	
<u>over</u>(*varlist* [, <u>nolabel</u>])	identify multiple subpopulations

Description

svy: ratio produces estimates of ratios of finite-population totals from survey data; see [R] **ratio** for a description of sample ratios from nonsurvey data.

Options

svy_options; see [SVY] **svy**.

    ⌐‾‾⌐Model⌐‾‾‾

stdize(*varname*) specifies that the point estimates be adjusted by direct standardization across the strata identified by *varname*. This option requires the stdweight() option.

stdweight(*varname*) specifies the weight variable associated with the standard strata identified in the stdize() option. The standardization weights must be constant within the standard strata.

nostdrescale prevents the standardization weights from being rescaled within the over() groups. This option requires stdize() but is ignored if the over() option is not specified.

    ⌐‾‾⌐if/in/over⌐‾‾‾

over(*varlist* [, <u>nolabel</u>]) specifies that estimates be computed for multiple subpopulations.

The subpopulations are identified by the different values of the variables in *varlist*.

When over() is supplied with a single variable name, such as over(*varname*), the value labels of *varname* are used to identify the subpopulations. If *varname* does not have labeled values (or there are unlabeled values), the values themselves are used, provided that they are non-negative integers. Non-integer values, negative values, and labels that are not valid Stata names will be substituted with a default identifier.

When supplied with multiple variable names, a subpopulation index (starting at 1) is used to identify subpopulations. In this case, the index is listed with the values that identify the subpopulations.

nolabel requests that value labels attached to the variables identifying the subpopulations be ignored.

Remarks

svy: ratio will produce the ratio of finite-population totals for one or more pairs of variables and over multiple subpopulations. svy: ratio also produces a full covariance matrix, enabling the use of postestimation commands to draw inferences and make comparisons of ratios (and functions of ratios), even between subpopulations.

▷ Example 1

In our NHANES II dataset, the variable tcresult contains total serum cholesterol and the variable hdresult contains serum levels of high-density lipoproteins (HDL). We can use svy: ratio to estimate the ratio of the total of hdresult to the total of tcresult.

```
. use http://www.stata-press.com/data/r9/nhanes2c
. svy: ratio hdresult/tcresult
(running ratio on estimation sample)
Survey: Ratio estimation
Number of strata =      30        Number of obs     =      8720
Number of PSUs   =      60        Population size   = 9.9e+07
                                  Design df         =        30

      _ratio_1: hdresult/tcresult
```

		Linearized		
	Ratio	Std. Err.	[95% Conf. Interval]	
_ratio_1	.2336173	.0024621	.228589	.2386457

Out of the 10,351 NHANES II subjects with a tcresult reading, only 8,720 had an hdresult reading. Consequently, svy: ratio used only the 8,720 observations that had nonmissing values for both variables. In your own datasets, if you encounter substantial missing-data rates, it is generally a good idea to look into the reasons for the missing-data phenomenon and to consider the potential for problems with nonresponse bias in your analysis.

◁

❏ Technical Note

Note that the slash / is optional. We could have typed

```
. svy: ratio hdresult tcresult
(output omitted)
```

❏

(*Continued on next page*)

▷ Example 2: Multiple ratios

We must use parentheses when estimating multiple ratios. Here is an example with two ratios, labeled R1 and R2.

```
. use http://www.stata-press.com/data/r9/yx

. svy: ratio (R1: y1/x1) (R2: y2/x2)
(running ratio on estimation sample)

Survey: Ratio estimation

Number of strata =      31          Number of obs    =     10351
Number of PSUs   =      62          Population size  = 1.2e+08
                                    Design df        =        31

            R1: y1/x1
            R2: y2/x2
```

	Ratio	Linearized Std. Err.	[95% Conf. Interval]	
R1	.9918905	.0102386	.9710087	1.012772
R2	.9962729	.0083088	.9793269	1.013219

◁

▷ Example 3: Multiple subpopulations

We can use the over() option to compare subpopulation ratios. Here we estimate the ratio of HDL to total serum cholesterol over age group.

```
. use http://www.stata-press.com/data/r9/nhanes2c

. svy: ratio hd2tc: hdresult/tcresult, over(agegrp)
(running ratio on estimation sample)

Survey: Ratio estimation

Number of strata =      30          Number of obs    =      8720
Number of PSUs   =      60          Population size  = 9.9e+07
                                    Design df        =        30

        hd2tc: hdresult/tcresult

    _subpop_1: agegrp = age20-29
    _subpop_2: agegrp = age30-39
    _subpop_3: agegrp = age40-49
    _subpop_4: agegrp = age50-59
    _subpop_5: agegrp = age60-69
    _subpop_6: agegrp = age 70+
```

Over	Ratio	Linearized Std. Err.	[95% Conf. Interval]	
hd2tc				
_subpop_1	.2651725	.0039043	.257199	.2731461
_subpop_2	.2408933	.0027581	.2352606	.246526
_subpop_3	.2225631	.0038232	.2147551	.2303711
_subpop_4	.2146759	.0027853	.2089875	.2203642
_subpop_5	.2116907	.0022942	.2070054	.216376
_subpop_6	.2144071	.004051	.2061339	.2226804

◁

▷ Example 4

svy: ratio or svy: mean can be used to estimate means for subpopulations.

In our NHANES II dataset, we have a variable female (equal to 1 if female and 0 otherwise) and a variable iron containing iron levels. Suppose that we wish to estimate the ratio of total iron levels in females to total number of females in the population. We can do this by first creating a new variable firon that represents iron levels in females; i.e., the variable equals iron level if the subject is female and zero if male. We can then use svy: ratio to estimate the ratio of the total of firon to the total of female.

```
. use http://www.stata-press.com/data/r9/nhanes2b
. gen firon = female*iron
. svy: ratio firon/female
(running ratio on estimation sample)

Survey: Ratio estimation

Number of strata =      31          Number of obs    =     10351
Number of PSUs   =      62          Population size  = 1.2e+08
                                    Design df        =        31

        _ratio_1: firon/female
```

		Linearized		
	Ratio	Std. Err.	[95% Conf. Interval]	
_ratio_1	97.16247	.6743344	95.78715	98.53778

This estimate can be obtained more easily by using svy: mean with the subpop option. The computation is identical.

```
. svy, subpop(female): mean iron
(running mean on estimation sample)

Survey: Mean estimation

Number of strata =      31          Number of obs    =     10351
Number of PSUs   =      62          Population size  = 1.2e+08
                                    Subpop. no. obs  =      5436
                                    Subpop. size     = 6.1e+07
                                    Design df        =        31
```

		Linearized		
	Mean	Std. Err.	[95% Conf. Interval]	
iron	97.16247	.6743344	95.78715	98.53778

◁

(Continued on next page)

Saved Results

svy: ratio saves in e(). In addition to the items documented in [SVY] **svy**, svy: ratio also saves the following:

Scalars
    e(N_over)   number of subpopulations

Macros

e(cmd)	ratio	e(varlist)	*varlist*
e(over)	*varlist* from over()	e(stdize)	*varname* from stdize()
e(over_labels)	labels from over() variables	e(stdweight)	*varname* from stdweight()
e(over_namelist)	names from e(over_labels)	e(namelist)	ratio identifiers

Matrices
    e(_N)   vector of sample sizes
    e(_N_subp)   vector of subpopulation size estimates

Methods and Formulas

svy: ratio is implemented as an ado-file.

See [SVY] **variance estimation**, [SVY] **direct standardization**, and [SVY] **poststratification** for discussions that provide background information for the following formulas.

The ratio estimator

Let Y_j and X_j be survey items for the jth individual in the population, where $j = 1, \ldots, M$ and M is the size of the population. The associated population ratio for the items of interest is $R = Y/X$ where

$$Y = \sum_{j=1}^{M} Y_j \qquad \text{and} \qquad X = \sum_{j=1}^{M} X_j$$

Let y_j and x_j be the corresponding survey items for the jth sampled individual from the population, where $j = 1, \ldots, m$ and m is the number of observations in the sample.

The estimator $\widehat{R}$ for the population ratio R is $\widehat{R} = \widehat{Y}/\widehat{X}$, where

$$\widehat{Y} = \sum_{j=1}^{m} w_j y_j \qquad \text{and} \qquad \widehat{X} = \sum_{j=1}^{m} w_j x_j$$

and w_j is a sampling weight. The score variable for the ratio estimator is

$$z_j(\widehat{R}) = \frac{y_j - \widehat{R} x_j}{\widehat{X}} = \frac{\widehat{X} y_j - \widehat{Y} x_j}{\widehat{X}^2}$$

The standardized ratio estimator

Let D_g denote the set of sampled observations that belong to the gth standard stratum and define $I_{D_g}(j)$ to indicate if the jth observation is a member of the gth standard stratum; where $g = 1$, $\ldots$, L_D and L_D is the number of standard strata. Also let π_g denote the fraction of the population that belongs to the gth standard stratum, thus $\pi_1 + \cdots + \pi_{L_D} = 1$. Note that π_g is derived from the stdweight() option.

The estimator for the standardized ratio is

$$\widehat{R}^D = \sum_{g=1}^{L_D} \pi_g \frac{\widehat{Y}_g}{\widehat{X}_g}$$

where

$$\widehat{Y}_g = \sum_{j=1}^{m} I_{D_g}(j)\, w_j y_j$$

and $\widehat{X}_g$ is similarly defined. The score variable for the standardized ratio is

$$z_j(\widehat{R}^D) = \sum_{g=1}^{L_D} \pi_g I_{D_g}(j) \frac{\widehat{X}_g y_j - \widehat{Y}_g x_j}{\widehat{X}_g^2}$$

The poststratified ratio estimator

Let P_k denote the set of sampled observations that belong to poststratum k and define $I_{P_k}(j)$ to indicate if the jth observation is a member of poststratum k; where $k = 1, \ldots, L_P$ and L_P is the number of poststrata. Also let M_k denote the population size for poststratum k. P_k and M_k are identified by specifying the poststrata() and postweight() options on svyset.

The estimator for the poststratified ratio is

$$\widehat{R}^P = \frac{\widehat{Y}^P}{\widehat{X}^P}$$

where

$$\widehat{Y}^P = \sum_{k=1}^{L_P} \frac{M_k}{\widehat{M}_k} \widehat{Y}_k = \sum_{k=1}^{L_P} \frac{M_k}{\widehat{M}_k} \sum_{j=1}^{m} I_{P_k}(j)\, w_j y_j$$

and $\widehat{X}^P$ is similarly defined. The score variable for the poststratified ratio is

$$z_j(\widehat{R}^P) = \frac{z_j(\widehat{Y}^P) - \widehat{R}^P z_j(\widehat{X}^P)}{\widehat{X}^P} = \frac{\widehat{X}^P z_j(\widehat{Y}^P) - \widehat{Y}^P z_j(\widehat{X}^P)}{(\widehat{X}^P)^2}$$

where

$$z_j(\widehat{Y}^P) = \sum_{k=1}^{L_P} I_{P_k}(j) \frac{M_k}{\widehat{M}_k} \left(y_j - \frac{\widehat{Y}_k}{\widehat{M}_k} \right)$$

and $z_j(\widehat{X}^P)$ is similarly defined.

The standardized poststratified ratio estimator

The estimator for the standardized poststratified ratio is

$$\widehat{R}^{DP} = \sum_{g=1}^{L_D} \pi_g \frac{\widehat{Y}_g^P}{\widehat{X}_g^P}$$

where

$$\widehat{Y}_g^P = \sum_{k=1}^{L_P} \frac{M_k}{\widehat{M}_k} \widehat{Y}_{g,k} = \sum_{k=1}^{L_P} \frac{M_k}{\widehat{M}_k} \sum_{j=1}^{m} I_{D_g}(j) I_{P_k}(j)\, w_j y_j$$

and $\widehat{X}_g^P$ is similarly defined. The score variable for the standardized poststratified ratio is

$$z_j(\widehat{R}^{DP}) = \sum_{g=1}^{L_D} \pi_g \frac{\widehat{X}_g^P z_j(\widehat{Y}_g^P) - \widehat{Y}_g^P z_j(\widehat{X}_g^P)}{(\widehat{X}_g^P)^2}$$

where

$$z_j(\widehat{Y}_g^P) = \sum_{k=1}^{L_P} I_{P_k}(j) \frac{M_k}{\widehat{M}_k} \left\{ I_{D_g}(j) y_j - \frac{\widehat{Y}_{g,k}}{\widehat{M}_k} \right\}$$

and $z_j(\widehat{X}_g^P)$ is similarly defined.

Subpopulation estimation

Let S denote the set of sampled observations that belong to the subpopulation of interest, and define $I_S(j)$ to indicate if the jth observation falls within the subpopulation.

The estimator for the subpopulation ratio is $\widehat{R}^S = \widehat{Y}^S / \widehat{X}^S$, where

$$\widehat{Y}^S = \sum_{j=1}^{m} I_S(j)\, w_j y_j \qquad \text{and} \qquad \widehat{X}^S = \sum_{j=1}^{m} I_S(j)\, w_j x_j$$

Its score variable is

$$z_j(\widehat{R}^S) = I_S(j) \frac{y_j - \widehat{R}^S x_j}{\widehat{X}^S} = I_S(j) \frac{\widehat{X}^S y_j - \widehat{Y}^S x_j}{(\widehat{X}^S)^2}$$

The estimator for the standardized subpopulation ratio is

$$\widehat{R}^{DS} = \sum_{g=1}^{L_D} \pi_g \frac{\widehat{Y}_g^S}{\widehat{X}_g^S}$$

where

$$\widehat{Y}_g^S = \sum_{j=1}^{m} I_{D_g}(j) I_S(j)\, w_j y_j$$

and $\widehat{X}_g^S$ is similarly defined. Its score variable is

$$z_j(\widehat{R}^{DS}) = \sum_{g=1}^{L_D} \pi_g I_{D_g}(j) I_S(j) \frac{\widehat{X}_g^S y_j - \widehat{Y}_g^S x_j}{(\widehat{X}_g^S)^2}$$

The estimator for the poststratified subpopulation ratio is

$$\widehat{R}^{PS} = \frac{\widehat{Y}^{PS}}{\widehat{X}^{PS}}$$

where

$$\widehat{Y}^{PS} = \sum_{k=1}^{L_P} \frac{M_k}{\widehat{M}_k} \widehat{Y}_k^S = \sum_{k=1}^{L_P} \frac{M_k}{\widehat{M}_k} \sum_{j=1}^{m} I_{P_k}(j) I_S(j) w_j y_j$$

and $\widehat{X}^{PS}$ is similarly defined. Its score variable is

$$z_j(\widehat{R}^{PS}) = \frac{\widehat{X}^{PS} z_j(\widehat{Y}^{PS}) - \widehat{Y}^{PS} z_j(\widehat{X}^{PS})}{(\widehat{X}^{PS})^2}$$

where

$$z_j(\widehat{Y}^{PS}) = \sum_{k=1}^{L_P} I_{P_k}(j) \frac{M_k}{\widehat{M}_k} \left\{ I_S(j) y_j - \frac{\widehat{Y}_k^S}{\widehat{M}_k} \right\}$$

and $z_j(\widehat{X}^{PS})$ is similarly defined.

The estimator for the standardized poststratified subpopulation ratio is

$$\widehat{R}^{DPS} = \sum_{g=1}^{L_D} \pi_g \frac{\widehat{Y}_g^{PS}}{\widehat{X}_g^{PS}}$$

where

$$\widehat{Y}_g^{PS} = \sum_{k=1}^{L_p} \frac{M_k}{\widehat{M}_k} \widehat{Y}_{g,k}^S = \sum_{k=1}^{L_p} \frac{M_k}{\widehat{M}_k} \sum_{j=1}^{m} I_{D_g}(j) I_{P_k}(j) I_S(j) w_j y_j$$

and $\widehat{X}_g^{PS}$ is similarly defined. Its score variable is

$$z_j(\widehat{R}^{DPS}) = \sum_{g=1}^{L_D} \pi_g \frac{\widehat{X}_g^{PS} z_j(\widehat{Y}_g^{PS}) - \widehat{Y}_g^{PS} z_j(\widehat{X}_g^{PS})}{(\widehat{X}_g^{PS})^2}$$

where

$$z_j(\widehat{Y}_g^{PS}) = \sum_{k=1}^{L_P} I_{P_k}(j) \frac{M_k}{\widehat{M}_k} \left\{ I_{D_g}(j) I_S(j) y_j - \frac{\widehat{Y}_{g,k}^S}{\widehat{M}_k} \right\}$$

and $z_j(\widehat{X}_g^{PS})$ is similarly defined.

References

Cochran, W. G. 1977. *Sampling Techniques*. 3rd ed. New York: Wiley.

Eltinge, J. L. and W. M. Sribney. 1996. svy2: Estimation of means, totals, ratios, and proportions for survey data. *Stata Technical Bulletin* 31: 6–23. Reprinted in *Stata Technical Bulletin Reprints*, vol. 6, pp. 213–235.

Kish, L. 1965. *Survey Sampling*. New York: Wiley.

McDowell, A., A. Engel, J. T. Massey, and K. Maurer. 1981. Plan and operation of the Second National Health and Nutrition Examination Survey, 1976–1980. *Vital and Health Statistics* 15(1). Hyattsville, MD: National Center for Health Statistics.

Wolter, K. M. 1985. *Introduction to Variance Estimation*. New York: Springer.

Also See

Complementary:	[SVY] **svy: ratio postestimation**
Related:	[R] **ratio**;
	[SVY] **svy: mean**, [SVY] **svy: proportion**, [SVY] **svy: total**
Background:	[U] **20 Estimation and postestimation commands**,
	[SVY] **estimation options**, [SVY] **direct standardization**,
	[SVY] **poststratification**, [SVY] **subpopulation estimation**,
	[SVY] **svy**, [SVY] **variance estimation**

Title

svy: ratio postestimation — Postestimation tools for svy: ratio

Description

The following postestimation commands are available for svy: ratio:

command	description
estat	postestimation statistics for survey data
estimates	cataloging estimation results
lincom	point estimates, standard errors, testing, and inference for linear combinations of descriptive statistics
nlcom	point estimates, standard errors, testing, and inference for nonlinear combinations of descriptive statistics
test	Wald tests for simple and composite linear hypotheses
testnl	Wald tests of nonlinear hypotheses

See [SVY] estat.

See the corresponding entries in the *Stata Base Reference Manual* for details on the other postestimation commands.

predict is not allowed after svy: ratio.

Remarks

▷ Example 1

Continuing with example 2 from [SVY] **svy: ratio**, we can perform a test of equality of the two ratios.

```
. test _b[R1] = _b[R2]
Adjusted Wald test
 ( 1)  R1 - R2 = 0
       F(  1,     31) =     0.12
             Prob > F =     0.7302
```

Instead of testing equality, we can use lincom to estimate the difference.

```
. lincom _b[R1] - _b[R2]
 ( 1)  R1 - R2 = 0
```

	Coef.	Std. Err.	t	P>|t|	[95% Conf. Interval]
(1)	-.0043824	.0125921	-0.35	0.730	-.0300641 .0212993

◁

197

▷ Example 2

Continuing with example 3 from [SVY] **svy: ratio**, we can test the equality of the ratio from the subpopulation of individuals in their twenties to the ratio from the subpopulation of individuals in their fifties.

```
. test [hd2tc]_subpop_1 = [hd2tc]_subpop_4

Adjusted Wald test

 ( 1)  [hd2tc]_subpop_1 - [hd2tc]_subpop_4 = 0

       F(  1,    30) =   164.69
            Prob > F =    0.0000
```

◁

Methods and Formulas

All postestimation commands listed above are implemented as ado-files.

Also See

Complementary:	[SVY] **svy: ratio**, [SVY] **estat**;
	[R] **estimates**, [R] **lincom**, [R] **nlcom**, [R] **test**, [R] **testnl**
Background:	[U] **13.5 Accessing coefficients and standard errors**,
	[U] **20 Estimation and postestimation commands**

Title

svy: regress — Linear regression for survey data

Syntax

svy [*vcetype*] [, *svy_options*] : regress *depvar* [*indepvars*] [*if*] [*in*] [, *options*]

vcetype	description
SE	
linearized	Taylor linearized variance estimation
brr	BRR variance estimation; see [SVY] **svy brr**
jackknife	jackknife variance estimation; see [SVY] **svy jackknife**

Specifying a *vcetype* overrides the default from svyset.

svy_options	description
if/in	
subpop()	identify a subpopulation
SE	
brr_options	additional options allowed with BRR variance estimation; see [SVY] *brr_options*
jackknife_options	additional options allowed with jackknife variance estimation; see [SVY] *jackknife_options*
Reporting	
level(#)	set confidence level; default is level(95)
noheader	suppress the table header
nolegend	suppress the table legend
noadjust	do not adjust model Wald statistic

svy requires that the survey-design variables be identified using svyset; see [SVY] **svyset**.

xi is allowed; see [R] **xi**.

See [U] **20 Estimation and postestimation commands** for additional capabilities of estimation commands.

Warning: Using *if* or *in* restrictions will not produce correct variance estimates for subpopulations in many cases. To compute estimates for a subpopulation, use the subpop() option. The full specification for subpop() is

subpop([*varname*] [*if*])

options	description
Model	
noconstant	suppress the constant term

Description

svy: regress fits linear regression models for complex survey data; see [R] **regress** for a description of this model using nonsurvey data, [SVY] **svy: ivreg** for instrumental variables regression, and [SVY] **svy: intreg** for interval regression for survey data.

Options

svy_options; see [SVY] **svy**.

⌐ Model ⌐

noconstant; see [SVY] **estimation options**.

Remarks

svy: regress performs linear regression via weighted least squares for survey data. For a general discussion of linear regression, see Draper and Smith (1998), Johnston and DiNardo (1997), or Kmenta (1997). See Skinner, Holt, and Smith (1989, chapter 3) for a discussion of linear regression for survey data.

▷ Example 1

Once the data are svyset, we can use svy: regress just as we would use regress with nonsurvey data. Here we use the NHANES II dataset to model the logarithm of lead concentration in people's blood.

```
. use http://www.stata-press.com/data/r9/nhanes2a
. svyset psuid [pweight=leadwt], strata(stratid)
      pweight: leadwt
          VCE: linearized
    Strata 1: stratid
       SU 1: psuid
      FPC 1: <zero>
```

(Continued on next page)

```
. svy: regress loglead age female black orace region2-region4 smsa1 smsa2
(running regress on estimation sample)

Survey: Linear regression

Number of strata   =        31            Number of obs    =       4948
Number of PSUs     =        62            Population size  = 1.129e+08
                                          Design df        =         31
                                          F(  9,     23)   =     134.62
                                          Prob > F         =     0.0000
                                          R-squared        =     0.2443
```

loglead	Coef.	Linearized Std. Err.	t	P>|t|	[95% Conf. Interval]	
age	.0028425	.0004282	6.64	0.000	.0019691	.0037159
female	-.3641964	.0112612	-32.34	0.000	-.3871637	-.3412291
black	.1462126	.0277811	5.26	0.000	.0895527	.2028725
orace	-.0754489	.0370151	-2.04	0.050	-.1509418	.0000439
region2	-.0206953	.0456639	-0.45	0.654	-.1138274	.0724369
region3	-.1272598	.0528061	-2.41	0.022	-.2349586	-.0195611
region4	-.0374591	.0422001	-0.89	0.382	-.1235268	.0486085
smsa1	.1038586	.0432539	2.40	0.023	.0156417	.1920755
smsa2	.0995561	.0365985	2.72	0.011	.0249129	.1741993
_cons	2.623901	.0421096	62.31	0.000	2.538018	2.709784

◁

Saved Results

svy: regress saves in e(). In addition to the items documented in [SVY] svy, svy: regress also saves the following:

Macros
  e(cmd)   regress
  e(depvar)   name of dependent variable
  e(predict)   program used to implement predict

Methods and Formulas

svy: regress is implemented as an ado-file.

Let j index the individuals in the population. The regression coefficients $\beta' = (\beta_0, \beta_1, \ldots, \beta_k)$ are viewed as fixed finite-population parameters that we wish to estimate. These parameters are defined with respect to an outcome variable Y_j and a $(k+1)$-dimensional row vector of explanatory variables $X_j = (X_{j0}, \ldots, X_{jk})$. As in nonsurvey work, we often have X_{j0} identically equal to unity so that β_0 is an intercept coefficient. Within a finite-population context, we can formally define the regression coefficient vector β as the solution to the vector-estimating equation:

$$G(\beta) = X'Y - X'X\beta = 0 \tag{1}$$

where Y is the vector of outcomes for the full population and X is the matrix of explanatory variables for the full population. Assuming that $(X'X)^{-1}$ exists, the solution to (1) is $\beta = (X'X)^{-1}X'Y$.

Given observations (y_j, x_j), collected through a complex sample design, we need to estimate β in a way that accounts for the sample design. To do this, note that the matrix factors $X'X$ and $X'Y$ can be viewed as matrix population totals. For example, $X'Y = \sum_j X_j Y_j$. Thus we estimate $X'X$ and $X'Y$ with the weighted estimators

$$\widehat{X'X} = \sum_j w_j x'_j x_j = X'_s W X_s$$

and

$$\widehat{X'Y} = \sum_j w_j x'_j y_j = X'_s W Y_s$$

where X_s is the matrix of explanatory variables for the sample, Y_s is the outcome vector for the sample, and $W = \mathrm{diag}(w_j)$ is a diagonal matrix containing the sampling weights w_j. The corresponding coefficient estimator is

$$\widehat{\beta} = (\widehat{X'X})^{-1} \widehat{X'Y} = (X'_s W X_s)^{-1} X'_s W Y_s \tag{2}$$

Note that (2) is what the `regress` command with `aweights` or `iweights` computes for point estimates.

The coefficient estimator $\widehat{\beta}$ can also be defined as the solution to a vector-estimating equation

$$\widehat{G}(\beta) = \widehat{X'Y} - \widehat{X'X}\beta = X'_s W Y_s - X'_s W X_s \beta = 0$$

See [SVY] **variance estimation** for details regarding the linearized variance estimator for linear regression.

References

Draper, N. and H. Smith. 1998. *Applied Regression Analysis.* 3rd ed. New York: Wiley.

Eltinge, J. L. and W. M. Sribney. 1996. svy4: Linear, logistic, and probit regressions for survey data. *Stata Technical Bulletin* 31: 26–31. Reprinted in *Stata Technical Bulletin Reprints*, vol. 6, pp. 239–245.

Fuller, W. A. 1975. Regression analysis for sample survey. *Sankhyā, Series C* 37: 117–132.

Johnston, J. and J. DiNardo. 1997. *Econometric Methods.* 4th ed. New York: McGraw–Hill.

Kmenta, J. 1997. *Elements of Econometrics.* 2nd ed. Ann Arbor: University of Michigan Press.

McDowell, A., A. Engel, J. T. Massey, and K. Maurer. 1981. Plan and operation of the Second National Health and Nutrition Examination Survey, 1976–1980. *Vital and Health Statistics* 15(1). Hyattsville, MD: National Center for Health Statistics.

Skinner, C. J., D. Holt, and T. M. F. Smith. 1989. *Analysis of Complex Surveys.* New York: Wiley.

Also See

Complementary:	[SVY] **svy: regress postestimation**
Related:	[R] **regress**;
	[SVY] **svy: ivreg**, [SVY] **svy: intreg**
Background:	[U] **20 Estimation and postestimation commands**,
	[SVY] **estimation options**, [SVY] **poststratification**,
	[SVY] **subpopulation estimation**, [SVY] **svy**, [SVY] **variance estimation**

Title

svy: regress postestimation — Postestimation tools for svy: regress

Description

The following postestimation commands are available for svy: regress:

command	description
estat	postestimation statistics for survey data
estimates	cataloging estimation results
lincom	point estimates, standard errors, testing, and inference for linear combinations of coefficients
mfx	marginal effects or elasticities
nlcom	point estimates, standard errors, testing, and inference for nonlinear combinations of coefficients
predict	predictions, residuals, influence statistics, and other diagnostic measures
predictnl	point estimates, standard errors, testing, and inference for generalized predictions
suest	seemingly unrelated estimation
test	Wald tests for simple and composite linear hypotheses
testnl	Wald tests of nonlinear hypotheses

See [SVY] **estat**.

See the corresponding entries in the *Stata Base Reference Manual* for details.

Syntax for predict

predict [*type*] *newvarname* [*if*] [*in*] [, *statistic*]

statistic	description
xb	linear prediction, $x_j\beta$; the default
residuals	residuals
score	score; equivalent to residuals
stdp	standard error of the linear prediction

These statistics are available both in and out of sample; type predict ... if e(sample) ... if wanted only for the estimation sample.

Options for predict

xb, the default, calculates the linear prediction $x_j\beta$.

residuals calculates the residuals, i.e., the value of the dependent variable minus the predicted value of the dependent variable.

score is a synonym for residuals.

stdp calculates the standard error of the prediction.

Remarks

▷ Example 1

Continuing with our example from [SVY] **svy: regress**, we use `predict` to compute the residuals and save their values in the new variable `resid`.

```
. predict resid, residuals
. describe resid
```

variable name	storage type	display format	value label	variable label
resid	float	%9.0g		Residuals

◁

Methods and Formulas

All postestimation commands listed above are implemented as ado-files.

Also See

Complementary:	[SVY] **svy: regress**, [SVY] **estat**;
	[R] **estimates**, [R] **lincom**, [R] **mfx**, [R] **nlcom**, [R] **predict**,
	[R] **predictnl**, [R] **suest**, [R] **test**, [R] **testnl**
Background:	[U] **13.5 Accessing coefficients and standard errors**,
	[U] **20 Estimation and postestimation commands**

Title

> **svy: tabulate oneway** — One-way tables for survey data

Syntax

Basic syntax

> svy: ta̲bulate *varname*

Full syntax

> svy [*vcetype*] [, *svy_options*] : ta̲bulate *varname* [*if*] [*in*]
>
>   [, *tabulate_options display_items display_options*]

Syntax to report results

> svy [, *display_items display_options*]

vcetype	description
SE	
li̲nearized	Taylor linearized variance estimation
brr	BRR variance estimation; see [SVY] **svy brr**
ja̲ckknife	jackknife variance estimation; see [SVY] **svy jackknife**

Specifying a *vcetype* overrides the default from svyset.

svy_options	description
if/in	
su̲bpop( )	identify a subpopulation
SE	
brr_options	additional options allowed with BRR variance estimation; see [SVY] ***brr_options***
jackknife_options	additional options allowed with jackknife variance estimation; see [SVY] ***jackknife_options***

svy requires that the survey design variables be identified using svyset; see [SVY] **svyset**.

See [U] **20 Estimation and postestimation commands** for additional capabilities of estimation commands.

Warning: Using *if* or *in* restrictions will not produce correct variance estimates for subpopulations in many cases. To compute estimates for a subpopulation, use the subpop() option. The full specification for subpop() is

> su̲bpop([*varname*] [*if*])

(Continued on next page)

205

tabulate_options	description
Model	
<u>stdize</u>(*varname*)	variable identifying strata for standardization
<u>stdweight</u>(*varname*)	weight variable for standardization
<u>tab</u>(*varname*)	variable to compute cell totals/proportions of
<u>miss</u>ing	treat missing values like other values

display_items	description
Table items	
<u>cell</u>	cell proportions
<u>count</u>	weighted cell counts
se	standard errors
ci	confidence intervals
deff	display the DEFF design effects
deft	display the DEFT design effects
<u>srssubpop</u>	report design effects assuming SRS within subpopulation
obs	cell observations

When any of se, ci, deff, deft, or srssubpop are specified, only one of cell or count can be specified. If none of se, ci, deff, deft, or srssubpop is specified, both cell and count can be specified.

display_options	description
Reporting	
<u>level</u>(*#*)	set confidence level; default is level(95)
† <u>proportion</u>	display proportions (default)
<u>percent</u>	display percentages instead of proportions
<u>nomarginal</u>	suppress column marginal
<u>nolabel</u>	suppress displaying the value labels
<u>format</u>(*%fmt*)	cell format, default format(%6.0g)
<u>cellwidth</u>(*#*)	cell width
<u>csepwidth</u>(*#*)	cell separation width
<u>stubwidth</u>(*#*)	stub width

† proportion is not shown in the dialog box.

Description

svy: tabulate produces one-way tabulations for complex survey data. See [SVY] **svy: tabulate twoway** for two-way tabulations for complex survey data.

Options

svy_options; see [SVY] **svy**.

> **⌐ Model ⌐**

stdize(*varname*) specifies that the point estimates be adjusted by direct standardization across the strata identified by *varname*. This option requires the stdweight() option.

stdweight(*varname*) specifies the weight variable associated with the strata identified in the stdize() option. The standardization weights must be constant within the standard strata.

tab(*varname*) specifies that counts be cell totals of this variable and that proportions (or percentages) be relative to (i.e., weighted by) this variable. For example, if this variable denotes income, then the cell "counts" are instead totals of income for each cell, and the cell proportions are proportions of income for each cell.

missing specifies that missing values in *varname* be treated as another row category, rather than be omitted from the analysis (the default).

> **⌐ Table items ⌐**

cell requests that cell proportions (or percentages) be displayed. This is the default if count is not specified.

count requests that weighted cell counts be displayed.

se requests that the standard errors of cell proportions (the default) or weighted counts be displayed. When se (or ci, deff, or deft) is specified, only one of cell or count can be selected. The standard error computed is the standard error of the one selected.

ci requests confidence intervals for cell proportions or weighted counts.

deff and deft request that the design-effect measures DEFF and DEFT be displayed for each cell proportion or weighted count. See [SVY] **estat** for details.

> Note that options deff and deft are not allowed with estimation results that employed direct standardization or poststratification.

srssubpop requests that DEFF and DEFT be computed using an estimate of SRS (simple random sampling) variance for sampling within a subpopulation. By default DEFF and DEFT are computed using an estimate of the SRS variance for sampling from the entire population. Typically, srssubpop would be given when computing subpopulation estimates by strata or by groups of strata.

obs requests that the number of observations for each cell be displayed.

> **⌐ Reporting ⌐**

level(*#*); see [SVY] **estimation options**.

proportion, the default, requests that proportions be displayed.

percent requests that percentages be displayed instead of proportions.

nomarginal requests that the column marginal not be displayed.

nolabel requests that variable labels and value labels be ignored.

format(%*fmt*) specifies a format for the items in the table. The default is %6.0g. See [U] **12.5 Formats: controlling how data are displayed**.

cellwidth(*#*), csepwidth(*#*), and stubwidth(*#*) specify widths of table elements in the output; see [P] **tabdisp**. Acceptable values for the stubwidth() option range from 4 to 32.

Note that svy: tabulate uses the tabdisp command (see [P] **tabdisp**) to produce the table. Only five items can be displayed in the table at one time, where the ci option implies 2 items. If too many items are selected, a warning will appear immediately. To view additional items, redisplay the table while specifying different options.

Remarks

Despite the long list of options for svy: tabulate, it is a simple command to use. Using the svy: tabulate command is just like using tabulate to produce one-way tables for ordinary data. The main difference is that svy: tabulate computes standard errors appropriate for complex survey data.

Standard errors and confidence intervals can optionally be displayed for weighted counts or cell proportions. The confidence intervals for proportions are constructed using a logit transform so that their endpoints always lie between 0 and 1; see [SVY] **svy: tabulate twoway**. Associated design effects (DEFF and DEFT) can be viewed for the variance estimates.

▷ Example 1

In the following example, we use svy: tabulate to estimate the distribution of the race category variable from our NHANES II dataset (McDowell et al. 1981). Before calling svy: tabulate, we use svyset to declare the survey structure of the data.

```
. use http://www.stata-press.com/data/r9/nhanes2b
. svyset psuid [pweight=finalwgt], strata(stratid)
      pweight: finalwgt
          VCE: linearized
    Strata 1: stratid
        SU 1: psuid
       FPC 1: <zero>
. svy: tabulate race
(running tabulate on estimation sample)
```

Number of strata	=	31	Number of obs	=	10351
Number of PSUs	=	62	Population size	=	1.172e+08
			Design df	=	31

1=white, 2=black, 3=other	proportions
White	.8792
Black	.0955
Other	.0253
Total	1

Key: proportions = cell proportions

Here we display weighted counts for each category of `race` along with the 95% confidence bounds, and design effects DEFF and DEFT. We also use the `format()` option to improve the look of the table.

```
. svy: tabulate race, format(%11.3g) count ci deff deft
(running tabulate on estimation sample)
Number of strata   =      31        Number of obs       =      10351
Number of PSUs     =      62        Population size     = 1.172e+08
                                    Design df           =         31
```

1=white, 2=black, 3=other	count	lb	ub	deff	deft
White	102999549	97060400	108938698	60.2	7.76
Black	11189236	8213964	14164508	18.6	4.31
Other	2968728	414930	5522526	47.9	6.92
Total	117157513				

```
Key:  count   =  weighted counts
      lb      =  lower 95% confidence bounds for weighted counts
      ub      =  upper 95% confidence bounds for weighted counts
      deff    =  deff for variances of weighted counts
      deft    =  deft for variances of weighted counts
```

From the above results, we can conclude with 95% confidence that the number of people in the population that fall within the `White` category is between 97060400 and 108938698.

◁

Saved Results

In addition to the items documented in [SVY] **svy**, `svy: tabulate` also saves in `e()` the following:

Scalars

`e(r)`	number of rows	`e(total)`	weighted sum of `tab()` variable

Macros

`e(cmd)`	tabulate	`e(rowvar)`	*varname*, the row variable
`e(tab)`	`tab()` variable	`e(setype)`	cell or count

Matrices

`e(Prop)`	matrix of cell proportions	`e(Obs)`	matrix of observation counts
`e(Deff)`	DEFF vector for `e(setype)` items	`e(Deft)`	DEFT vector for `e(setype)` items

Methods and Formulas

`svy: tabulate` is implemented as an ado-file.

See the *Methods and Formulas* section in [SVY] **svy: tabulate twoway** for a discussion that details how table items and confidence intervals are computed. Note that a one-way table is really just a two-way table that has a single row or column.

References

Cochran, W. G. 1977. *Sampling Techniques*. 3rd ed. New York: Wiley.

Kish, L. 1965. *Survey Sampling*. New York: Wiley.

McDowell, A., A. Engel, J. T. Massey, and K. Maurer. 1981. Plan and operation of the Second National Health and Nutrition Examination Survey, 1976–1980. *Vital and Health Statistics* 15(1). Hyattsville, MD: National Center for Health Statistics.

Also See

Complementary: [SVY] **svy: tabulate postestimation**, [SVY] **svydes**

Related: [R] **tabulate oneway**;
[SVY] **svy: mean**, [SVY] **svy: ratio**,
[SVY] **svy: tabulate twoway**, [SVY] **svy: total**

Background: [U] **20 Estimation and postestimation commands**,
[SVY] **estimation options**, [SVY] **direct standardization**,
[SVY] **poststratification**, [SVY] **subpopulation estimation**,
[SVY] **svy**, [SVY] **variance estimation**

Title

svy: tabulate postestimation — Postestimation tools for svy: tabulate

Description

The following postestimation commands are available for `svy: tabulate`:

command	description
estat	postestimation statistics for survey data
estimates	cataloging estimation results
lincom	point estimates, standard errors, testing, and inference for linear combinations of descriptive statistics
nlcom	point estimates, standard errors, testing, and inference for nonlinear combinations of descriptive statistics
test	Wald tests for simple and composite linear hypotheses
testnl	Wald tests of nonlinear hypotheses

See [SVY] **estat**.

See the corresponding entries in the *Stata Base Reference Manual* for details on the other postestimation commands.

Methods and Formulas

All postestimation commands listed above are implemented as ado-files.

Also See

Complementary:	[SVY] **estat**, [SVY] **svy: tabulate oneway**, [SVY] **svy: tabulate twoway**; [R] **estimates**, [R] **lincom**, [R] **nlcom**, [R] **test**, [R] **testnl**
Background:	[U] **13.5 Accessing coefficients and standard errors**, [U] **20 Estimation and postestimation commands**

Title

svy: tabulate twoway — Two-way tables for survey data

Syntax

Basic syntax

svy: <u>tab</u>ulate *varname*$_1$ *varname*$_2$

Full syntax

svy [*vcetype*] [, *svy_options*] : <u>tab</u>ulate *varname*$_1$ *varname*$_2$ [*if*] [*in*]

[, *tabulate_options display_items display_options statistic_options*]

Syntax to report results

svy [, *display_items display_options statistic_options*]

vcetype	description
SE	
<u>linear</u>ized	Taylor linearized variance estimation
brr	BRR variance estimation; see [SVY] **svy brr**
<u>jack</u>knife	jackknife variance estimation; see [SVY] **svy jackknife**

Specifying a *vcetype* overrides the default from svyset.

svy_options	description
if/in	
<u>sub</u>pop()	identify a subpopulation
SE	
brr_options	additional options allowed with BRR variance estimation; see [SVY] ***brr_options***
jackknife_options	additional options allowed with jackknife variance estimation; see [SVY] ***jackknife_options***

svy requires that the survey design variables be identified using svyset; see [SVY] **svyset**.

See [U] **20 Estimation and postestimation commands** for additional capabilities of estimation commands.

Warning: Using *if* or *in* restrictions will not produce correct variance estimates for subpopulations in many cases. To compute estimates for a subpopulation, use the subpop() option. The full specification for subpop() is

<u>sub</u>pop([*varname*] [*if*])

212

_tabulate_options_	description
Model	
<u>std</u>ize(_varname_)	variable identifying strata for standardization
<u>stdw</u>eight(_varname_)	weight variable for standardization
tab(_varname_)	variable for which to compute cell totals/proportions
<u>miss</u>ing	treat missing values like other values

_display_items_	description
Table items	
<u>cel</u>l	cell proportions
<u>cou</u>nt	weighted cell counts
<u>col</u>umn	within-column proportions
row	within-row proportions
se	standard errors
ci	confidence intervals
deff	display the DEFF design effects
deft	display the DEFT design effects
<u>srs</u>subpop	report design effects assuming SRS within subpopulation
obs	cell observations

When any of se, ci, deff, deft, or srssubpop are specified, only one of cell, count, column, or row can be specified. If none of se, ci, deff, deft, or srssubpop is specified, any or all of cell, count, column, and row can be specified.

_display_options_	description
Reporting	
<u>le</u>vel(#)	set confidence level; default is level(95)
† <u>pro</u>portion	display proportions (default)
<u>per</u>cent	display percentages instead of proportions
<u>ver</u>tical	stack confidence interval endpoints vertically
<u>nom</u>arginals	suppress row and column marginals
<u>nol</u>abel	suppress displaying the value labels
† <u>not</u>able	suppress displaying the table
<u>f</u>ormat(%_fmt_)	cell format, default format(%6.0g)
<u>cellw</u>idth(#)	cell width
<u>csep</u>width(#)	cell-separation width
<u>stubw</u>idth(#)	stub width

† proportion and notable are not shown in the dialog box.

statistic_options	description
Test statistics	
pearson	Pearson's chi-squared
lr	likelihood ratio
null	display null-based statistics
wald	adjust Wald
llwald	adjusted log-linear Wald
noadjust	Report unadjusted model Wald statistics

Description

svy: tabulate produces two-way tabulations with tests of independence for complex survey data. See [SVY] **svy: tabulate oneway** for one-way tabulations for complex survey data.

Options

svy_options; see [SVY] **svy**.

Model

stdize(*varname*) specifies that the point estimates be adjusted by direct standardization across the strata identified by *varname*. This option requires the stdweight() option.

stdweight(*varname*) specifies the weight variable associated with the standard strata identified in the stdize() option. The standardization weights must be constant within the standard strata.

tab(*varname*) specifies that counts be cell totals of this variable and that proportions (or percentages) be relative to (i.e., weighted by) this variable. For example, if this variable denotes income, the cell "counts" are instead totals of income for each cell, and the cell proportions are proportions of income for each cell.

missing specifies that missing values in *varname*$_1$ and *varname*$_2$ be treated as another row or column category, rather than be omitted from the analysis (the default).

Table items

cell requests that cell proportions (or percentages) be displayed. This is the default if none of count, row, or column is specified.

count requests that weighted cell counts be displayed.

row or column requests that row or column proportions (or percentages) be displayed.

se requests that the standard errors of cell proportions (the default), weighted counts, or row or column proportions be displayed. When se (or ci, deff, or deft) is specified, only one of cell, count, row, or column can be selected. The standard error computed is the standard error of the one selected.

ci requests confidence intervals for cell proportions, weighted counts, or row or column proportions.

deff and deft request that the design-effect measures DEFF and DEFT be displayed for each cell proportion, count, or row or column proportion. See [SVY] **estat** for details. The mean generalized DEFF is also displayed when deff, deft, or subpop is requested; see *Methods and Formulas* for an explanation.

Note that options `deff` and `deft` are not allowed with estimation results that employed direct standardization or poststratification.

`srssubpop` requests that DEFF and DEFT be computed using an estimate of SRS (simple random sampling) variance for sampling within a subpopulation. By default, DEFF and DEFT are computed using an estimate of the SRS variance for sampling from the entire population. Typically, `srssubpop` would be given when computing subpopulation estimates by strata or by groups of strata.

`obs` requests that the number of observations for each cell be displayed.

Reporting

`level(#)`; see [SVY] **estimation options**.

`proportion`, the default, requests that proportions be displayed.

`percent` requests that percentages be displayed instead of proportions.

`vertical` requests that the endpoints of confidence intervals be stacked vertically on display.

`nomarginals` requests that row and column marginals not be displayed.

`nolabel` requests that variable labels and value labels be ignored.

`notable` prevents the header and table from being displayed in the output. When specified, only the results of the requested test statistics are displayed. This option may not be specified with any of the options in *display_options* except the `level()` option.

`format(%fmt)` specifies a format for the items in the table. The default is `%6.0g`. See [U] **12.5 Formats: controlling how data are displayed**.

`cellwidth(#)`, `csepwidth(#)`, and `stubwidth(#)` specify widths of table elements in the output; see [P] **tabdisp**. Acceptable values for the `stubwidth()` option range from 4 to 32.

Test statistics

`pearson` requests that the Pearson χ^2 statistic be computed. By default, this is the test of independence that is displayed. The Pearson χ^2 statistic is corrected for the survey design using the second-order correction of Rao and Scott (1984) and is converted into an F statistic. One term in the correction formula can be calculated using either observed cell proportions or proportions under the null hypothesis (i.e., the product of the marginals). By default, observed cell proportions are used. If the `null` option is selected, then a statistic corrected using proportions under the null hypothesis is displayed as well. See the following discussion for details.

`lr` requests that the likelihood-ratio test statistic for proportions be computed. Note that this statistic is not defined when there are one or more zero cells in the table. The statistic is corrected for the survey design using exactly the same correction procedure that is used with the `pearson` statistic. Again either observed cell proportions or proportions under the null hypothesis can be used in the correction formula. By default, the former is used; specifying the `null` option gives both the former and the latter. Neither variant of this statistic is recommended for sparse tables. For nonsparse tables, the `lr` statistics are similar to the corresponding `pearson` statistics.

`null` modifies the `pearson` and `lr` options only. If `null` is specified, two corrected statistics are displayed. The statistic labeled "D-B (null)" ("D-B" stands for design-based) uses proportions under the null hypothesis (i.e., the product of the marginals) in the Rao and Scott (1984) correction. The statistic labeled merely "Design-based" uses observed cell proportions. If `null` is not specified, only the correction that uses observed proportions is displayed. See the following discussion for details.

wald requests a Wald test of whether observed weighted counts equal the product of the marginals (Koch, Freeman, and Freeman 1975). By default, an adjusted F statistic is produced; an unadjusted statistic can be produced by specifying noadjust. The unadjusted F statistic can yield extremely anticonservative p-values (i.e., p-values that are too small) when the degrees of freedom of the variance estimates (the number of sampled PSUs minus the number of strata) are small relative to the $(R - 1)(C - 1)$ degrees of freedom of the table (where R is the number of rows and C is the number of columns). Hence, the statistic produced by wald and noadjust should not be used for inference unless it is essentially identical to the adjusted statistic.

llwald requests a Wald test of the log-linear model of independence (Koch, Freeman, and Freeman 1975). Note that the statistic is not defined when there are one or more zero cells in the table. The adjusted statistic (the default) can produce anticonservative p-values, especially for sparse tables, when the degrees of freedom of the variance estimates are small relative to the degrees of freedom of the table. Specifying noadjust yields a statistic with more severe problems. Neither the adjusted nor the unadjusted statistic is recommended for inference; the statistics are only made available for comparative and pedagogical purposes.

noadjust modifies the wald and llwald options only. It requests that an unadjusted F statistic be displayed in addition to the adjusted statistic.

Note that svy: tabulate uses the tabdisp command (see [P] **tabdisp**) to produce the table. Only five items can be displayed in the table at one time. If too many items are selected, a warning will appear immediately. To view additional items, redisplay the table while specifying different options.

Remarks

Remarks are presented under the headings

Introduction
The Rao and Scott correction
Wald statistics
Properties of the statistics

Introduction

Despite the long list of options for svy: tabulate, it is a simple command to use. Using the svy: tabulate command is just like using tabulate to produce two-way tables for ordinary data. The main difference is that svy: tabulate computes a test of independence that is appropriate for complex survey data.

The test of independence that is displayed by default is based on the usual Pearson χ^2 statistic for two-way tables. To account for the survey design, the statistic is turned into an F statistic with noninteger degrees of freedom using a second-order Rao and Scott (1981, 1984) correction. Although the theory behind the Rao and Scott correction is complicated, the p-value for the corrected F statistic can be interpreted in the same way as a p-value for the Pearson χ^2 statistic for "ordinary" data (i.e., data that are assumed independent and identically distributed [i.i.d.]).

svy: tabulate, in fact, computes four statistics for the test of independence with two variants of each, for a total of eight statistics. The options that give these eight statistics are pearson (the default), lr, null (a toggle for displaying variants of the pearson and lr statistics), wald, llwald, and noadjust (a toggle for displaying variants of the wald and llwald statistics). The options wald and llwald with noadjust yield the statistics developed by Koch, Freeman, and Freeman (1975), which have been implemented in the CROSSTAB procedure of the SUDAAN software (Shah, Barnwell, and Bieler 1997, Release 7.5).

These eight statistics, along with other variants, have been evaluated in simulations (Sribney 1998). Based on these simulations, we advise researchers to use the default statistic (the `pearson` option) in all situations. We recommend that the other statistics only be used for comparative or pedagogical purposes. Sribney (1998) gives a detailed comparison of the statistics; a summary of his conclusions is provided later in this entry.

Other than the test-statistic options (*statistic_options*) and the survey-design options (*svy_options*), most of the other options of `svy: tabulate` simply relate to different choices for what can be displayed in the body of the table. By default, cell proportions are displayed, but in most circumstances, it makes more sense to view either row or column proportions or weighted counts.

Standard errors and confidence intervals can optionally be displayed for weighted counts or cell, row, or column proportions. The confidence intervals for proportions are constructed using a logit transform so that their endpoints always lie between 0 and 1. Associated design effects (DEFF and DEFT) can be viewed for the variance estimates. The mean generalized DEFF (Rao and Scott 1984) is also displayed when option `deff`, `deft`, or `srssubpop` is specified. The mean generalized DEFF is essentially a design effect for the asymptotic distribution of the test statistic; see the *Methods and Formulas* section at the end of this entry.

▷ Example 1

We use data from the Second National Health and Nutrition Examination Survey (NHANES II) (McDowell et al. 1981). The `strata`, `psu`, and `pweight` variables are first set using the `svyset` command; see [SVY] **svyset** for details.

```
. use http://www.stata-press.com/data/r9/nhanes2b
. svyset psuid [pweight=finalwgt], strata(stratid)
      pweight: finalwgt
          VCE: linearized
    Strata 1: stratid
       SU 1: psuid
      FPC 1: <zero>
. svy: tabulate race diabetes
(running tabulate on estimation sample)
```

Number of strata	=	31		Number of obs	=	10349
Number of PSUs	=	62		Population size	=	1.171e+08
				Design df	=	31

1=white, 2=black, 3=other	diabetes, 1=yes, 0=no		
	0	1	Total
White	.851	.0281	.8791
Black	.0899	.0056	.0955
Other	.0248	5.2e-04	.0253
Total	.9658	.0342	1

```
Key:  cell proportions

Pearson:
    Uncorrected   chi2(2)         =   21.3483
    Design-based  F(1.52, 47.26)  =   15.0056    P = 0.0000
```

The default table displays only cell proportions, and this makes it very difficult to compare the incidence of diabetes in white, black, and "other" racial groups. It would be better to look at row proportions. This can be done by redisplaying the results (i.e., reissuing the command without specifying any variables) with the `row` option.

```
. svy: tabulate, row
Number of strata    =        31         Number of obs     =       10349
Number of PSUs      =        62         Population size   = 1.171e+08
                                        Design df         =          31

  1=white,     diabetes, 1=yes,
  2=black,            0=no
  3=other        0        1   Total

     White    .968     .032        1
     Black    .941     .059        1
     Other   .9797   .0203         1

     Total   .9658   .0342         1

Key:  row proportions

Pearson:
  Uncorrected    chi2(2)              =    21.3483
  Design-based   F(1.52, 47.26)    =    15.0056    P = 0.0000
```

This table is much easier to interpret. A larger proportion of blacks have diabetes than do whites or persons in the "other" racial category. Note that the test of independence for a two-way contingency table is equivalent to the test of homogeneity of row (or column) proportions. Hence, we can conclude that there is a highly significant difference between the incidence of diabetes among the three racial groups.

We may now wish to compute confidence intervals for the row proportions. If we try to redisplay specifying ci along with row, we get the following result:

```
. svy: tabulate, row ci
confidence intervals are only available for cells to compute row confidence
intervals, rerun command with row and ci options
r(111);
```

There are limits to what svy: tabulate can redisplay. Basically, any of the options relating to variance estimation (i.e., se, ci, deff, and deft) must be specified at run time along with the single item (i.e., count, cell, row, or column) for which we want standard errors, confidence intervals, DEFF, or DEFT. So to get confidence intervals for row proportions, we must rerun the command. We do so below, requesting not only ci, but also se.

```
. svy: tabulate race diabetes, row se ci format(%7.4f)
(running tabulate on estimation sample)
Number of strata   =        31         Number of obs      =      10349
Number of PSUs     =        62         Population size    = 1.171e+08
                                       Design df          =         31
```

1=white, 2=black, 3=other	diabetes, 1=yes, 0=no		Total
	0	1	
White	0.9680 (0.0020) [0.9638,0.9718]	0.0320 (0.0020) [0.0282,0.0362]	1.0000
Black	0.9410 (0.0061) [0.9271,0.9523]	0.0590 (0.0061) [0.0477,0.0729]	1.0000
Other	0.9797 (0.0076) [0.9566,0.9906]	0.0203 (0.0076) [0.0094,0.0434]	1.0000
Total	0.9658 (0.0018) [0.9619,0.9693]	0.0342 (0.0018) [0.0307,0.0381]	1.0000

```
Key:  row proportions
      (linearized standard errors of row proportions)
      [95% confidence intervals for row proportions]

Pearson:
    Uncorrected    chi2(2)         =    21.3483
    Design-based   F(1.52, 47.26)  =    15.0056      P = 0.0000
```

In the above table, we specified a %7.4f format rather than using the default %6.0g format. Note that the single format applies to every item in the table. We can omit the marginal totals by specifying nomarginal. If the above style for displaying the confidence intervals is obtrusive—and it can be in a wider table—we can use the vertical option to stack the endpoints of the confidence interval, one over the other, and omit the brackets (the parentheses around the standard errors are also omitted when vertical is specified). To express results as percentages, as with the tabulate command (see [R] **tabulate twoway**), we can use the percent option. Or we can play around with these display options until we get a table that we are satisfied with, first making changes to the options on redisplay (i.e., omitting the cross-tabulated variables when we issue the command).

◁

❏ Technical Note

The standard errors computed by svy: tabulate are exactly the same as those produced by svy: mean, svy: proportion, and svy: ratio. Indeed, svy: tabulate uses these commands as subroutines to produce its table.

In the previous example, the estimate of the proportion of African–Americans with diabetes (the second proportion in the second row of the preceding table) is simply a ratio estimate; hence, we can also obtain the same estimates using svy: ratio:

```
. gen black = (race==2) if !missing(race)
. gen diablk = diabetes*black
(2 missing values generated)
```

```
. svy: ratio diablk/black
(running ratio on estimation sample)

Survey: Ratio estimation

Number of strata =      31           Number of obs     =     10349
Number of PSUs   =      62           Population size   = 1.2e+08
                                     Design df         =        31

        _ratio_1: diablk/black
```

		Linearized		
	Ratio	Std. Err.	[95% Conf. Interval]	
_ratio_1	.0590349	.0061443	.0465035	.0715662

Although the standard errors are exactly the same, the confidence intervals are slightly different. The svy: tabulate command produced the confidence interval $[0.0477, 0.0729]$, and svy: ratio gave $[0.0465, 0.0716]$. The difference is due to the fact that svy: tabulate uses a logit transform to produce confidence intervals whose endpoints are always between 0 and 1. This transformation also shifts the confidence intervals slightly toward the null (i.e., 0.5), which is beneficial since the untransformed confidence intervals tend to be, on average, biased away from the null. See *Methods and Formulas* for details.

❑

▷ Example 2: The tab option

The tab() option allows us to compute proportions relative to a certain variable. For example, suppose that we wish to compare the proportion of total income among different racial groups in males with that of females. We do so below with fictitious data:

```
. svy: tabulate gender race, tab(income) row
(running tabulate on estimation sample)

Number of strata   =        31        Number of obs     =       10351
Number of PSUs     =        62        Population size   =  1.172e+08
                                      Design df         =          31
```

		Race		
Gender	White	Black	Other	Total
Male	.8857	.0875	.0268	1
Female	.884	.094	.022	1
Total	.8848	.0909	.0243	1

```
Tabulated variable:  income

Key:  row proportions

Pearson:
  Uncorrected   chi2(2)            =     3.6241
  Design-based  F(1.91, 59.12)  =     0.8626       P = 0.4227
```

◁

The Rao and Scott correction

svy: tabulate can produce eight different statistics for the test of independence. By default, svy: tabulate displays the Pearson χ^2 statistic with the Rao and Scott (1981, 1984) second-order correction. Based on simulations (Sribney 1998), we recommend that you use this statistic in all situations. The statistical literature, however, contains several alternatives, along with other possibilities for the implementation of the Rao and Scott correction. Hence, for comparative or pedagogical purposes, you may want to view some of the other statistics computed by svy: tabulate. This section briefly describes the differences among these statistics; for a more detailed discussion, see Sribney (1998).

Two statistics commonly used for independent, identically distributed (i.i.d.) data for the test of independence of $R \times C$ tables (R rows and C columns) are the Pearson χ^2 statistic

$$X_{\mathrm{P}}^2 = m \sum_{r=1}^{R} \sum_{c=1}^{C} \left(\widehat{p}_{rc} - \widehat{p}_{0rc} \right)^2 / \widehat{p}_{0rc}$$

and the likelihood-ratio χ^2 statistic

$$X_{\mathrm{LR}}^2 = 2m \sum_{r=1}^{R} \sum_{c=1}^{C} \widehat{p}_{rc} \ln \left(\widehat{p}_{rc} / \widehat{p}_{0rc} \right)$$

where m is the total number of sampled individuals, $\widehat{p}_{rc}$ is the estimated proportion for the cell in the rth row and cth column of the table, and $\widehat{p}_{0rc}$ is the estimated proportion under the null hypothesis of independence; i.e., $\widehat{p}_{0rc} = \widehat{p}_{r\cdot} \widehat{p}_{\cdot c}$, the product of the row and column marginals: $\widehat{p}_{r\cdot} = \sum_{c=1}^{C} \widehat{p}_{rc}$ and $\widehat{p}_{\cdot c} = \sum_{r=1}^{R} \widehat{p}_{rc}$.

For i.i.d. data, both of these statistics are distributed asymptotically as $\chi^2_{(R-1)(C-1)}$. Note that the likelihood-ratio statistic is not defined when one or more of the cells in the table are empty. The Pearson statistic, however, can be calculated when one or more cells in the table are empty—the statistic may not have good properties in this case, but the statistic still has a computable value.

For survey data, X_{P}^2 and X_{LR}^2 can be computed using weighted estimates of $\widehat{p}_{rc}$ and $\widehat{p}_{0rc}$. However, for a complex sampling design, one can no longer claim that they are distributed as $\chi^2_{(R-1)(C-1)}$, but you can estimate the variance of $\widehat{p}_{rc}$ under the sampling design. For instance, in Stata, this variance can be estimated via linearization methods by using svy: mean or svy: ratio.

Rao and Scott (1981, 1984) derived the asymptotic distribution of X_{P}^2 and X_{LR}^2 in terms of the variance of $\widehat{p}_{rc}$. Unfortunately, the result (see (1) in *Methods and Formulas*) is not computationally feasible, but it can be approximated using correction formulas. svy: tabulate uses the second-order correction developed by Rao and Scott (1984). By default, or when the pearson option is specified, svy: tabulate displays the second-order correction of the Pearson statistic. The lr option gives the second-order correction of the likelihood-ratio statistic. Because it is the default of svy: tabulate, the correction computed with $\widehat{p}_{rc}$ is referred to as the default correction.

The Rao and Scott papers, however, left some details outstanding about the computation of the correction. One term in the correction formula can be computed using either $\widehat{p}_{rc}$ or $\widehat{p}_{0rc}$. Since under the null hypothesis both are asymptotically equivalent, theory offers no guidance about which is best. By default, svy: tabulate uses $\widehat{p}_{rc}$ for the corrections of the Pearson and likelihood-ratio statistics. If the null option is specified, the correction is computed using $\widehat{p}_{0rc}$. For nonsparse tables, these two correction methods yield almost identical results. However, in simulations of sparse tables, Sribney (1998) found that the null-corrected statistics were extremely anticonservative for 2×2 tables (i.e., under the null, "significance" was declared too often) and were too conservative for other tables. The default correction, however, had better properties. Hence, we do not recommend using null option.

For the computational details of the Rao and Scott corrected statistics, see *Methods and Formulas*.

Wald statistics

Prior to the work by Rao and Scott (1981, 1984), Wald tests for the test of independence for two-way tables were developed by Koch, Freeman, and Freeman (1975). Two Wald statistics have been proposed. The first is similar to the Pearson statistic in that it is based on

$$\widehat{Y}_{rc} = \widehat{N}_{rc} - \widehat{N}_{r.}\widehat{N}_{.c}/\widehat{N}_{..}$$

where $\widehat{N}_{rc}$ is the estimated weighted count for the r, cth cell. The delta method can be used to approximate the variance of $\widehat{Y}_{rc}$, and a Wald statistic can be calculated in the usual manner. A second Wald statistic can be constructed based on a log-linear model for the table. Like the likelihood-ratio statistic, this statistic is undefined when there is a zero proportion in the table.

These Wald statistics are initially χ^2 statistics, but they have better properties when converted into F statistics with denominator degrees of freedom that account for the degrees of freedom of the variance estimator. They can be converted to F statistics in one of two ways. One method is the standard manner: divide by the χ^2 degrees of freedom $d_0 = (R-1)(C-1)$ to get an F statistic with d_0 numerator degrees of freedom and $\nu = n - L$ denominator degrees of freedom. This is the form of the F statistic suggested by Koch, Freeman, and Freeman (1975) and implemented in the CROSSTAB procedure of the SUDAAN software (Shah, Barnwell, and Bieler 1997, Release 7.5), and it is the method used by svy: tabulate when the noadjust option is specified with wald or llwald.

Another technique is to adjust the F statistic by using

$$F_{\text{adj}} = (\nu - d_0 + 1)W/(\nu d_0) \qquad \text{with} \qquad F_{\text{adj}} \sim F(d_0, \nu - d_0 + 1)$$

This is the default adjustment for svy: tabulate. Note that test and the other svy estimation commands produce adjusted F statistics by default, using exactly the same adjustment procedure. See Korn and Graubard (1990) for a justification of the procedure.

The adjusted F statistic is identical to the unadjusted F statistic when $d_0 = 1$, that is, for 2×2 tables.

As Thomas and Rao (1987) point out (also see Korn and Graubard, 1990), the unadjusted F statistics can become extremely anticonservative as d_0 increases when ν is small or moderate; i.e., under the null, the statistics are "significant" far more often than they should be. Because the unadjusted statistics behave so poorly for larger tables when ν is not large, their use can only be justified for small tables or when ν is large. But when the table is small or when ν is large, the unadjusted statistic is essentially identical to the adjusted statistic. Hence, for the purpose of statistical inference, there is no point in looking at the unadjusted statistics.

The adjusted "Pearson" Wald F statistic behaves reasonably under the null in most cases. However, even the adjusted F statistic for the log-linear Wald test tends to be moderately anticonservative when ν is not large (Thomas and Rao 1987, Sribney 1998).

▷ Example 3

With the NHANES II data, we tabulate, for the male subpopulation, high blood pressure (highbp) versus a variable (sizplace) that indicates the degree of urban/ruralness. We request that all eight statistics for the test of independence be displayed.

```
. use http://www.stata-press.com/data/r9/nhanes2b
. gen male = (sex==1) if !missing(sex)
```

```
. svy, subpop(male): tabulate highbp sizplace, col obs pearson lr null wald
> llwald noadj
(running tabulate on estimation sample)
```

Number of strata = 31	Number of obs = 10351
Number of PSUs = 62	Population size = 1.172e+08
	Subpop. no. of obs = 4915
	Subpop. size = 56159480
	Design df = 31

1 if BP > 140/90, 0 otherwise	1=urban,..., 8=rural								
	1	2	3	4	5	6	7	8	Total
0	.8489	.8929	.9213	.8509	.8413	.9242	.8707	.8674	.8764
	431	527	558	371	186	210	314	1619	4216
1	.1511	.1071	.0787	.1491	.1587	.0758	.1293	.1326	.1236
	95	80	64	74	36	20	57	273	699
Total	1	1	1	1	1	1	1	1	1
	526	607	622	445	222	230	371	1892	4915

```
  Key:  column proportions
        number of observations

Pearson:
  Uncorrected   chi2(7)           =   64.4581
  D-B (null)    F(5.30, 164.45) =    2.2078      P = 0.0522
  Design-based  F(5.54, 171.87) =    2.6863      P = 0.0189

Likelihood ratio:
  Uncorrected   chi2(7)           =   68.2365
  D-B (null)    F(5.30, 164.45) =    2.3372      P = 0.0408
  Design-based  F(5.54, 171.87) =    2.8437      P = 0.0138

Wald (Pearson):
  Unadjusted    chi2(7)           =   21.2704
  Unadjusted    F(7, 31)          =    3.0386      P = 0.0149
  Adjusted      F(7, 25)          =    2.4505      P = 0.0465

Wald (log-linear):
  Unadjusted    chi2(7)           =   25.7644
  Unadjusted    F(7, 31)          =    3.6806      P = 0.0052
  Adjusted      F(7, 25)          =    2.9683      P = 0.0208
```

The p-values from the null-corrected Pearson and likelihood-ratio statistics (lines labeled "D-B (null)"; "D-B" stands for "design-based") are bigger than the corresponding default-corrected statistics (lines labeled "Design-based"). Simulations (Sribney 1998) show that the null-corrected statistics are overly conservative for many sparse tables (except 2×2 tables); this appears to be the case here, although this table is hardly sparse. The default-corrected Pearson statistic has good properties under the null for both sparse and nonsparse tables; hence, the smaller p-value for it should be considered reliable.

The default-corrected likelihood-ratio statistic is usually similar to the default-corrected Pearson statistic except for very sparse tables, when it tends to be anticonservative. This example follows this pattern, with its p-value being slightly smaller than that of the default-corrected Pearson statistic.

For tables of these dimensions (2×8), the unadjusted "Pearson" Wald and log-linear Wald F statistics are extremely anticonservative under the null when the variance degrees of freedom are small. Here the variance degrees of freedom are only 31 (62 PSUs minus 31 strata), so we expect that the unadjusted Wald F statistics yield smaller p-values than the adjusted F statistics. Because of their poor behavior under the null for small variance degrees of freedom, they cannot be trusted in this case. Simulations show that although the adjusted "Pearson" Wald F statistic has good properties under the null, it is often less powerful than the default Rao-and-Scott corrected statistics. That is likely the explanation for the larger p-value for the adjusted "Pearson" Wald F statistic than that for the default-corrected Pearson and likelihood-ratio statistics.

The p-value for the adjusted log-linear Wald F statistic is about the same as that for the trustworthy default-corrected Pearson statistic. However, that is likely due to the anticonservatism of the log-linear Wald under the null balancing out its lower power under alternative hypotheses.

Note that the "uncorrected" χ^2 Pearson and likelihood-ratio statistics displayed in the table are misspecified statistics; that is, they are based on an i.i.d. assumption, which is not valid for complex survey data. Hence, they are not correct, even asymptotically. The "unadjusted" Wald χ^2 statistics, on the other hand, are completely different. They are valid asymptotically as the variance degrees of freedom become large.

◁

Properties of the statistics

This section briefly summarizes the properties of the eight statistics computed by svy: tabulate. For details, see Sribney (1998), Rao and Thomas (1989), Thomas and Rao (1987), and Korn and Graubard (1990).

pearson is the Rao and Scott (1984) second-order corrected Pearson statistic, computed using $\widehat{p}_{rc}$ in the correction (default correction). It is displayed by default. Simulations show it to have good properties under the null for both sparse and nonsparse tables. Its power is similar to the lr statistic in most situations. It appears to be more powerful than the adjusted "Pearson" Wald F statistic (wald option) in many situations, especially for larger tables. We recommend the use of this statistic in all situations.

pearson null is the Rao and Scott (1984) second-order corrected Pearson statistic, computed using $\widehat{p}_{0rc}$ in the correction. It is numerically similar to the pearson statistic for nonsparse tables. For sparse tables, it can be erratic. Under the null, it can be anticonservative for sparse 2×2 tables but conservative for larger sparse tables.

lr is the Rao and Scott second-order corrected likelihood-ratio statistic, computed using $\widehat{p}_{rc}$ in the correction (default correction). The correction is identical to that for pearson. It is numerically similar to the pearson statistic for nonsparse tables. It can be anticonservative (p-values too small) in very sparse tables. If there is a zero cell, it cannot be computed.

lr null is the Rao and Scott second-order corrected likelihood-ratio statistic, computed using $\widehat{p}_{0rc}$ in the correction. The correction is identical to that for pearson null. It is numerically similar to the lr statistic for nonsparse tables. For sparse tables, it can be overly conservative. If there is a zero cell, it cannot be computed.

wald statistic is the adjusted "Pearson" Wald F statistic. It has good properties under the null for nonsparse tables. It can be erratic for sparse 2×2 tables and some sparse large tables. The pearson statistic appears to be more powerful in many situations.

wald noadjust is the unadjusted "Pearson" Wald F statistic. It can be extremely anticonservative under the null when the table degrees of freedom (number of rows minus one times the number of columns minus one) approaches the variance degrees of freedom (number of sampled PSUs minus the number of strata). It is exactly the same as the adjusted wald statistic for 2×2 tables. It is similar to the adjusted wald statistic for small tables and/or large variance degrees of freedom.

llwald statistic is the adjusted log-linear Wald F statistic. It can be anticonservative for both sparse and nonsparse tables. If there is a zero cell, it cannot be computed.

llwald noadjust statistic is the unadjusted log-linear Wald F statistic. Like wald noadjust, it can be extremely anticonservative under the null when the table degrees of freedom approach the variance degrees of freedom. It also suffers from the same general anticonservatism of the llwald statistic. If there is a zero cell, it cannot be computed.

Saved Results

svy: tabulate saves in e(): In addition to the items documented in [SVY] **svy**, svy: tabulate also saves the following:

Scalars

e(r)	number of rows	e(c)	number of columns
e(cvgdeff)	c.v. of generalized DEFF eigenvalues	e(mgdeff)	mean generalized DEFF
e(total)	weighted sum of tab() variable		
e(F_Pear)	default-corrected Pearson F	e(F_Penl)	null-corrected Pearson F
e(df1_Pear)	numerator d.f. for e(F_Pear)	e(df1_Penl)	numerator d.f. for e(F_Penl)
e(df2_Pear)	denominator d.f. for e(F_Pear)	e(df2_Penl)	denominator d.f. for e(F_Penl)
e(p_Pear)	p-value for e(F_Pear)	e(p_Penl)	p-value for e(F_Penl)
e(cun_Pear)	uncorrected Pearson χ^2		
e(F_LR)	default-corrected likelihood-ratio F	e(F_LRnl)	null-corrected likelihood-ratio F
e(df1_LR)	numerator d.f. for e(F_LR)	e(df1_LRnl)	numerator d.f. for e(F_LRnl)
e(df2_LR)	denominator d.f. for e(F_LR)	e(df2_LRnl)	denominator d.f. for e(F_LRnl)
e(p_LR)	p-value for e(F_LR)	e(p_LRnl)	p-value for e(F_LRnl)
e(cun_LR)	uncorrected likelihood-ratio χ^2		
e(F_Wald)	adjusted "Pearson" Wald F	e(F_LLW)	adjusted log-linear Wald F
e(p_Wald)	p-value for e(F_Wald)	e(p_LLW)	p-value for e(F_LLW)
e(Fun_Wald)	unadjusted "Pearson" Wald F	e(Fun_LLW)	unadjusted log-linear Wald F
e(pun_Wald)	p-value for e(Fun_Wald)	e(pun_LLW)	p-value for e(Fun_LLW)
e(cun_Wald)	unadjusted "Pearson" Wald χ^2	e(cun_LLW)	unadjusted log-linear Wald χ^2

Macros

e(cmd)	tabulate		
e(rowvar)	$varname_1$, the row variable	e(tab)	tab() variable
e(colvar)	$varname_2$, the column variable	e(setype)	cell, count, column, or row

Matrices

e(Prop)	matrix of cell proportions	e(Obs)	matrix of observation counts
e(Deff)	DEFF vector for e(setype) items	e(Deft)	DEFT vector for e(setype) items

Methods and Formulas

svy: tabulate is implemented as an ado-file.

The table items

For a table of R rows by C columns with cells indexed by r, c, let

$$y_{(rc)j} = \begin{cases} 1 & \text{if the } j\text{th observation of the data is in the } r, c\text{th cell} \\ 0 & \text{otherwise} \end{cases}$$

where $j = 1, \ldots, m$ indexes individuals in the sample. Weighted cell counts (the count option) are

$$\widehat{N}_{rc} = \sum_{j=1}^{m} w_j\, y_{(rc)j}$$

where w_j is a sampling weight. If a variable x_j is specified with the tab() option, $\widehat{N}_{rc}$ becomes

$$\widehat{N}_{rc} = \sum_{j=1}^{m} w_j\, x_j\, y_{(rc)j}$$

Let

$$\widehat{N}_{r\cdot} = \sum_{c=1}^{C} \widehat{N}_{rc}, \qquad \widehat{N}_{\cdot c} = \sum_{r=1}^{R} \widehat{N}_{rc}, \qquad \text{and} \qquad \widehat{N}_{\cdot\cdot} = \sum_{r=1}^{R}\sum_{c=1}^{C} \widehat{N}_{rc}$$

Estimated cell proportions are $\widehat{p}_{rc} = \widehat{N}_{rc}/\widehat{N}_{\cdot\cdot}$; estimated row proportions (row option) are $\widehat{p}_{\mathrm{row}\,rc} = \widehat{N}_{rc}/\widehat{N}_{r\cdot}$; estimated column proportions (column option) are $\widehat{p}_{\mathrm{col}\,rc} = \widehat{N}_{rc}/\widehat{N}_{\cdot c}$; estimated row marginals are $\widehat{p}_{r\cdot} = \widehat{N}_{r\cdot}/\widehat{N}_{\cdot\cdot}$; and estimated column marginals are $\widehat{p}_{\cdot c} = \widehat{N}_{\cdot c}/\widehat{N}_{\cdot\cdot}$.

$\widehat{N}_{rc}$ is a total, the proportion estimators are ratios, and their variances can be estimated using linearization methods as outlined in [SVY] **variance estimation**. svy: tabulate computes the variance estimates using svy: mean, svy: ratio, and svy: total.

Confidence intervals

Confidence intervals for proportions are calculated using a logit transform so that the endpoints lie between 0 and 1. Let $\widehat{p}$ be an estimated proportion and $\widehat{s}$ be an estimate of its standard error. Let

$$f(\widehat{p}) = \ln\left(\frac{\widehat{p}}{1-\widehat{p}}\right)$$

be the logit transform of the proportion. In this metric, an estimate of the standard error is

$$\widehat{\mathrm{SE}}\{f(\widehat{p})\} = f'(\widehat{p})\widehat{s} = \frac{\widehat{s}}{\widehat{p}(1-\widehat{p})}$$

Thus a $100(1-\alpha)\%$ confidence interval in this metric is

$$\ln\left(\frac{\widehat{p}}{1-\widehat{p}}\right) \pm \frac{t_{1-\alpha/2,\nu}\,\widehat{s}}{\widehat{p}(1-\widehat{p})}$$

where $t_{1-\alpha/2,\nu}$ is the $(1-\alpha/2)$th quantile of Student's t distribution with ν degrees of freedom. The endpoints of this confidence interval are transformed back to the proportion metric using the inverse of the logit transform

$$f^{-1}(y) = \frac{e^y}{1+e^y}$$

Hence, the displayed confidence intervals for proportions are

$$f^{-1}\left\{\ln\left(\frac{\widehat{p}}{1-\widehat{p}}\right) \pm \frac{t_{1-\alpha/2,\nu}\,\widehat{s}}{\widehat{p}(1-\widehat{p})}\right\}$$

Confidence intervals for weighted counts are untransformed and are identical to the intervals produced by svy: total.

The test statistics

The uncorrected Pearson χ^2 statistic is

$$X_{\mathrm{P}}^2 = m \sum_{r=1}^{R} \sum_{c=1}^{C} (\widehat{p}_{rc} - \widehat{p}_{0rc})^2 / \widehat{p}_{0rc}$$

and the uncorrected likelihood-ratio χ^2 statistic is

$$X_{\mathrm{LR}}^2 = 2m \sum_{r=1}^{R} \sum_{c=1}^{C} \widehat{p}_{rc} \ln (\widehat{p}_{rc}/\widehat{p}_{0rc})$$

where m is the total number of sampled individuals, $\widehat{p}_{rc}$ is the estimated proportion for the cell in the rth row and cth column of the table as defined earlier, and $\widehat{p}_{0rc}$ is the estimated proportion under the null hypothesis of independence; i.e., $\widehat{p}_{0rc} = \widehat{p}_{r\cdot}\widehat{p}_{\cdot c}$, the product of the row and column marginals.

Rao and Scott (1981, 1984) showed that, asymptotically, X_{P}^2 and X_{LR}^2 are distributed as

$$X^2 \sim \sum_{k=1}^{(R-1)(C-1)} \delta_k W_k \tag{1}$$

where the W_k are independent χ_1^2 variables and the δ_k are the eigenvalues of

$$\Delta = (\widetilde{\mathbf{X}}_2' \mathbf{V}_{\mathrm{srs}} \widetilde{\mathbf{X}}_2)^{-1} (\widetilde{\mathbf{X}}_2' \mathbf{V} \widetilde{\mathbf{X}}_2) \tag{2}$$

where $\mathbf{V}$ is the variance of the $\widehat{p}_{rc}$ under the survey design and $\mathbf{V}_{\mathrm{srs}}$ is the variance of the $\widehat{p}_{rc}$ that you would have if the design were simple random sampling; namely, $\mathbf{V}_{\mathrm{srs}}$ has diagonal elements $p_{rc}(1 - p_{rc})/m$ and off-diagonal elements $-p_{rc}p_{st}/m$.

$\widetilde{\mathbf{X}}_2$ is calculated as follows. Rao and Scott do their development in a log-linear modeling context, so consider $[\, 1 \mid \mathbf{X_1} \mid \mathbf{X_2} \,]$ as predictors for the cell counts of the $R \times C$ table in a log-linear model. The $\mathbf{X_1}$ matrix of dimension $RC \times (R + C - 2)$ contains the $R - 1$ "main effects" for the rows and the $C - 1$ "main effects" for the columns. The $\mathbf{X_2}$ matrix of dimension $RC \times (R - 1)(C - 1)$ contains the row and column "interactions". Hence, fitting $[\, 1 \mid \mathbf{X_1} \mid \mathbf{X_2} \,]$ gives the fully saturated model (i.e., fits the observed values perfectly) and $[\, 1 \mid \mathbf{X_1} \,]$ gives the independence model. The $\widetilde{\mathbf{X}}_2$ matrix is the projection of $\mathbf{X_2}$ onto the orthogonal complement of the space spanned by the columns of $\mathbf{X}_1$, where the orthogonality is defined with respect to $\mathbf{V}_{\mathrm{srs}}$; i.e., $\widetilde{\mathbf{X}}_2' \mathbf{V}_{\mathrm{srs}} \mathbf{X}_1 = \mathbf{0}$.

See Rao and Scott (1984) for the proof justifying (1) and (2). However, even without a full understanding, you can get a feeling for Δ. It is like a "ratio" (although remember that it is a matrix) of two variances. The variance in the "numerator" involves the variance under the true survey design, and the variance in the "denominator" involves the variance assuming that the design was simple random sampling. Recall that the design effect DEFF for an estimated proportion (see [SVY] **estat**) is defined as

$$\mathrm{DEFF} = \frac{\widehat{V}(\widehat{p}_{rc})}{\widetilde{V}_{\mathrm{srsor}}(\widetilde{p}_{rc})}$$

Hence, Δ can be regarded as a design-effects matrix, and Rao and Scott call its eigenvalues, the δ_ks, the "generalized design effects".

It is easy to compute an estimate for Δ using estimates for $\mathbf{V}$ and $\mathbf{V}_{\mathrm{srs}}$. Rao and Scott (1984) derive a simpler formula for $\widehat{\Delta}$:

$$\widehat{\Delta} = \left(\mathbf{C}'\mathbf{D}_{\widehat{\mathbf{p}}}^{-1}\widehat{V}_{\mathrm{srs}}\mathbf{D}_{\widehat{\mathbf{p}}}^{-1}\mathbf{C}\right)^{-1}\left(\mathbf{C}'\mathbf{D}_{\widehat{\mathbf{p}}}^{-1}\widehat{V}\mathbf{D}_{\widehat{\mathbf{p}}}^{-1}\mathbf{C}\right)$$

Here $\mathbf{C}$ is a contrast matrix that is any $RC \times (R-1)(C-1)$ full-rank matrix that is orthogonal to $[\mathbf{1} \mid \mathbf{X}_1]$; i.e., $\mathbf{C}'\mathbf{1} = \mathbf{0}$ and $\mathbf{C}'\mathbf{X}_1 = \mathbf{0}$. $\mathbf{D}_{\widehat{\mathbf{p}}}$ is a diagonal matrix with the estimated proportions $\widehat{p}_{rc}$ on the diagonal. Note that when one of the $\widehat{p}_{rc}$ is zero, the corresponding variance estimate is also zero; hence, the corresponding element for $\mathbf{D}_{\widehat{\mathbf{p}}}^{-1}$ is immaterial for computing $\widehat{\Delta}$.

Unfortunately, (1) is not practical for the computation of a p-value. However, you can compute simple first-order and second-order corrections based on it. A first-order correction is based on downweighting the i.i.d. statistics by the average eigenvalue of $\widehat{\Delta}$; namely, you compute

$$X_{\mathrm{P}}^2(\widehat{\delta}.) = X_{\mathrm{P}}^2/\widehat{\delta}. \qquad \text{and} \qquad X_{\mathrm{LR}}^2(\widehat{\delta}.) = X_{\mathrm{LR}}^2/\widehat{\delta}.$$

where $\widehat{\delta}.$ is the mean-generalized DEFF

$$\widehat{\delta}. = \frac{1}{(R-1)(C-1)} \sum_{k=1}^{(R-1)(C-1)} \delta_k$$

These corrected statistics are asymptotically distributed as $\chi^2_{(R-1)(C-1)}$. Thus to first-order, you can view the i.i.d. statistics X_{P}^2 and X_{LR}^2 as being "too big" by a factor of $\widehat{\delta}.$ for true survey design.

A better second-order correction can be obtained by using the Satterthwaite approximation to the distribution of a weighted sum of χ_1^2 variables. Here the Pearson statistic becomes

$$X_{\mathrm{P}}^2(\widehat{\delta}., \widehat{a}) = \frac{X_{\mathrm{P}}^2}{\widehat{\delta}.(\widehat{a}^2 + 1)} \tag{3}$$

where $\widehat{a}$ is the coefficient of variation of the eigenvalues:

$$\widehat{a}^2 = \frac{\sum \widehat{\delta}_k^2}{(R-1)(C-1)\widehat{\delta}.^2} - 1$$

Since $\sum \widehat{\delta}_k = \mathrm{tr}\,\widehat{\Delta}$ and $\sum \widehat{\delta}_k^2 = \mathrm{tr}\,\widehat{\Delta}^2$, (3) can be written in an easily computable form as

$$X_{\mathrm{P}}^2(\widehat{\delta}., \widehat{a}) = \frac{\mathrm{tr}\,\widehat{\Delta}}{\mathrm{tr}\,\widehat{\Delta}^2} X_{\mathrm{P}}^2$$

These corrected statistics are asymptotically distributed as χ_d^2, with

$$d = \frac{(R-1)(C-1)}{\widehat{a}^2 + 1} = \frac{(\mathrm{tr}\,\widehat{\Delta})^2}{\mathrm{tr}\,\widehat{\Delta}^2}$$

i.e., a χ^2 with, in general, noninteger degrees of freedom. The likelihood-ratio X_{LR}^2 statistic can also be given this second-order correction in an identical manner.

We would be done if it were not for two outstanding issues. First, there are two possible ways to compute the variance estimate $\widehat{V}_{\mathrm{srs}}$, which is used to compute $\widehat{\Delta}$. $\mathbf{V}_{\mathrm{srs}}$ has diagonal elements $p_{rc}(1-p_{rc})/m$ and off-diagonal elements $-p_{rc}p_{st}/m$, but note that here p_{rc} is the true, not estimated, proportion. Hence, the question is, what to use to estimate p_{rc}: the observed proportions $\widehat{p}_{rc}$ or the proportions estimated under the null hypothesis of independence $\widehat{p}_{0rc} = \widehat{p}_{r\cdot}\widehat{p}_{\cdot c}$? Rao and Scott (1984, 53) leave this as an open question.

Because of the question of using $\widehat{p}_{rc}$ or $\widehat{p}_{0rc}$ to compute $\widehat{V}_{\mathrm{srs}}$, svy: tabulate can compute both corrections. By default, when the null option is not specified, only the correction based on $\widehat{p}_{rc}$ is displayed. If null is specified, two corrected statistics and corresponding p-values are displayed, one computed using $\widehat{p}_{rc}$ and the other using $\widehat{p}_{0rc}$.

The second outstanding issue concerns the degrees of freedom resulting from the variance estimate $\widehat{V}$ of the cell proportions under the survey design. The customary degrees of freedom for t statistics resulting from this variance estimate are $\nu = n - L$, where n is the number of PSUs in the sample and L is the number of strata.

Rao and Thomas (1989) suggest turning the corrected χ^2 statistic into an F statistic by dividing it by its degrees of freedom $d_0 = (R-1)(C-1)$. The F statistic is then taken to have numerator degrees of freedom equal to d_0 and denominator degrees of freedom equal to νd_0. Hence, the corrected Pearson F statistic is

$$F_{\mathrm{P}} = \frac{X_{\mathrm{P}}^2}{\operatorname{tr}\widehat{\Delta}} \quad \text{with} \quad F_{\mathrm{P}} \sim F(d, \nu d) \quad \text{where} \quad d = \frac{(\operatorname{tr}\widehat{\Delta})^2}{\operatorname{tr}\widehat{\Lambda}^2} \quad \text{and} \quad \nu = n - L \tag{4}$$

This is the corrected statistic that svy: tabulate displays by default or when the pearson option is specified. When the lr option is specified, an identical correction is produced for the likelihood-ratio statistic X_{LR}^2. When null is specified, (4) is also used. For the statistic labeled "D-B (null)", $\widehat{\Delta}$ is computed using $\widehat{p}_{0rc}$. For the statistic labeled "Design-based", $\widehat{\Delta}$ is computed using $\widehat{p}_{rc}$.

The Wald statistics computed by svy: tabulate with the wald and llwald options were developed by Koch, Freeman, and Freeman (1975). The statistic given by the wald option is similar to the Pearson statistic since it is based on

$$\widehat{Y}_{rc} = \widehat{N}_{rc} - \widehat{N}_{r\cdot}\widehat{N}_{\cdot c}/\widehat{N}_{\cdot\cdot}$$

where $r = 1, \ldots, R-1$ and $c = 1, \ldots, C-1$. The delta method can be used to estimate the variance of $\widehat{\mathbf{Y}}$ (which is $\widehat{Y}_{rc}$ stacked into a vector), and a Wald statistic can be constructed in the usual manner:

$$W = \widehat{\mathbf{Y}}'\left\{\mathbf{J_N}\widehat{V}(\widehat{\mathbf{N}})\mathbf{J_N}'\right\}^{-1}\widehat{\mathbf{Y}} \qquad \text{where} \qquad \mathbf{J_N} = \partial\widehat{\mathbf{Y}}/\partial\widehat{\mathbf{N}}'$$

The statistic given by the llwald option is based on the log-linear model with predictors $[\mathbf{1}|\mathbf{X}_1|\mathbf{X}_2]$ that was mentioned earlier. This Wald statistic is

$$W_{\mathrm{LL}} = \left(\mathbf{X}_2'\ln\widehat{\mathbf{p}}\right)'\left\{\mathbf{X}_2'\mathbf{J_p}\widehat{V}(\widehat{\mathbf{p}})\mathbf{J_p}'\mathbf{X}_2\right\}^{-1}\left(\mathbf{X}_2'\ln\widehat{\mathbf{p}}\right)$$

where $\mathbf{J_p}$ is the matrix of first derivatives of $\ln\widehat{\mathbf{p}}$ with respect to $\widehat{\mathbf{p}}$, which is, of course, just a matrix with $\widehat{p}_{rc}^{-1}$ on the diagonal and zero elsewhere. Note that this log-linear Wald statistic is undefined when there is a zero cell in the table.

Unadjusted F statistics (noadjust option) are produced using

$$F_{\text{unadj}} = W/d_0 \qquad \text{with} \qquad F_{\text{unadj}} \sim F(d_0, \nu)$$

Adjusted F statistics are produced using

$$F_{\text{adj}} = (\nu - d_0 + 1)W/(\nu d_0) \qquad \text{with} \qquad F_{\text{adj}} \sim F(d_0, \nu - d_0 + 1)$$

The other svy estimators also use this adjustment procedure for F statistics. See Korn and Graubard (1990) for a justification of the procedure.

References

Fuller, W. A., W. Kennedy, D. Schnell, G. Sullivan, H. J. Park. 1986. PC CARP. Ames, IA: Statistical Laboratory, Iowa State University.

Koch, G. G., D. H. Freeman, Jr., and J. L. Freeman. 1975. Strategies in the multivariate analysis of data from complex surveys. *International Statistical Review* 43: 59–78.

Korn, E. L. and B. I. Graubard. 1990. Simultaneous testing of regression coefficients with complex survey data: use of Bonferroni t statistics. *The American Statistician* 44: 270–276.

McDowell, A., A. Engel, J. T. Massey, and K. Maurer. 1981. Plan and operation of the Second National Health and Nutrition Examination Survey, 1976–1980. *Vital and Health Statistics* 15(1). Hyattsville, MD: National Center for Health Statistics.

Rao, J. N. K. and A. J. Scott. 1981. The analysis of categorical data from complex sample surveys: chi-squared tests for goodness of fit and independence in two-way tables. *Journal of the American Statistical Association* 76: 221–230.

——. 1984. On chi-squared tests for multiway contingency tables with cell proportions estimated from survey data. *Annals of Statistics* 12: 46–60.

Rao, J. N. K. and D. R. Thomas. 1989. Chi-squared tests for contingency tables. In *Analysis of Complex Surveys*, ed. C. J. Skinner, D. Holt, and T. M. F. Smith, Ch. 4, 89–114. New York: Wiley.

Shah, B. V., B. G. Barnwell, and G. S. Bieler. 1997. *SUDAAN User's Manual, Release 7.5*. Research Triangle Park, NC: Research Triangle Institute.

Sribney, W. M. 1998. svy7: Two-way contingency tables for survey or clustered data. *Stata Technical Bulletin* 45: 33–49. Reprinted in *Stata Technical Bulletin Reprints*, vol. 8, pp. 297–322.

Thomas, D. R. and J. N. K. Rao. 1987. Small-sample comparisons of level and power for simple goodness-of-fit statistics under cluster sampling. *Journal of the American Statistical Association* 82: 630–636.

Also See

Complementary:	[SVY] **svy: tabulate postestimation**, [SVY] **svydes**
Related:	[R] **tabulate twoway**, [R] **test**,
	[SVY] **svy: mean**, [SVY] **svy: ratio**,
	[SVY] **svy: tabulate oneway**, [SVY] **svy: total**
Background:	[U] **20 Estimation and postestimation commands**,
	[SVY] **estimation options**, [SVY] **direct standardization**,
	[SVY] **poststratification**, [SVY] **subpopulation estimation**,
	[SVY] **svy**, [SVY] **variance estimation**

Title

svy: **total** — Estimate totals for survey data

Syntax

svy [*vcetype*] [, *svy_options*] : total *varlist* [*if*] [*in*] [, *options*]

vcetype	description
SE	
linearized	Taylor linearized variance estimation
brr	BRR variance estimation; see [SVY] **svy brr**
jackknife	jackknife variance estimation; see [SVY] **svy jackknife**

Specifying a *vcetype* overrides the default from svyset.

svy_options	description
if/in/over	
subpop()	identify a subpopulation
SE	
brr_options	additional options allowed with BRR variance estimation; see [SVY] ***brr_options***
jackknife_options	additional options allowed with jackknife variance estimation; see [SVY] ***jackknife_options***
Reporting	
level(#)	set confidence level; default is level(95)
noheader	suppress the table header
nolegend	suppress the table legend

svy requires that the survey-design variables be identified using svyset; see [SVY] **svyset**.

See [U] **20 Estimation and postestimation commands** for additional capabilities of estimation commands.

Warning: Using *if* or *in* restrictions will not produce correct variance estimates for subpopulations in many cases. To compute estimates for a subpopulation, use the subpop() option. The full specification for subpop() is

subpop([*varname*] [*if*])

options	description
if/in/over	
over(*varlist* [, nolabel])	identify multiple subpopulations

Description

svy: total produces estimates of finite-population totals; see [R] **total** for a description of sample totals from nonsurvey data.

Options

svy_options; see [SVY] **svy**.

> if/in/over

over(*varlist* [, nolabel]) specifies that estimates be computed for multiple subpopulations.

The subpopulations are identified by the different values of the variables in *varlist*.

When over() is supplied with a single variable name, such as over(*varname*), the value labels of *varname* are used to identify the subpopulations. If *varname* does not have labeled values (or there are unlabeled values), the values themselves are used, provided that they are non-negative integers. Non-integer values, negative values, and labels that are not valid Stata names will be substituted with a default identifier.

When supplied with multiple variable names, a subpopulation index (starting at 1) is used to identify subpopulations. In this case, the index is listed with the values that identify the subpopulations.

nolabel requests that value labels attached to the variables identifying the subpopulations be ignored.

Remarks

svy: total will produce finite-population totals for one or more variables and over multiple subpopulations. svy: total also produces a full covariance matrix, enabling the use of postestimation commands to draw inferences and make comparisons of totals (and functions of totals) between variables and subpopulations.

▷ Example 1

In our NHANES II dataset, heartatk is a variable that is 1 if a person has ever had a heart attack and 0 otherwise. We estimate the total number of persons who have had heart attacks in the population represented by our data.

```
. use http://www.stata-press.com/data/r9/nhanes2
. svy: total heartatk
(running total on estimation sample)

Survey: Total estimation

Number of strata =      31          Number of obs    =    10349
Number of PSUs   =      62          Population size  = 1.2e+08
                                    Design df        =       31
```

		Linearized		
	Total	Std. Err.	[95% Conf.	Interval]
heartatk	3483276	236179.8	3001584	3964968

◁

▷ Example 2: Subpopulation totals

We can use the `over()` option to compare subpopulation totals. Here we estimate the total number of persons who have had heart attacks over the `sex` variable in the population represented by our data.

```
. svy: total heartatk, over(sex)
(running total on estimation sample)

Survey: Total estimation

Number of strata =        31        Number of obs   =     10349
Number of PSUs   =        62        Population size = 1.2e+08
                                    Design df       =        31

          Male: sex = Male
        Female: sex = Female
```

Over	Total	Linearized Std. Err.	[95% Conf. Interval]	
heartatk				
Male	2304839	200231.3	1896465	2713213
Female	1178437	109020.5	956088.2	1400786

◁

Saved Results

`svy: total` saves in `e()`:

Scalars
    e(N_over)   number of subpopulations

Macros
    e(cmd)   total   e(varlist)   *varlist*
    e(over)   *varlist* from over()   e(over_labels)   labels from over() variables
    e(over_namelist)   names from e(over_labels)

Matrices
    e(_N)   vector of sample sizes
    e(_N_subp)   vector of subpopulation size estimates

Methods and Formulas

`svy: total` is implemented as an ado-file.

See [SVY] **variance estimation** and [SVY] **poststratification** for discussions that provide background information for the following formulas.

The total estimator

Let Y_j be a survey item for the jth individual in the population, where $j = 1, \ldots, M$ and M is the size of the population. The associated population total for the item of interest is

$$Y = \sum_{j=1}^{M} Y_j$$

Let y_j be the survey item for the jth sampled individual from the population, where $j = 1, \ldots, m$ and m is the number of observations in the sample.

The estimator $\widehat{Y}$ for the population total Y is

$$\widehat{Y} = \sum_{j=1}^{m} w_j y_j$$

where w_j is a sampling weight. The estimator for the number of individuals in the population is

$$\widehat{M} = \sum_{j=1}^{m} w_j$$

The score variable for the total estimator is the variable itself,

$$z_j(\widehat{Y}) = y_j$$

The poststratified total estimator

Let P_k denote the set of sampled observations that belong to poststratum k and define $I_{P_k}(j)$ to indicate if the jth observation is a member of poststratum k; where $k = 1, \ldots, L_P$ and L_P is the number of poststrata. Also let M_k denote the population size for poststratum k. P_k and M_k are identified by specifying the poststrata() and postweight() options on svyset.

The estimator for the poststratified total is

$$\widehat{Y}^P = \sum_{k=1}^{L_P} \frac{M_k}{\widehat{M}_k} \widehat{Y}_k = \sum_{k=1}^{L_P} \frac{M_k}{\widehat{M}_k} \sum_{j=1}^{m} I_{P_k}(j) w_j y_j$$

where

$$\widehat{M}_k = \sum_{j=1}^{m} I_{P_k}(j) w_j$$

The score variable for the poststratified total is

$$z_j(\widehat{Y}^P) = \sum_{k=1}^{L_P} I_{P_k}(j) \frac{M_k}{\widehat{M}_k} \left(y_j - \frac{\widehat{Y}_k}{\widehat{M}_k} \right)$$

Subpopulation estimation

Let S denote the set of sampled observations that belong to the subpopulation of interest, and define $I_S(j)$ to indicate if the jth observation falls within the subpopulation.

The estimator for the subpopulation total is

$$\widehat{Y}^S = \sum_{j=1}^{m} I_S(j)\, w_j y_j$$

and its score variable is

$$z_j(\widehat{Y}^S) = I_S(j)\, y_j$$

The estimator for the poststratified subpopulation total is

$$\widehat{Y}^{PS} = \sum_{k=1}^{L_P} \frac{M_k}{\widehat{M}_k} \widehat{Y}_k^S = \sum_{k=1}^{L_P} \frac{M_k}{\widehat{M}_k} \sum_{j=1}^{m} I_{P_k}(j) I_S(j)\, w_j y_j$$

and its score variable is

$$z_j(\widehat{Y}^{PS}) = \sum_{k=1}^{L_P} I_{P_k}(j) \frac{M_k}{\widehat{M}_k} \left\{ I_S(j)\, y_j - \frac{\widehat{Y}_k^S}{\widehat{M}_k} \right\}$$

References

Cochran, W. G. 1977. *Sampling Techniques.* 3rd ed. New York: Wiley.

Eltinge, J. L. and W. M. Sribney. 1996. svy2: Estimation of means, totals, ratios, and proportions for survey data. *Stata Technical Bulletin* 31: 6–23. Reprinted in *Stata Technical Bulletin Reprints*, vol. 6, pp. 213–235.

Kish, L. 1965. *Survey Sampling.* New York: Wiley.

McDowell, A., A. Engel, J. T. Massey, and K. Maurer. 1981. Plan and operation of the Second National Health and Nutrition Examination Survey, 1976–1980. *Vital and Health Statistics* 15(1). Hyattsville, MD: National Center for Health Statistics.

Wolter, K. M. 1985. *Introduction to Variance Estimation.* New York: Springer.

Also See

Complementary:	[SVY] **svy: total postestimation**
Related:	[R] **total**,
	[SVY] **svy: mean**, [SVY] **svy: proportion**, [SVY] **svy: ratio**
Background:	[U] **20 Estimation and postestimation commands**,
	[SVY] **estimation options**, [SVY] **poststratification**,
	[SVY] **subpopulation estimation**, [SVY] **svy**, [SVY] **variance estimation**

Title

svy: total postestimation — Postestimation tools for svy: total

Description

The following postestimation commands are available for svy: total:

command	description
estat	postestimation statistics for survey data
estimates	cataloging estimation results
lincom	point estimates, standard errors, testing, and inference for linear combinations of descriptive statistics
nlcom	point estimates, standard errors, testing, and inference for nonlinear combinations of descriptive statistics
test	Wald tests for simple and composite linear hypotheses
testnl	Wald tests of nonlinear hypotheses

See [SVY] **estat**.

See the corresponding entries in the *Stata Base Reference Manual* for details on the other postestimation commands.

predict is not allowed after svy: total.

Remarks

▷ Example 1

Continuing with example 2 from [SVY] **svy: total**, we can perform a test of equality of the totals between the two subpopulations.

```
. test [heartatk]Male = [heartatk]Female
Adjusted Wald test
 ( 1)  [heartatk]Male - [heartatk]Female = 0
       F(  1,    31) =   26.34
            Prob > F =    0.0000
```

◁

Methods and Formulas

All postestimation commands listed above are implemented as ado-files.

Also See

Complementary:	[SVY] **svy: total**, [SVY] **estat**;
	[R] **estimates**, [R] **lincom**, [R] **nlcom**, [R] **test**, [R] **testnl**
Background:	[U] **13.5 Accessing coefficients and standard errors**,
	[U] **20 Estimation and postestimation commands**

Title

svydes — Describe survey data

Syntax

svydes [*varlist*] [*if*] [*in*] [, *options*]

options	description
Main	
stage(*#*)	sampling stage to describe; default is stage(1)
<u>final</u>stage	display information per sampling unit in the final stage
single	display only the strata with a single sampling unit
<u>gen</u>erate(*newvar*)	generate a variable identifying strata with a single sampling unit

svydes requires that the survey-design variables be identified using svyset; see [SVY] **svyset**.

Description

svydes displays a table that describes the strata and the sampling units for a given sampling stage in a survey dataset.

Options

⌐ Main ⌐

stage(*#*) specifies the sampling stage to describe. The default is stage(1).

finalstage specifies that results be displayed for each sampling unit in the final sampling stage; that is, a separate line of output is produced for every sampling unit in the final sampling stage. This option is not allowed with stage(), single, or generate().

single specifies that only the strata containing a single sampling unit be displayed in the table.

generate(*newvar*) stores a variable that identifies strata containing a single sampling unit for a given sampling stage.

Remarks

Survey datasets are typically the result of a stratified survey design with cluster sampling in one or more stages. Within a stratum for a given sampling stage, there are sampling units, which may be either clusters of observations or individual observations.

svydes displays a table that describes the strata and sampling units for a given sampling stage. One row of the table is produced for each stratum. Each row contains the number of sampling units, the range and mean of the number of observations per sampling unit, and the total number of observations. If the finalstage option is specified, one row of the table is produced for each sampling unit of the final stage. In this case, each row contains the number of observations for the respective sampling unit.

If a *varlist* is specified, svydes reports the number of sampling units that contain at least one observation with complete data (i.e., no missing values) for all variables in the *varlist*. These are the sampling units that would be used to compute point estimates using the variables in *varlist* with a given svy estimation commands.

▷ Example 1: Strata with a single sampling unit

We use data from the Second National Health and Nutrition Examination Survey (NHANES II) (McDowell et al. 1981) as our example. First, we set the strata, PSU, and pweight variables.

```
. use http://www.stata-press.com/data/r9/nhanes2b
. svyset psuid [pweight=finalwgt], strata(stratid)
      pweight: finalwgt
          VCE: linearized
    Strata 1: stratid
        SU 1: psuid
       FPC 1: <zero>
```

svydes will display the strata and PSU arrangement of the dataset.

```
. svydes
Survey: Describing stage 1 sampling units
      pweight: finalwgt
          VCE: linearized
    Strata 1: stratid
        SU 1: psuid
       FPC 1: <zero>
```

			#Obs per Unit		
Stratum	#Units	#Obs	min	mean	max
1	2	380	165	190.0	215
2	2	185	67	92.5	118
3	2	348	149	174.0	199
(output omitted)					
31	2	308	143	154.0	165
32	2	450	211	225.0	239
31	62	10351	67	167.0	288

Our NHANES II dataset has 31 strata (stratum 19 is missing) and 2 PSUs per stratum.

The variable hdresult contains serum levels of high-density lipoproteins (HDL). If we try to estimate the mean of hdresult, we get a missing value for the standard-error estimate and a note explaining why.

```
. svy: mean hdresult
(running mean on estimation sample)
Survey: Mean estimation
Number of strata =      31         Number of obs   =     8720
Number of PSUs   =      60         Population size = 9.9e+07
                                   Design df       =       29
```

	Mean	Linearized Std. Err.	[95% Conf. Interval]	
hdresult	49.67141	.	.	.

```
Note: Missing standard error due to stratum with single sampling unit; see
      help svydes.
```

Running svydes with hdresult and the single option will show us which strata have only one PSU.

```
. svydes hdresult, single
Survey: Describing strata with a single sampling unit in stage 1
      pweight: finalwgt
          VCE: linearized
     Strata 1: stratid
        SU 1: psuid
       FPC 1: <zero>
```

			#Obs with	#Obs with	#Obs per included Unit		
	#Units	#Units	complete	missing			
Stratum	included	omitted	data	data	min	mean	max
1	1*	1	114	266	114	114.0	114
2	1*	1	98	87	98	98.0	98
	2						

Both stratid = 1 and stratid = 2 have only one PSU with nonmissing values of hdresult. Since this dataset has only 62 PSUs, the finalstage option produces a manageable amount of output:

```
. svydes hdresult, finalstage
Survey: Describing final stage sampling units
      pweight: finalwgt
          VCE: linearized
     Strata 1: stratid
        SU 1: psuid
       FPC 1: <zero>
```

		#Obs with	#Obs with
		complete	missing
Stratum	Unit	data	data
1	1	0	215
1	2	114	51
2	1	98	20
2	2	0	67
3	1	161	38
3	2	116	33
(output omitted)			
32	1	180	59
32	2	203	8
31	62	8720	1631

                          10351

It is rather striking that there are two PSUs without any values for hdresult. All other PSUs have only a moderate number of missing values. Obviously, in a case such as this, a data analyst should first try to ascertain the reason why these data are missing. The answer here (Johnson 1995) is that HDL measurements could not be collected until the third survey location. Thus there are no hdresult data for the first two locations: stratid = 1, psuid = 1 and stratid = 2, psuid = 2.

Assuming that we wish to go ahead and analyze the hdresult data, we must "collapse" strata—that is, merge them together—so that every stratum has at least two PSUs with some nonmissing values. We can accomplish this by collapsing stratid = 1 into stratid = 2. To perform the stratum collapse, we create a new strata identifier newstr and a new PSU identifier newpsu.

```
. gen newstr = stratid
. gen newpsu = psuid
. replace newpsu = psuid + 2 if stratid == 1
(380 real changes made)
. replace newstr = 2 if stratid == 1
(380 real changes made)
```

We set the new strata and PSU variables.

```
. svyset newpsu [pweight=finalwgt], strata(newstr)
      pweight: finalwgt
          VCE: linearized
    Strata 1: newstr
       SU 1: newpsu
      FPC 1: <zero>
```

We use svydes to check what we have done.

```
. svydes hdresult, finalstage
Survey: Describing final stage sampling units
      pweight: finalwgt
          VCE: linearized
    Strata 1: newstr
       SU 1: newpsu
      FPC 1: <zero>
```

Stratum	Unit	#Obs with complete data	#Obs with missing data
2	1	98	20
2	2	0	67
2	3	0	215
2	4	114	51
3	1	161	38
3	2	116	33
(output omitted)			
32	1	180	59
32	2	203	8
30	62	8720	1631

```
                          10351
```

The new stratum, newstr $= 2$, has 4 PSUs, 2 of which contain some nonmissing values of hdresult. This is sufficient to allow us to estimate the mean of hdresult and get a nonmissing standard error estimate.

```
. svy: mean hdresult
(running mean on estimation sample)

Survey: Mean estimation

Number of strata =     30        Number of obs   =     8720
Number of PSUs   =     60        Population size = 9.9e+07
                                 Design df       =       30
```

	Mean	Linearized Std. Err.	[95% Conf. Interval]
hdresult	49.67141	.3830147	48.88919 50.45364

◁

▷ Example 2: Using e(sample) to find strata with a single sampling unit

Some estimation commands drop observations from the estimation sample when they encounter collinear predictors or perfect predictors. As such, it can be difficult to ascertain which strata contain a single sampling unit. In such cases, we can use if e(sample) instead of *varlist* when faced with the problem of strata with a single sampling unit. We revisit the previous analysis to illustrate.

```
. use http://www.stata-press.com/data/r9/nhanes2b

. svy: mean hdresult
(running mean on estimation sample)

Survey: Mean estimation

Number of strata =      31        Number of obs    =    8720
Number of PSUs   =      60        Population size  = 9.9e+07
                                  Design df        =      29
```

		Linearized	
	Mean	Std. Err.	[95% Conf. Interval]
hdresult	49.67141	.	. .

```
Note: Missing standard error due to stratum with single sampling unit; see
      help svydes.
. svydes if e(sample), single

Survey: Describing strata with a single sampling unit in stage 1

      pweight: finalwgt
          VCE: linearized
    Strata 1: stratid
        SU 1: psu
       FPC 1: <zero>
```

			#Obs per Unit		
Stratum	#Units	#Obs	min	mean	max
1	1*	114	114	114.0	114
2	1*	98	98	98.0	98
	2				

◁

Methods and Formulas

svydes is implemented as an ado-file.

References

Eltinge, J. L. and W. M. Sribney. 1996. svy3: Describing survey data: sampling design and missing data. *Stata Technical Bulletin* 31: 23–26. Reprinted in *Stata Technical Bulletin Reprints*, vol. 6, pp. 235–239.

Johnson, C. L. 1995. Personal communication.

McDowell, A., A. Engel, J. T. Massey, and K. Maurer. 1981. Plan and operation of the Second National Health and Nutrition Examination Survey, 1976–1980. *Vital and Health Statistics* 15(1). Hyattsville, MD: National Center for Health Statistics.

Also See

Complementary:	[SVY] **svy**, [SVY] **svyset**
Background:	[SVY] **survey**, [SVY] **variance estimation**

Title

svymarkout — Mark observations for exclusion based on survey characteristics

Syntax

svymarkout [*markvar*]

Description

svymarkout is a programmer's command that resets the values of *markvar* to contain 0 wherever any of the survey-characteristic variables (previously set by svyset) contain missing values.

svymarkout assumes that *markvar* was created by marksample or mark; see [P] **mark**. svymarkout is for use in programs designed for use with svy commands; see [P] **program properties** for a discussion of how to write programs to be used with svy.

▷ Example 1

```
program mysvyprogram, ...
    ...
    syntax ...
    marksample touse
    svymarkout 'touse'
    ...
end
```

◁

Saved Results

svymarkout saves in s():

Macros
    s(weight)   weight variable set by svyset

Also See

Complementary: [P] **mark**

Background: [P] **program properties**

Title

svyset — Declare survey design for dataset

Syntax

Single-stage design

svyset [*psu*] [*weight*] [, *design_options options*]

Multiple-stage design

svyset *psu* [*weight*] [, *design_options*] [|| *ssu, design_options*] ... [*options*]

Report or clear the current settings

svyset [, clear]

design_options	description
Main	
strata(*varname*)	variable identifying strata
fpc(*varname*)	finite-population correction

options	description
Weights	
brrweight(*varlist*)	balanced repeated replication (BRR) weights
jkrweight(*varlist*, ...)	jackknife replication weights
SE	
vce(linearized)	Taylor linearized variance estimation
vce(brr)	balanced repeated replication (BRR) variance estimation
vce(jacknife)	jackknife variance estimation
mse	use the MSE formula with vce(brr) or vce(jacknife)
Poststrata	
poststrata(*varname*)	variable identifying poststrata
postweight(*varname*)	poststratum population sizes
†noclear	change some of the settings without clearing the others
†clear(*opname*)	clear the specified settings; implies noclear

† noclear and clear() are not shown in the dialog box.

pweights and iweights are allowed; see [U] **11.1.6 weight**.

The full specification for jkrweight() is

jkrweight(*varlist* [, stratum(# [# ...]) fpc(# [# ...]) multiplier(# [# ...]) reset])

Description

svyset declares the data to be complex survey data, designates variables that contain information about the survey design, and specifies the default method for variance estimation. You must svyset your data before using any svy command; see [SVY] **svy**.

psu is _n or the name of a variable (numeric or string) that contains identifiers for the primary sampling units (clusters). Use _n to indicate that individuals (instead of clusters) were randomly sampled if the design does not involve clustered sampling. In the single-stage syntax, *psu* is optional and defaults to _n.

ssu is _n or the name of a variable (numeric or string) that contains identifiers for sampling units (clusters) in subsequent stages of the survey design. Use _n to indicate that individuals were randomly sampled within the last sampling stage.

Settings made by svyset are saved with a dataset. So, if a dataset is saved after it has been svyset, it does not have to be set again.

The current settings are reported when svyset is called without arguments:

    . svyset

Use the clear option to remove the current settings:

    . svyset, clear

Options

```
        Main
```

strata(*varname*) specifies the name of a variable (numeric or string) that contains stratum identifiers.

fpc(*varname*) requests a finite-population correction for the variance estimates. If *varname* has values less than or equal to 1, it is interpreted as a stratum sampling rate $f_h = n_h/N_h$, where n_h = number of units sampled from stratum h and N_h = total number of units in the population belonging to stratum h. If *varname* has values greater than or equal to n_h, it is interpreted as containing N_h. It is an error for *varname* to have values between 1 and n_h.

```
        Weights
```

brrweight(*varlist*) specifies the replicate weight variables to be used with vce(brr).

jkrweight(*varlist*, ...) specifies the replicate weight variables to be used with vce(jackknife).

The following options set characteristics on the jackknife replicate weight variables. If a single value is specified, all the specified jackknife replicate weight variables will be supplied with the same characteristic. If multiple values are specified, each replicate weight variable will be supplied with the corresponding value according to the order specified. These options are not shown in the dialog box.

  stratum(# [# ...]) specifies an identifier for the stratum in which the sampling weights have been adjusted.

  fpc(# [# ...]) specifies the FPC value to be added as a characteristic of the jackknife replicate weight variables. The values set by this suboption have the same interpretation as the fpc(*varname*) option.

  multiplier(# [# ...]) specifies the value of a jackknife multiplier to be added as a characteristic of the jackknife replicate weight variables.

reset indicates that the characteristics for the replicate weight variables may be overwritten or reset to the default, if they exist.

─────┌ SE ┐──

vce(*vcetype*) specifies the default method for variance estimation; see [SVY] **variance estimation**.

vce(linearized) sets the default to Taylor linearization.

vce(brr) sets the default to balanced repeated replication; also see [SVY] **svy brr**.

vce(jackknife) sets the default to the jackknife; also see [SVY] **svy jackknife**.

mse specifies that the MSE formula be used when vce(brr) or vce(jackknife) is specified. This option requires vce(brr) or vce(jackknife).

─────┌ Poststrata ┐───

poststrata(*varname*) specifies the name of the variable (numeric or string) that contains poststratum identifiers.

postweight(*varname*) specifies the name of the numeric variable that contains poststratum population totals (or sizes), i.e., the number of elementary sampling units in the population within each poststratum. These totals are assumed to be specific to the design strata (the statum identifiers from the strata() option).

The following options are available with svyset but are not shown in the dialog box:

clear clears all the settings from the data. Typing

> . svyset, clear

clears the survey design characteristics from the data in memory. Although this option may be specified with some of the other svyset options, it is redundant since svyset automatically clears the previous settings before setting new survey design characteristics.

noclear allows some of the options in *options* to be changed without clearing all the other settings. This option is not allowed with *psu*, *ssu*, *design_options*, or clear

clear(*opname*) allows some of the options in *options* to be cleared without clearing all the other settings. *opname* refers to an option name and may be one or more of the following:

> weight   vce   mse   brrweight   jkrweight   poststrata

This option implies the noclear option.

Remarks

▷ Example 1

We use the svyset command to set the stratification and sampling weight variables of the NMIHS dataset.

```
. use http://www.stata-press.com/data/r9/nmihs
. svyset [pweight=finwgt], strata(stratan)
      pweight: finwgt
          VCE: linearized
     Strata 1: stratan
        SU 1: <observations>
       FPC 1: <zero>
```

If we save the dataset, these settings will be remembered the next time we use this dataset.

```
. save mynmihs
file mynmihs.dta saved
. use mynmihs, clear
. svyset
      pweight: finwgt
          VCE: linearized
   Strata 1: stratan
      SU 1: <observations>
     FPC 1: <zero>
```

We can now use the svy prefix with estimation commands.

```
. svy: mean birthwgt
(running mean on estimation sample)

Survey: Mean estimation

Number of strata =        6        Number of obs    =     9946
Number of PSUs   =     9946        Population size  = 3.9e+06
                                   Design df        =     9940
```

		Linearized		
	Mean	Std. Err.	[95% Conf. Interval]	
birthwgt	3355.452	6.402741	3342.902	3368.003

We can change some settings without changing others by specifying the noclear and clear() options. By default, svyset clears all the previous settings before applying new settings.

```
. generate adjwgt = 2*finwgt
. svyset [pweight=adjwgt], noclear
      pweight: adjwgt
          VCE: linearized
   Strata 1: stratan
      SU 1: <observations>
     FPC 1: <zero>
. svyset [pweight=finwgt]
      pweight: finwgt
          VCE: linearized
   Strata 1: <one>
      SU 1: <observations>
     FPC 1: <zero>
```

◁

(*Continued on next page*)

▷ Example 2: Finite-population correction (FPC)

A finite-population correction (FPC) accounts for the reduction in variance that occurs when sampling *without* replacement from a finite population compared to sampling *with* replacement from the same population.

Consider the following dataset:

```
. use http://www.stata-press.com/data/r9/fpc
. list
```

	stratid	psuid	weight	nh	Nh	x
1.	1	1	3	5	15	2.8
2.	1	2	3	5	15	4.1
3.	1	3	3	5	15	6.8
4.	1	4	3	5	15	6.8
5.	1	5	3	5	15	9.2
6.	2	1	4	3	12	3.7
7.	2	2	4	3	12	6.6
8.	2	3	4	3	12	4.2

In this dataset, the variable nh is the number of PSUs per stratum that were sampled, Nh is the total number of PSUs per stratum in the sampling frame (i.e., the population), and x is our survey item of interest.

If we wish to use a finite-population correction in our computations, we must set the FPC when we identify the sampling weights, PSUs, and strata. Here we estimate the population mean of x, assuming sampling without replacement.

```
. svyset psuid [pw=weight], strata(stratid) fpc(Nh)
      pweight: weight
          VCE: linearized
    Strata 1: stratid
        SU 1: psuid
       FPC 1: Nh
. svy: mean x
(running mean on estimation sample)
Survey: Mean estimation
Number of strata =      2      Number of obs   =      8
Number of PSUs   =      8      Population size =     27
                               Design df       =      6
```

		Mean	Linearized Std. Err.	[95% Conf. Interval]	
x		5.448148	.6160407	3.940751	6.955545

We must respecify the survey design before estimating the population mean of x, assuming sampling with replacement.

```
. svyset psuid [pw=weight], strata(stratid)

    pweight: weight
        VCE: linearized
  Strata 1: stratid
      SU 1: psuid
     FPC 1: <zero>

. svy: mean x
(running mean on estimation sample)

Survey: Mean estimation

Number of strata =       2          Number of obs    =       8
Number of PSUs   =       8          Population size  =      27
                                    Design df        =       6
```

	Mean	Linearized Std. Err.	[95% Conf. Interval]
x	5.448148	.7412683	3.63433 7.261966

Including an FPC always reduces the variance estimate. However, the reduction in the variance estimates will be small when the N_h are large relative to the n_h.

Rather than having a variable that represents the total number of PSUs per stratum in the sampling frame, we sometimes have a variable that represents a sampling rate $f_h = n_h/N_h$. In this case, we set the variable of sampling rates the same way to get an FPC. The survey variance-estimation routines in Stata are smart. If the FPC variable is less than or equal to 1, it is interpreted as a sampling rate; if it is greater than or equal to n_h, it is interpreted as containing N_h. It is an error for the FPC variable to have values between 1 and n_h or to have a mixture of sampling rates and stratum sizes.

◁

▷ Example 3: Designs with multiple stages of clustering

In the following example, we will illustrate how to use svyset for various survey designs, from simple random sampling (SRS) to multistage designs with stratification in one or more stages.

SRS without sampling weights:

```
. use http://www.stata-press.com/data/r9/stage5a, clear

. svyset _n
    pweight: <none>
        VCE: linearized
  Strata 1: <one>
      SU 1: <observations>
     FPC 1: <zero>
```

SRS with poststratification:

```
. svyset _n, poststrata(postid) postweight(postw)
    pweight: <none>
        VCE: linearized
  Poststrata: postid
  Postweight: postw
    Strata 1: <one>
        SU 1: <observations>
       FPC 1: <zero>
```

Stratified SRS:

```
. svyset _n [pweight=pw], strata(strata)
      pweight: pw
          VCE: linearized
     Strata 1: strata
        SU 1: <observations>
       FPC 1: <zero>
```

Stratified SRS, sampled without replacement:

```
. svyset _n [pweight=pw], strata(strata) fpc(fpc1)
      pweight: pw
          VCE: linearized
     Strata 1: strata
        SU 1: <observations>
       FPC 1: fpc1
```

Stratified and clustered, sampled without replacement, sampling individuals with replacement within PSUs:

```
. svyset su1 [pweight=pw], strata(strata) fpc(fpc1) || _n
      pweight: pw
          VCE: linearized
     Strata 1: strata
        SU 1: su1
       FPC 1: fpc1
     Strata 2: <one>
        SU 2: <observations>
       FPC 2: <zero>
```

Clustered sampling in two stages, stratified in the first stage, sampling without replacement in the first stage, sampling with replacement in the second stage:

```
. svyset su1 [pweight=pw], strata(strata) fpc(fpc1) || su2
      pweight: pw
          VCE: linearized
     Strata 1: strata
        SU 1: su1
       FPC 1: fpc1
     Strata 2: <one>
        SU 2: su2
       FPC 2: <zero>
```

Clustered sampling without replacement in two stages, stratified in the first stage:

```
. svyset su1 [pweight=pw], strata(strata) fpc(fpc1) || su2, fpc(fpc2)
      pweight: pw
          VCE: linearized
     Strata 1: strata
        SU 1: su1
       FPC 1: fpc1
     Strata 2: <one>
        SU 2: su2
       FPC 2: fpc2
```

Clustered sampling without replacement in five stages, stratified in the first stage, with replacement sampling of individuals within the last stage clusters:

```
. svyset su1 [pweight=pw], strata(strata) fpc(fpc1)
>           || su2, fpc(fpc2) || su3, fpc(fpc3)
>           || su4, fpc(fpc4) || su5, fpc(fpc5) || _n

       pweight: pw
           VCE: linearized
      Strata 1: strata
          SU 1: su1
         FPC 1: fpc1
      Strata 2: <one>
          SU 2: su2
         FPC 2: fpc2
      Strata 3: <one>
          SU 3: su3
         FPC 3: fpc3
      Strata 4: <one>
          SU 4: su4
         FPC 4: fpc4
      Strata 5: <one>
          SU 5: su5
         FPC 5: fpc5
      Strata 6: <one>
          SU 6: <observations>
         FPC 6: <zero>
```

Clustered sampling without replacement in five stages, stratified in the first and third stage, with replacement sampling of individuals within the last stage clusters:

```
. svyset su1 [pweight=pw], strata(strata1) fpc(fpc1)
>           || su2, fpc(fpc2) || su3, fpc(fpc3) strata(strata3)
>           || su4, fpc(fpc4) || su5, fpc(fpc5) || _n
  (output omitted )
```

◁

▷ Example 4: Replication weights

Many groups that collect survey data for public use have taken steps to protect the privacy of the survey participants. This may result in datasets that have replicate weight variables instead of variables that identify the strata and sampling units from the sampling stages. These datasets require replication methods for variance estimation.

The `brrweight()` and `jkrweight()` options allow `svyset` to identify the set of replication weights for use with `vce(brr)` and `vce(jackknife)` (`svy brr` and `svy jackknife`), respectively. In addition to the weight variables, `svyset` also allows you to change the default *vcetype* from `vce(linearized)` to `vce(brr)` or `vce(jackknife)`. Here are a couple of simple examples using jackknife replication weights.

Here we have privacy-conscious data containing only sampling weights and jackknife replication weights, and we set the default variance estimator to the jackknife:

```
. svyset [pweight=pw], jkrweight(jkw_*) vce(jackknife)
       pweight: pw
           VCE: jackknife
           MSE: off
      jkrweight: jkw_1 jkw_2 jkw_3 jkw_4 jkw_5 jkw_6 jkw_7 jkw_8 jkw_9
      Strata 1: <one>
          SU 1: <observations>
         FPC 1: <zero>
```

In this example, we have privacy-conscious data containing only sampling weights and jackknife replication weights, and we set the default variance estimator to the jackknife using the MSE formula:

```
. svyset [pweight=pw], jkrweight(jkw_*) vce(jackknife) mse
         pweight: pw
             VCE: jackknife
             MSE: on
      jkrweight: jkw_1 jkw_2 jkw_3 jkw_4 jkw_5 jkw_6 jkw_7 jkw_8 jkw_9
        Strata 1: <one>
            SU 1: <observations>
           FPC 1: <zero>
```

◁

▷ Example 5: Characteristics for jackknife replicate weight variables

The `jkrweight()` option has suboptions that allow you to identify certain characteristics of the jackknife replicate weight variables. These characteristics are

1. An identifier for the stratum in which the sampling weights have been adjusted due to one of its PSUs being dropped. We use the `stratum()` suboption to set these values. The default is one stratum for all the replicate weight variables.

2. The FPC value. We use the `fpc()` suboption to set these values. The default value is zero.

   Note that this characteristic is ignored when the `mse` option is supplied to `svy jknife`.

3. A jackknife multiplier used in the formula for variance estimation. The multiplier for the standard leave-one-out jackknife method is

$$\frac{n_h - 1}{n_h}$$

where n_h is the number of PSUs sampled from stratum h. We use the `multiplier()` suboption to set these values. The default is derived from the above formula, assuming that n_h is equal to the number of replicate weight variables for stratum h.

Due to privacy concerns, public survey datasets may not contain stratum-specific information. However, the population size and an overall jackknife multiplier will likely be provided. In such cases, we must supply this information to `svyset` for the jackknife replicate weight variables. We will use the 1999–2000 NHANES data to illustrate how to set these characteristics.

The NHANES datasets for years 1999–2000 are available for download from the Centers for Disease Control and Prevention (CDC) web site `http://www.cdc.gov/`. This particular release of the NHANES data contains jackknife replication weights in addition to the usual PSU and stratum information. These variables are contained in the demographic dataset.

The 1999–2000 NHANES datasets are distributed in SAS Transport format, so we use Stata's `fdause` command to read the data into memory. Due to the nature of the survey design, the demographic dataset `demo.xpt` has two sampling-weight variables. `wtint2yr` contains the sampling weights appropriate for the interview data, and `wtmec2yr` contains the sampling weights appropriate for the MEC exam data. Consequently, there are two sets of jackknife replicate weight variables. The jackknife replicate weight variables for the interview data are named `wtirep01`, `wtirep02`, ... `wtirep52`. The jackknife replicate weight variables for the MEC exam data are named `wtmrep01`, `wtmrep02`, ... `wtmrep52`. The documentation published with the NHANES data gives guidance on which weight variables to use.

```
. fdause demo.xpt

. describe wtint2yr wtmec2yr wtirep01 wtmrep01

                storage  display   value
variable name   type     format    label     variable label
─────────────────────────────────────────────────────────────────────
wtint2yr        double   %10.0g              Full Sample 2 Year Interview
                                               Weight
wtmec2yr        double   %10.0g              Full Sample 2 Year Mec Exam
                                               Weight
wtirep01        double   %10.0g              Interview Weight Jack Knife
                                               Replicate 01
wtmrep01        double   %10.0g              Mec Exam Weight Jack Knife
                                               Replicate 01
```

The number of PSUs in the NHANES population is not apparent, so we will not set an FPC value, but we can set the standard jackknife multiplier for the 52 replicate weight variables and save the results as a Stata dataset for future use. Also note that the NHANES datasets all contain a variable called seqn. This variable has a respondent sequence number that allows the dataset users to merge the demographic dataset with other 1999–2000 NHANES datasets, so we sort on seqn before saving demo99_00.dta.

```
. local mult = 51/52

. svyset, jkrweight(wtmrep*, multiplier('mult'))
(output omitted)

. svyset, jkrweight(wtirep*, multiplier('mult'))
(output omitted)

. svyset, clear
no survey characteristics are set

. sort seqn

. save demo99_00
file demo99_00.dta saved
```

To complete this example, we will perform a simple analysis using the blood-pressure data; however, before we can perform any analysis, we have to merge the blood-pressure dataset, bpx.xpt, with our demographic dataset, demo99_00.dta. In the following, we use fdause to read in the blood-pressure data, sort on seqn, and save the resulting dataset to bpx99_00.dta. We then read in our copy of the demographic data, drop the irrelevant weight variables, and merge in the blood-pressure data from bpx99_00.dta. A quick call to tabulate on the _merge variable generated by merge indicates that 683 observations in the demographic data are not present in the blood-pressure data. Note that we do not drop these observations; otherwise, the estimate of the population size will be incorrect. Finally, we set the appropriate sampling and replicate weight variables using svyset before replacing bpx99_00.dta with a more complete copy of the blood-pressure data.

```
. fdause bpx.xpt

. sort seqn

. save bpx99_00
file bpx99_00.dta saved

. use demo99_00

. drop wtint?yr wtirep*

. merge seqn using bpx99_00

. tabulate _merge
```

_merge	Freq.	Percent	Cum.
1	683	6.85	6.85
3	9,282	93.15	100.00
Total	9,965	100.00	

```
. drop _merge

. svyset [pw=wtmec2yr], jkrweight(wtmrep*) vce(jackknife)
(output omitted )

. save bpx99_00, replace
file bpx99_00.dta saved
```

Here we estimate the mean systolic blood pressure for the population, using the MEC exam replication weights for jackknife variance estimation.

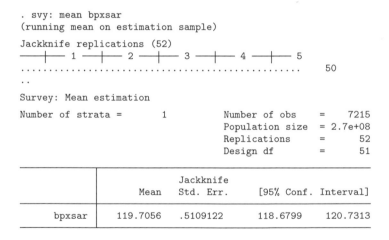

```
. svy: mean bpxsar
(running mean on estimation sample)

Jackknife replications (52)
───┼── 1 ──┼── 2 ──┼── 3 ──┼── 4 ──┼── 5
.................................................   50
..

Survey: Mean estimation

Number of strata =        1        Number of obs   =     7215
                                   Population size = 2.7e+08
                                   Replications    =       52
                                   Design df       =       51
```

	Mean	Jackknife Std. Err.	[95% Conf. Interval]
bpxsar	119.7056	.5109122	118.6799 120.7313

◁

▷ Example 6: Combining datasets from multiple surveys

The 2001–2002 NHANES datasets are also available from the CDC website. The guidelines that are published with these datasets recommend that the 1999–2000 and 2001–2002 NHANES datasets be combined to increase the accuracy of results. Combining datasets from multiple surveys is a complicated process, and Stata has no specific tools to help accomplish this task. However, the distributors of the NHANES datasets provide sampling-weight variables for the 1999–2002 combined data in the respective demographic datasets. They also provide some simple instructions on how to combine the datasets from these two surveys.

In the previous example, we worked with the 1999–2000 NHANES data. The 2001–2002 NHANES demographics data are contained in `demo_b.xpt`, and the blood-pressure data are contained in `bpx_b.xpt`. We follow the same steps as in the previous example to merge the blood-pressure data with the demographic data for years 2001–2002.

```
. fdause bpx_b.xpt
. sort seqn
. save bpx01_02
file bpx01_02.dta saved
. fdause demo_b.xpt
. drop wtint?yr
. sort seqn
. merge seqn using bpx01_02
. tabulate _merge
```

_merge	Freq.	Percent	Cum.
1	562	5.09	5.09
3	10,477	94.91	100.00
Total	11,039	100.00	

```
. drop _merge
. svyset sdmvpsu [pw=wtmec2yr], strata(sdmvstra)
      pweight: wtmec2yr
    Strata 1: sdmvstra
       SU 1: sdmvpsu
      FPC 1: <zero>
. save bpx01_02, replace
file bpx01_02.dta saved
```

The demographic dataset for years 2001–2002 does not contain replicate weight variables, but there are variables that provide information on PSUs and strata for variance estimation. The PSU information is contained in `sdmvpsu`, and the stratum information is in `sdmvstra`. See the documentation that comes with the NHANES datasets for the details regarding these variables.

This new blood-pressure dataset (`bpx01_02.dta`) is all we need if we are only interested in analyzing blood-pressure data for the data collected in the years 2001–2002. However, we want to use the 1999–2002 combined data, so we will follow the advice in the guidelines and just append the datasets from the two surveys.

For those concerned about overlapping stratum identifiers between the two survey datasets, it is a simple exercise to check that `sdmvstra` ranges from 1 to 13 for years 1999–2000 but ranges from 14 to 28 for years 2001–2002. Thus the stratum identifiers do not overlap, so we can simply append the data.

The 2001–2002 NHANES demographic dataset does not have any jackknife replicate weight variables, so we drop the replicate weight variables from the 1999–2000 dataset. The sampling-weight variable `wtmec2yr` is no longer appropriate for use with the combined data since its values are based on the survey designs individually, so we drop it from the combined dataset. Finally, we use `svyset` to identify the design variables for the combined surveys. Note that `wtmec4yr` is the sampling-weight variable for the MEC exam data developed by the data producers for the combined 1999–2002 NHANES data.

```
. use bpx99_00
. drop wt?rep*
. append using bpx01_02
. drop wtmec2yr
. svyset sdmvpsu [pw=wtmec4yr], strata(sdmvstra)
      pweight: wtmec4yr
    Strata 1: sdmvstra
        SU 1: sdmvpsu
       FPC 1: <zero>
. save bpx99_02
file bpx99_02.dta saved
```

Now we can estimate the mean systolic blood pressure for our population using the combined surveys and jackknife variance estimation.

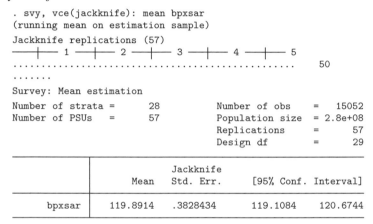

```
. svy, vce(jackknife): mean bpxsar
(running mean on estimation sample)
Jackknife replications (57)
───┼─── 1 ──┼── 2 ──┼── 3 ──┼── 4 ──┼── 5
..................................................  50
.......
Survey: Mean estimation
Number of strata =      28        Number of obs   =    15052
Number of PSUs   =      57        Population size = 2.8e+08
                                  Replications    =       57
                                  Design df       =       29
```

		Jackknife		
	Mean	Std. Err.	[95% Conf. Interval]	
bpxsar	119.8914	.3828434	119.1084	120.6744

◁

Saved Results

`svyset` saves in `r()`:

Scalars
    r(stages)   number of sampling stages

Macros
    r(wtype)   weight type
    r(wexp)   weight expression
    r(wvar)   weight variable name
    r(ssu#)   variable identifying sampling units for stage #
    r(strata#)   variable identifying strata for stage #
    r(fpc#)   FPC for stage #
    r(brrweight)   brrweight() variable list
    r(jkrweight)   jkrweight() variable list
    r(vce)   from vce() option
    r(mse)   from mse option
    r(poststrata)   poststrata() variable
    r(postweight)   postweight() variable
    r(settings)   svyset arguments to reproduce the current settings

Methods and Formulas

svyset is implemented as an ado-file.

References

Cochran, W. G. 1977. *Sampling Techniques.* 3rd ed. New York: Wiley.

Gonzalez J. F., Jr., N. Krauss, and C. Scott. 1992. Estimation in the 1988 National Maternal and Infant Health Survey. In *Proceedings of the Section on Statistics Education, American Statistical Association*, 343–348.

Johnson, W. 1995. Variance estimation for the NMIHS. Technical document. Hyattsville, MD: National Center for Health Statistics.

Also See

Complementary:	[SVY] **svy**, [SVY] **svydes**
Background:	[SVY] **survey**,
	[SVY] **poststratification**,
	[SVY] **subpopulation estimation**,
	[SVY] **variance estimation**

Title

> **variance estimation** — Variance estimation for survey data

Description

Stata's suite of estimation commands for survey data employ the three most-commonly used variance estimation techniques: balanced repeated replication, jackknife, and linearization. This entry discusses the details of these variance-estimation techniques.

Also see Cochran (1977) and Wolter (1985) for some methodological background on these variance estimators.

Remarks

Remarks are presented under the headings

> Variance of the total
> > Stratified single-stage design
> > Stratified two-stage design
>
> Variance for census data
> Ratios and other functions of survey data
> > Revisiting the total estimator
> > The ratio estimator
> > A note about score variables
>
> Linearized/robust variance estimation
> Balanced repeated replication (BRR)
> The jackknife
> > The delete-1 jackknife
> > The delete-k jackknife
>
> Confidence intervals

Variance of the total

This section describes the methods and formulas for svy: total. The variance estimators not employing replication methods use the variance of a total as an important ingredient; thus this section also serves as an introduction to variance estimation for survey data.

We will discuss the variance estimators for two complex survey designs:

1. The stratified single-stage design is the simplest design that has the elements present in most complex survey designs.

2. Adding a second stage of clustering to the previous design results in a variance estimator for designs with multiple stages of clustered sampling.

Stratified single-stage design

The population is partitioned into groups called *strata*. Clusters of observations are randomly sampled—with or without replacement—from within each stratum. These clusters are called *primary sampling units*, commonly abbreviated PSUs. In single-stage designs, data are collected from every individual member of the sampled PSUs. When the observed data are analyzed, sampling weights are used to account for the survey design. If the PSUs were sampled without replacement, a finite-population correction (FPC) is applied to the variance estimator.

The syntax to specify this design for svyset is

svyset *psu* [pweight=*weight*], strata(*strata*) fpc(*fpc*)

The stratum identifiers are contained in the variable named *strata*, PSU identifiers are contained in variable *psu*, the sampling weights are contained in variable *weight*, and the values for the FPC are contained in variable *fpc*.

Let $h = 1, \ldots, L$ enumerate the strata and (h, i) denote the ith PSU in stratum h; where $i = 1, \ldots, N_h$ and N_h is the number of PSUs in stratum h. Let (h, i, j) denote the jth individual from PSU (h, i) and M_{hi} be the number of individuals in PSU (h, i); then

$$M = \sum_{h=1}^{L} \sum_{i=1}^{N_h} M_{hi}$$

is the number of individuals in the population. Let Y_{hij} be a survey item for individual (h, i, j); for example, Y_{hij} might be income for adult j living in block i of county h. The associated population total is

$$Y = \sum_{h=1}^{L} \sum_{i=1}^{N_h} \sum_{j=1}^{M_{hi}} Y_{hij}$$

Let y_{hij} denote the items for individuals who are members of the sampled PSUs; here $h = 1$, $\ldots$, L; $i = 1, \ldots, n_h$; and $j = 1, \ldots, m_{hi}$. The number of individuals in the sample (number of observations) is

$$m = \sum_{h=1}^{L} \sum_{i=1}^{n_h} m_{hi}$$

The estimator for Y is

$$\widehat{Y} = \sum_{h=1}^{L} \sum_{i=1}^{n_h} \sum_{j=1}^{m_{hi}} w_{hij} y_{hij}$$

where w_{hij} is a sampling weight, and its unadjusted value for this design is $w_{hij} = N_h/n_h$. The estimator for the number of individuals in the population (population size) is

$$\widehat{M} = \sum_{h=1}^{L} \sum_{i=1}^{n_h} \sum_{j=1}^{m_{hi}} w_{hij}$$

The estimator for the variance of $\widehat{Y}$ is

$$\widehat{V}(\widehat{Y}) = \sum_{h=1}^{L} (1 - f_h) \frac{n_h}{n_h - 1} \sum_{i=1}^{n_h} (y_{hi} - \overline{y}_h)^2 \tag{1}$$

where y_{hi} is the weighted total for PSU (h, i)

$$y_{hi} = \sum_{j=1}^{m_{hi}} w_{hij} y_{hij}$$

and $\bar{y}_h$ is the mean of the PSU totals for stratum h:

$$\bar{y}_h = \frac{1}{n_h} \sum_{i=1}^{n_h} y_{hi}$$

The factor $(1 - f_h)$ is the FPC for stratum h, and f_h is the sampling rate for stratum h. The sampling rate f_h is derived from the variable specified in the `fpc()` option of `svyset`. If an FPC variable is not `svyset`, then $f_h = 0$. If an FPC variable is set and its values are greater than or equal to n_h, the variable is assumed to contain the values of N_h, and f_h is given by $f_h = n_h/N_h$. If its values are less than or equal to 1, the variable is assumed to contain the sampling rates f_h.

If multiple variables are supplied to `svy: total`, covariances are also computed. The estimator for the covariance between $\widehat{Y}$ and $\widehat{X}$ (notation for X is defined similarly to that of Y) is

$$\widehat{\mathrm{Cov}}(\widehat{Y}, \widehat{X}) = \sum_{h=1}^{L} (1 - f_h) \frac{n_h}{n_h - 1} \sum_{i=1}^{n_h} (y_{hi} - \bar{y}_h)(x_{hi} - \bar{x}_h)$$

Stratified two-stage design

The population is partitioned into strata. PSUs are randomly sampled without replacement from within each stratum. Clusters of observations are then randomly sampled—with or without replacement—from within the sampled PSUs. These clusters are called *secondary sampling units*, abbreviated as SSUs. Data is then collected from every individual member of the sampled SSUs. When the observed data are analyzed, sampling weights are used to account for the survey design. Each sampling stage provides a component to the variance estimator and has its own FPC.

The syntax to specify this design for `svyset` is

    `svyset` *psu* `[pweight=`*weight*`]`, `strata(`*strata*`) fpc(`*fpc₁*`) || ` *ssu*`, fpc(`*fpc₂*`)`

The stratum identifiers are contained in the variable named *strata*, PSU identifiers are contained in variable *psu*, the sampling weights are contained in variable *weight*, the values for the FPC for the first sampling stage are contained in variable *fpc₁*, SSU identifiers are contained in variable *ssu*, and the values for the FPC for the second sampling stage are contained in variable *fpc₂*.

The notation for this design is based on the previous notation. There still are L strata, and (h, i) identifies the ith PSU in stratum h. Let M_{hi} be the number of SSUs in PSU (h, i), M_{hij} is the number of individuals in SSU (h, i, j), and

$$M = \sum_{h=1}^{L} \sum_{i=1}^{N_h} \sum_{j=1}^{M_{hi}} M_{hij}$$

is the population size. Let Y_{hijk} be a survey item for individual (h, i, j, k); for example, Y_{hijk} might be income for adult k living in block j of county i of state h. The associated population total is

$$Y = \sum_{h=1}^{L} \sum_{i=1}^{N_h} \sum_{j=1}^{M_{hi}} \sum_{k=1}^{M_{hij}} Y_{hijk}$$

Let y_{hijk} denote the items for individuals who are members of the sampled SSUs; here $h = 1$, $\ldots$, L; $i = 1, \ldots, n_h$; $j = 1, \ldots, m_{hi}$; and $k = 1, \ldots, m_{hij}$. The number of observations is

$$m = \sum_{h=1}^{L} \sum_{i=1}^{n_h} \sum_{j=1}^{m_{hi}} m_{hij}$$

The estimator for Y is

$$\widehat{Y} = \sum_{h=1}^{L} \sum_{i=1}^{n_h} \sum_{j=1}^{m_{hi}} \sum_{k=1}^{m_{hij}} w_{hijk} y_{hijk}$$

where w_{hijk} is a sampling weight, and its unadjusted value for this design is

$$w_{hijk} = \frac{N_h}{n_h} \cdot \frac{M_{hi}}{m_{hi}}$$

The estimator for the population size is

$$\widehat{M} = \sum_{h=1}^{L} \sum_{i=1}^{n_h} \sum_{j=1}^{m_{hi}} \sum_{k=1}^{m_{hij}} w_{hijk}$$

The estimator for the variance of $\widehat{Y}$ is

$$\widehat{V}(\widehat{Y}) = \sum_{h=1}^{L} (1 - f_h) \frac{n_h}{n_h - 1} \sum_{i=1}^{n_h} (y_{hi} - \overline{y}_h)^2$$

$$+ \sum_{h=1}^{L} f_h \sum_{i=1}^{n_h} (1 - f_{hi}) \frac{m_{hi}}{m_{hi} - 1} \sum_{j=1}^{m_{hi}} (y_{hij} - \overline{y}_{hi})^2$$

(2)

where y_{hi} is the weighted total for PSU (h, i), $\overline{y}_h$ is the mean of the PSU totals for stratum h, y_{hij} is the weighted total for SSU (h, i, j)

$$y_{hij} = \sum_{k=1}^{m_{hij}} w_{hijk} y_{hijk}$$

and $\overline{y}_{hi}$ is the mean of the SSU totals for PSU (h, i)

$$\overline{y}_{hi} = \frac{1}{m_{hi}} \sum_{j=1}^{m_{hi}} y_{hij}$$

Note that (2) is equivalent to (1) with an added term representing the increase in variability due to the second stage of sampling. The factor $(1 - f_h)$ is the FPC, and f_h is the sampling rate for the first stage of sampling. The factor $(1 - f_{hi})$ is the FPC, and f_{hi} is the sampling rate for PSU (h, i). The sampling rate f_{hi} is derived in the same manner as f_h.

If multiple variables are supplied to svy: total, covariances are also computed. For estimated totals $\widehat{Y}$ and $\widehat{X}$ (notation for X is defined similarly to that of Y), the covariance estimator is

$$\widehat{\mathrm{Cov}}(\widehat{Y}, \widehat{X}) = \sum_{h=1}^{L}(1 - f_h)\frac{n_h}{n_h - 1}\sum_{i=1}^{n_h}(y_{hi} - \overline{y}_h)(x_{hi} - \overline{x}_h)$$

$$+ \sum_{h=1}^{L} f_h \sum_{i=1}^{n_h}(1 - f_{hi})\frac{m_{hi}}{m_{hi} - 1}\sum_{j=1}^{m_{hi}}(y_{hij} - \overline{y}_{hi})(x_{hij} - \overline{x}_{hi})$$

Based on the formulas (1) and (2), writing down the variance estimator for a survey design with three or more stages is a matter of deriving the variance component for each sampling stage. It helps to notice that the sampling units from a given stage pose as strata for the next sampling stage.

Note that all but the last stage must be sampled without replacement in order to get nonzero variance components from each stage of clustered sampling. For example, if $f_h = 0$ in (2), the second stage contributes nothing to the variance estimator.

Variance for census data

The point estimates that result from the analysis of census data, in which the entire population was sampled without replacement, are the population's parameters instead of random variables. As such, there is no sample-to-sample variation if we consider the population fixed. In this case the sampling fraction is 1, thus if the FPC variable you svyset for the first sampling stage is 1, Stata will report a standard error of 0.

Ratios and other functions of survey data

Shah (2004) points out a simple procedure for deriving the linearized variance for functions of survey data that are continuous functions of the sampling weights. Let θ be a (possibly vector-valued) function of the population data and $\widehat{\theta}$ be its associated estimator based on survey data.

1. Define the jth observation of the score variable by

$$z_j = \frac{\partial\widehat{\theta}}{\partial w_j}$$

   If $\widehat{\theta}$ is implicitly defined through estimating equations, z_j can be computed by taking the partial derivative of the estimating equations with respect to w_j.

2. Define the weighted total of the score variable by

$$\widehat{Z} = \sum_{j=1}^{m} w_j z_j$$

3. Estimate the variance $V(\widehat{Z})$ using the design-based variance estimator for the total $\widehat{Z}$. This variance estimator is an approximation to $V(\widehat{\theta})$.

Revisiting the total estimator

As a first example, we derive the variance of the total from a stratified single-stage design. In this case, you have $\widehat{\theta} = \widehat{Y}$, and deriving the score variable for $\widehat{Y}$ results in the original values of the variable of interest.

$$z_j(\widehat{\theta}) = z_j(\widehat{Y}) = \frac{\partial \widehat{Y}}{\partial w_j} = y_j$$

Thus you trivially recover the variance of the total given in (1) and (2).

The ratio estimator

The estimator for the population ratio is

$$\widehat{R} = \frac{\widehat{Y}}{\widehat{X}}$$

and its score variable is

$$z_j(\widehat{R}) = \frac{\partial \widehat{R}}{\partial w_j} = \frac{y_j - \widehat{R}\,x_j}{\widehat{X}}$$

Plugging this into (1) or (2) results in a variance estimator that is algebraically equivalent to the variance estimator derived from directly applying the delta method (a first-order Taylor expansion with respect to y and x)

$$\widehat{V}(\widehat{R}) = \frac{1}{\widehat{X}^2}\left\{\widehat{V}(\widehat{Y}) - 2\widehat{R}\,\widehat{\mathrm{Cov}}(\widehat{Y}, \widehat{X}) + \widehat{R}^2\,\widehat{V}(\widehat{X})\right\}$$

A note about score variables

The functional form of the score variable for each estimation command is detailed in the *Methods and Formulas* section of its manual entry; see [SVY] **svy: total**, [SVY] **svy: ratio**, and [SVY] **svy: mean**.

While Deville (1999) and Demnati and Rao (2004) refer to z_j as the *linearized variable*, here it is referred to as the *score variable* to tie it more closely to the model-based estimators discussed in the following section.

Linearized/robust variance estimation

The regression models for survey data that allow the vce(linearized) option use "linearization"-based variance estimators that are natural extensions of the variance estimator for totals. For general methodological background on regression and generalized-linear-model analysis of complex survey data; see, for example, Binder (1983), Cochran (1977), Fuller (1975), Godambe (1991), Kish and Frankel (1974), Särndal, Swensson, Wretman (1992), Shao (1996), and Skinner (1989).

Suppose that you observed $(Y_j, \mathbf{x}_j)$ for the entire population and are interested in modeling the relationship between Y_j and $\mathbf{x}_j$ by the vector of parameters $\boldsymbol{\beta}$ that solve the following estimating equations:

$$G(\boldsymbol{\beta}) = \sum_{j=1}^{M} S(\boldsymbol{\beta}; Y_j, \mathbf{x}_j) = 0$$

For ordinary least squares, $G(\beta)$ is the normal equations

$$G(\beta) = X'Y - X'X\beta = 0$$

where Y is the vector of outcomes for the full population and X is the matrix of explanatory variables for the full population. For a pseudolikelihood model—such as logistic regression—$G(\beta)$ is the first derivative of the log-pseudolikelihood function with respect to β. Estimate β by solving for $\widehat{\beta}$ from the weighted sample-estimating equations

$$\widehat{G}(\beta) = \sum_{j=1}^{m} w_j S(\beta; y_j, \mathbf{x}_j) = 0 \tag{3}$$

Note that the associated estimation command with `iweights` will produce point estimates $\widehat{\beta}$ equal to the solution of (3).

A first-order matrix Taylor series expansion yields

$$\widehat{\beta} - \beta \approx - \left\{ \frac{\partial \widehat{G}(\beta)}{\partial \beta} \right\}^{-1} \widehat{G}(\beta)$$

with the following variance estimator for $\widehat{\beta}$

$$\widehat{V}(\widehat{\beta}) = \left[\left\{ \frac{\partial \widehat{G}(\beta)}{\partial \beta} \right\}^{-1} \widehat{V}\{\widehat{G}(\beta)\} \left\{ \frac{\partial \widehat{G}(\beta)}{\partial \beta} \right\}^{-T} \right] \Bigg|_{\beta=\widehat{\beta}} = D\widehat{V}\{\widehat{G}(\beta)\} \Big|_{\beta=\widehat{\beta}} D'$$

where D is $(X'_s W X_s)^{-1}$ for linear regression (where W is a diagonal matrix of the sampling weights and X_s is the matrix of sampled explanatory variables) or the inverse of the negative Hessian matrix from the pseudolikelihood model. Write $\widehat{G}(\beta)$ as

$$\widehat{G}(\beta) = \sum_{j=1}^{m} w_j \mathbf{d}_j$$

where $\mathbf{d}_j = s_j \mathbf{x}_j$ and s_j is a residual for linear regression or an equation-level score from the pseudolikelihood model. The term *equation-level score* means the derivative of the log pseudolikelihood with respect to $\mathbf{x}_j\beta$. In either case, $\widehat{G}(\widehat{\beta})$ is an estimator for the total $G(\beta)$, and the variance estimator $\widehat{V}\{\widehat{G}(\beta)\}|_{\beta=\widehat{\beta}}$ is computed using the design-based variance estimator for a total.

Note that the above result is easily extended to models with ancillary parameters and/or multiple regression equations.

Balanced repeated replication (BRR)

Balanced repeated replication was first introduced by McCarthy (1966, 1969a, and 1969b) as a method of variance estimation for designs with two PSUs in every stratum. The BRR variance estimator tends to give more reasonable variance estimates for this design than the linearized variance estimator, which can result in large values and undesirably wide confidence intervals.

The model is fitted multiple times, once for each of a balanced set of combinations where one PSU is dropped (or downweighted) from each stratum. The variance is estimated using the resulting replicated point estimates (replicates). While the BRR method has since been generalized to include other designs, Stata's implementation of BRR requires two PSUs per stratum.

Let $\widehat{\theta}$ be the vector of point estimates computed using the sampling weights for a given stratified survey design (e.g., $\widehat{\theta}$ could be a vector of means, ratios, or regression coefficients). Each BRR replicate is produced by dropping (or downweighting) a PSU from every stratum. This could result in as many as 2^L replicates for a dataset with L strata; however, the BRR method uses Hadamard matrices to identify a balanced subset of the combinations from which to produce the replicates.

A Hadamard matrix is a square matrix, H_r (with r rows and columns), such that $H_r' H_r = rI$, where I is the identity matrix. The elements of H_r are $+1$ and -1; -1 causes the first PSU to be downweighted, $+1$ causes the second PSU to be downweighted; thus r must be greater than or equal to the number of strata.

Suppose that we are about to generate the adjusted-weight variable for the ith replication and w_j is the sampling weight attached to the jth observation, which happens to be in the first PSU of stratum h. The adjusted weight is

$$w_j^* = \begin{cases} fw_j, & \text{if } H_r[i,h] = -1 \\ (2-f)w_j, & \text{if } H_r[i,h] = +1 \end{cases}$$

where f is Fay's adjustment (Judkins 1990). Note that $f = 0$ by default.

Each replicate is produced by using an adjusted-weight variable with the estimation command that computed $\widehat{\theta}$. The adjusted-weight variables can be generated by Stata or supplied to svyset using the brrweight() option. We call the variables supplied to the brrweight() option "BRR replicate weight variables".

Let $\widehat{\theta}_{(i)}$ be the vector of point estimates from the ith replication. When the mse option is specified, the variance estimator is

$$\widehat{V}(\widehat{\theta}) = \frac{1}{r} \sum_{i=1}^{r} \{\widehat{\theta}_{(i)} - \widehat{\theta}\}\{\widehat{\theta}_{(i)} - \widehat{\theta}\}'$$

Otherwise, the variance estimator is

$$\widehat{V}(\widehat{\theta}) = \frac{1}{r} \sum_{i=1}^{r} \{\widehat{\theta}_{(i)} - \overline{\theta}_{(.)}\}\{\widehat{\theta}_{(i)} - \overline{\theta}_{(.)}\}'$$

where $\overline{\theta}_{(.)}$ is the BRR mean

$$\overline{\theta}_{(.)} = \frac{1}{r} \sum_{i=1}^{r} \widehat{\theta}_{(i)}$$

The jackknife

The jackknife method for variance estimation is appropriate for many models and survey designs. The model is fitted multiple times, and each time one or more PSUs are dropped from the estimation sample. The variance is estimated using the resulting replicates (replicated point estimates).

Let $\widehat{\boldsymbol{\theta}}$ be the vector of point estimates computed using the sampling weights for a given survey design (e.g., $\widehat{\boldsymbol{\theta}}$ could be a vector of means, ratios, or regression coefficients). The dataset is resampled by dropping one or more PSUs from a single stratum and adjusting the sampling weights before recomputing a replicate for $\widehat{\boldsymbol{\theta}}$.

Let w_{hij} be the sampling weight for the jth individual from PSU i in stratum h. Suppose that you are about to generate the adjusted weights for the replicate resulting from dropping k PSUs from stratum h. The adjusted weight is

$$
w^*_{abj} = \begin{cases} 0, & \text{if } a = h \text{ and } b \text{ is dropped} \\ \dfrac{n_h}{n_h - k} w_{abj}, & \text{if } a = h \text{ and } b \text{ is not dropped} \\ w_{abj}, & \text{otherwise} \end{cases}
$$

Each replicate is produced by using the adjusted-weight variable with the estimation command that produced $\widehat{\boldsymbol{\theta}}$. For the delete-1 jackknife (where one PSU is dropped for each replicate), adjusted weights can be generated by Stata or supplied to svyset using the jkrweight() option. For the delete-k jackknife (where $k > 1$ PSUs are dropped for each replicate), the adjusted-weight variables must be supplied to svyset using the jkrweight() option. The variables supplied to the jkrweight() option are called *jackknife replicate weight variables*.

The delete-1 jackknife

Let $\widehat{\boldsymbol{\theta}}_{(h,i)}$ be the point estimates (replicate) from leaving out the ith PSU from stratum h. The pseudovalue for replicate (h, i) is

$$
\widehat{\boldsymbol{\theta}}^*_{h,i} = \widehat{\boldsymbol{\theta}}_{(h,i)} + n_h\{\widehat{\boldsymbol{\theta}} - \widehat{\boldsymbol{\theta}}_{(h,i)}\}
$$

When the mse option is specified, the variance estimator is

$$
\widehat{V}(\widehat{\boldsymbol{\theta}}) = \sum_{h=1}^{L}(1 - f_h)\, m_h \sum_{i=1}^{n_h}\{\widehat{\boldsymbol{\theta}}_{(h,i)} - \widehat{\boldsymbol{\theta}}\}\{\widehat{\boldsymbol{\theta}}_{(h,i)} - \widehat{\boldsymbol{\theta}}\}'
$$

and the jackknife mean is

$$
\overline{\boldsymbol{\theta}}_{(.)} = \frac{1}{n}\sum_{h=1}^{L}\sum_{i=1}^{n_h}\widehat{\boldsymbol{\theta}}_{(h,i)}
$$

where f_h is the sampling rate and m_h is the jackknife multiplier associated with stratum h. Otherwise, the variance estimator is

$$
\widehat{V}(\widehat{\boldsymbol{\theta}}) = \sum_{h=1}^{L}(1 - f_h)\, m_h \sum_{i=1}^{n_h}\{\widehat{\boldsymbol{\theta}}_{(h,i)} - \overline{\boldsymbol{\theta}}_h\}\{\widehat{\boldsymbol{\theta}}_{(h,i)} - \overline{\boldsymbol{\theta}}_h\}', \qquad \overline{\boldsymbol{\theta}}_h = \frac{1}{n_h}\sum_{i=1}^{n_h}\widehat{\boldsymbol{\theta}}_{(h,i)}
$$

and the jackknife mean is

$$\overline{\theta}^* = \frac{1}{n} \sum_{h=1}^{L} \sum_{i=1}^{n_h} \widehat{\theta}_{h,i}^*$$

The multiplier for the delete-1 jackknife is

$$m_h = \frac{n_h - 1}{n_h}$$

The delete-k jackknife

Let $\widetilde{\theta}_{(h,d)}$ be one of the point estimates that resulted from leaving out k PSUs from stratum h. Let c_h be the number of such combinations that were used to generate a replicate for stratum h; then $d = 1, \ldots, c_h$. If all combinations were used, then

$$c_h = \frac{n_h!}{(n_h - k)! k!}$$

The pseudovalue for replicate (h, d) is

$$\widetilde{\theta}_{h,d}^* = \widetilde{\theta}_{(h,d)} + c_h \{ \widehat{\theta} - \widetilde{\theta}_{(h,d)} \}$$

When the mse option is specified, the variance estimator is

$$\widehat{V}(\widehat{\theta}) = \sum_{h=1}^{L} (1 - f_h) \, m_h \sum_{d=1}^{c_h} \{ \widetilde{\theta}_{(h,d)} - \widehat{\theta} \} \{ \widetilde{\theta}_{(h,d)} - \widehat{\theta} \}'$$

and the jackknife mean is

$$\overline{\theta}_{(.)} = \frac{1}{C} \sum_{h=1}^{L} \sum_{d=1}^{c_h} \widetilde{\theta}_{(h,d)}, \quad C = \sum_{h=1}^{L} c_h$$

Otherwise, the variance estimator is

$$\widehat{V}(\widehat{\theta}) = \sum_{h=1}^{L} (1 - f_h) \, m_h \sum_{d=1}^{c_h} \{ \widetilde{\theta}_{(h,d)} - \overline{\theta}_h \} \{ \widetilde{\theta}_{(h,d)} - \overline{\theta}_h \}', \qquad \overline{\theta}_h = \frac{1}{c_h} \sum_{d=1}^{c_h} \widetilde{\theta}_{(h,d)}$$

and the jackknife mean is

$$\overline{\theta}^* = \frac{1}{C} \sum_{h=1}^{L} \sum_{d=1}^{c_h} \widetilde{\theta}_{h,d}^*$$

The multiplier for the delete-k jackknife is

$$m_h = \frac{n_h - k}{n_h k}$$

Variables containing the values for the stratum identifier h, the sampling rate f_h, and the jackknife multiplier m_h can be svyset using the respective suboptions of the jkrweight() option: stratum(), fpc(), and multiplier().

Confidence intervals

In survey-data analysis, the customary number of degrees of freedom attributed to a test statistic is $d = n - L$, where n is the number of PSUs and L is the number of strata. Under regularity conditions, an approximate $100(1 - \alpha)\%$ confidence interval for a parameter θ (e.g., θ could be a total, ratio, or regression coefficient) is

$$\widehat{\theta} \pm t_{1-\alpha/2,d} \{\widehat{V}(\widehat{\theta})\}^{1/2}$$

Cochran (1977, section 2.8) and Korn and Graubard (1990) give some theoretical justification for using $d = n - L$ to compute univariate confidence intervals and p-values. However, for some cases, inferences based on the customary $n - L$ degrees-of-freedom calculation may be excessively liberal; the resulting confidence intervals may have coverage rates substantially less than the nominal $1 - \alpha$. This problem generally is of the greatest practical concern when the population of interest has a very skewed or heavy-tailed distribution or is concentrated in a small number of PSUs. In some of these cases, the user may want to consider constructing confidence intervals based on alternative degrees-of-freedom terms, based on the Satterthwaite (1941, 1946) approximation and modifications thereof; see, for example, Cochran (1977, section 5.4) and Eltinge and Jang (1996).

Sometimes there is no information on n or L for datasets that contain replicate weight variables but no PSU or strata variables. In this case, the number of degrees of freedom for `svy: brr` and `svy: jknife` is $d = r - 1$, where r is the number of replications.

References

Binder, D. A. 1983. On the variances of asymptotically normal estimators from complex surveys. *International Statistical Review* 51: 279–292.

Cochran, W. G. 1977. *Sampling Techniques*. 3rd ed. New York: Wiley.

Demnati, A. and J. N. K. Rao. 2004. Linearization variance estimators for survey data. *Survey Methodology* 30: 17–26.

Deville, J.-C. 1999. Variance estimation for complex statistics and estimators: Linearization and residual techniques. *Survey Methodology* 25: 193–203.

Eltinge, J. L. and D. S. Jang. 1996. Stability measures for variance component estimators under a stratified multistage design. *Survey Methodology* 22: 157–165.

Eltinge, J. L. and W. M. Sribney. 1996. svy4: Linear, logistic, and probit regressions for survey data. *Stata Technical Bulletin* 31: 26–31. Reprinted in *Stata Technical Bulletin Reprints*, vol. 6, pp. 239–245.

Fuller, W. A. 1975. Regression analysis for sample survey. *Sankhyā, Series C* 37: 117–132.

Godambe, V. P. ed. 1991. *Estimating Functions*. Oxford: Clarendon Press.

Gonzalez J. F., Jr., N. Krauss, and C. Scott. 1992. Estimation in the 1988 National Maternal and Infant Health Survey. In *Proceedings of the Section on Statistics Education, American Statistical Association*, 343–348.

Judkins, D. 1990. Fay's method for variance estimation. *Journal of Official Statistics* 16: 25–45.

Kish, L. and M. R. Frankel. 1974. Inference from complex samples. *Journal of the Royal Statistical Society* B 36: 1–37.

Korn, E. L. and B. I. Graubard. 1990. Simultaneous testing of regression coefficients with complex survey data: use of Bonferroni t statistics. *The American Statistician* 44: 270–276.

McCarthy, P. J. 1966. Replication: An Approach to the Analysis of Data from Complex Surveys. *Vital and Health Statistics* 2(14). Hyattsville, MD: National Center for Health Statistics.

———. 1969a. Pseudoreplication: Further Evaluation and Application of the Balanced Half-Sample Technique. *Vital and Health Statistics* 2(31). Hyattsville, MD: National Center for Health Statistics.

———. 1969b. Pseudoreplication: Half-Samples. *Review of the International Statistical Institute* 37: 239–264.

McDowell, A., A. Engel, J. T. Massey, and K. Maurer. 1981. Plan and operation of the Second National Health and Nutrition Examination Survey, 1976–1980. *Vital and Health Statistics* 15(1). Hyattsville, MD: National Center for Health Statistics.

Särndal, C.-E., B. Swensson, and J. Wretman. 1992. *Model Assisted Survey Sampling.* New York: Springer.

Satterthwaite, F. E. 1941. Synthesis of variance. *Psychometrika* 6: 309–316.

——. 1946. An approximate distribution of estimates of variance components. *Biometrics Bulletin* 2: 110–114.

Shah, B. V. 2004. Comment [on Demnati and Rao (2004)]. *Survey Methodology* 30: 29.

Shao, J. 1996. Resampling methods for sample surveys (with discussion). *Statistics* 27: 203–254.

Shao, J. and D. Tu 1995. *The Jackknife and Bootstrap.* New York: Springer.

Skinner, C. J. 1989. Introduction to Part A. In *Analysis of Complex Surveys,* ed. C. J. Skinner, D. Holt, and T. M. F. Smith, 23–58. New York: Wiley.

Also See

Complementary:	[SVY] **svy: mean**, [SVY] **svy: ratio**, [SVY] **svy: total**
Background:	[SVY] **svy**, [SVY] **svyset**, [SVY] **survey**,
	[P] **_robust**

Glossary

100% sample. See *census*.

balanced repeated replication. See *BRR*.

BRR. BRR is an acronym for *balance repeated replication*. BRR is a method of variance estimation for designs with two PSUs in every stratum. The BRR variance estimator tends to give more reasonable variance estimates for this design than the linearized variance estimator, which can result in large values and undesirably wide confidence intervals. The BRR variance estimator is described in [SVY] **variance estimation**.

census. When a census of the population is conducted, every individual in the population participates in the survey. Due to the time, cost, and other constraints the data collected in a census is typically limited to items that can be quickly and easily determined, usually through a questionnaire.

cluster. A cluster is a collection of individuals that are sampled as a group. Although the cost in time and money can be greatly decreased, cluster sampling usually results in larger variance estimates when compared with designs in which individuals are sampled independently.

DEFF and **DEFT**. DEFF and DEFT are design effects. Design effects compare the sample-to-sample variability from a given survey dataset with a hypothetical SRS design with the same number of individuals sampled from the population.

DEFF is the ratio of two variance estimates. The design-based variance is in the numerator, the hypothetical SRS variance is in the denominator.

DEFT is the ratio of two standard error estimates. The design-based standard error is in the numerator, the hypothetical SRS with-replacement standard error is in the denominator. If the given survey design is sampled with replacement, DEFT is the square root of DEFF.

design effects. See *DEFF* and *DEFT*.

direct standardization. Direct standardization is an estimation method that allows for the comparison of rates that come from different frequency distributions.

Estimated rates (means, proportions, and ratios) are adjusted according to the frequency distribution from a standard population. The standard population is partitioned into categories, called standard strata. The stratum frequencies for the standard population are called standard weights. The standardizing frequency distribution typically comes from census data, and the standard strata are most commonly identified by demographic information such as age, sex, and ethnicity.

FPC. FPC is an acronym for *finite-population correction*. An FPC is an adjustment applied to the variance of a point estimator due to sampling without replacement, resulting in variance estimates that are smaller than the variance estimates from comparable with-replacement sampling designs.

jackknife. The jackknife is a data-dependent way to estimate the variance of a statistic, such as a mean, ratio, or regression coefficient. Unlike BRR, the jackknife can be applied to practically any survey design. The jackknife variance estimator is described in [SVY] **variance estimation**.

linearization. Linearization is short for Taylor linearization. Also known as the delta method or the Huber/White/robust/sandwich variance estimator, linearization is a method for deriving an approximation to the variance of a point estimator, such as a ratio or regression coefficient. The linearized variance estimator is described in [SVY] **variance estimation**.

MEFF and **MEFT**. MEFF and MEFT are misspecification effects. Misspecification effects compare the variance estimate from a given survey dataset with the variance from a misspecified model. In Stata, the misspecified model is fitted without weighting, clustering, or stratification.

MEFF is the ratio of two variance estimates. The design-based variance is in the numerator, the misspecified variance is in the denominator.

MEFT is the ratio of two standard error estimates. The design-based standard error is in the numerator, the misspecified standard error is in the denominator. MEFT is the square root of MEFF.

misspecification effects. See *MEFF* and *MEFT*.

point estimate. A point estimate is another name for a statistic, such as a mean or regression coefficient.

poststratification. Poststratification is a method for adjusting sampling weights, usually to account for underrepresented groups in the population. This usually results in decreased bias due to nonresponse and underrepresented groups in the population. Poststratification also tends to result in smaller variance estimates.

The population is partitioned into categories, called poststrata. The sampling weights are adjusted so that the sum of the weights within each poststratum is equal to the respective poststratum size. The poststratum size is the number of individuals in the population that are in the poststratum. The frequency distribution of the poststrata typically comes from census data, and the poststrata are most commonly identified by demographic information such as age, sex, and ethnicity.

probability weight. Probability weight is another term for sampling weight.

pseudolikelihood. A pseudolikelihood is a weighted likelihood that is used for point estimation. Pseudolikelihoods are not true likelihoods because they do not represent the distribution function for the sample data from a survey. The sampling distribution is instead determined by the survey design.

PSU. PSU is an acronym for *primary sampling unit*. A PSU is a cluster that was sampled in the first sampling stage; see *cluster*.

replicate weight variable. A replicate weight variable contains sampling weight values that were adjusted for resampling the data; see [SVY] **variance estimation** for more details.

resampling. Resampling refers to the process of sampling from the dataset. In the delete-1 jackknife, the dataset is resampled by dropping one PSU and producing a replicate of the point estimates. In the BRR method, the dataset is resampled by dropping combinations of one PSU from each stratum. The resulting replicates of the point estimates are used to estimate their variances and covariances.

sample. A sample is the collection of individuals in the population that were chosen as part of the survey. Sample is also used to refer to the data, typically in the form of answered questions, collected from the sampled individuals.

sampling stage. Complex survey data are typically collected using multiple stages of clustered sampling. In the first stage, the PSUs are independently selected within each stratum. In the second stage, smaller sampling units are selected within the PSUs. In subsequent stages, smaller and smaller sampling units are selected within the clusters from the previous stage.

sampling unit. A sampling unit is an individual or collection of individuals from the population that can be selected in a specific stage of a given survey design. Examples of sampling units include: city blocks, high schools, hospitals, and houses.

sampling weight. Given a survey design, the sampling weight for an individual is the reciprocal of the probability of being sampled. The probability for being sampled is derived from stratification and clustering in the survey design. A sampling weight is typically considered to be the number of individuals in the population represented by the sampled individual.

sampling with and without replacement. Sampling units may be chosen more than once in designs that use sampling with replacement. Sampling units may be chosen at most once in designs that use sampling without replacement. Variance estimates from with-replacement designs tend to be larger than those from corresponding without-replacement designs.

SRS. SRS is an acronym for *simple random sample*. In a simple random sample, individuals are independently sampled—each with the same probability of being chosen.

SSU. SSU is an acronym for *secondary sampling unit*. An SSU is a cluster that was sampled from within a PSU in the second sampling stage. SSU is also used as a generic term unit to indicate any sampling unit that is not from the first sampling stage.

standard strata. See *direct standardization*.

standard weights. See *direct standardization*.

stratification. The population is partitioned into well-defined groups of individuals, called strata. In the first sampling stage, PSUs are independently sampled from within each stratum. In subsequent sampling stages, SSUs are independently sampled from within each stratum for that stage.

Survey designs that employ stratification typically result in smaller variance estimates than similar designs that do not. Stratification is most effective in decreasing variability when sampling units are more similar within the strata than between them.

subpopulation estimation. Subpopulation estimation focuses on computing point and variance estimates for a subset of the population. The variance estimates measure the sample-to-sample variability assuming that the same survey design is used to select individuals for observation from the population. This results in a different variance than measuring the sample-to-sample variability by restricting the samples to individuals within the subpopulation; see [SVY] **subpopulation estimation**.

survey data. Survey data consists of information about individuals that were sampled from a population according to a survey design. Survey data distinguishes itself from other forms of data due to the complex nature under which individuals are selected from the population.

In survey data analysis, the sample is used to draw inferences about the population. Furthermore the variance estimates measure the sample-to-sample variability that results from the survey design applied to the fixed population. This differs from standard statistical analysis in which the sample is used to draw inferences about a physical process and the variance measures the sample-to-sample variability that results from independently collecting the same number of observations from the same process.

survey design. A survey design describes how to sample individuals from the population. Survey designs typically include stratification and cluster sampling at one or more stages.

variance estimation. Variance estimation refers to the collection of methods used to measure the amount of sample–to–sample variation of point estimates; see [SVY] **variance estimation**.

Subject and author index

This is the subject and author index for the *Stata Survey Data Reference Manual*. Readers interested in topics other than survey data should see the combined subject index in the *Stata Quick Reference and Index*, which indexes the *Getting Started with Stata for Macintosh Manual*, the *Getting Started with Stata for Unix Manual*, the *Getting Started with Stata for Windows Manual*, the *Stata User's Guide*, the *Stata Base Reference Manual*, the *Stata Data Management Reference Manual*, the *Stata Graphics Reference Manual*, the *Stata Programming Reference Manual*, the *Stata Longitudinal/Panel Data Reference Manual*, the *Stata Multivariate Statistics Reference Manual*, the *Stata Survival Analysis and Epidemiological Tables Reference Manual*, the *Stata Time-Series Reference Manual*, and this manual.

Readers interested in Mata topics should see the index at the end of the *Mata Reference Manual*.

Semicolons set off the most important entries from the rest. Sometimes no entry will be set off with semicolons; this means all entries are equally important.